Skills *in*
COGNITIVE
BEHAVIOUR
THERAPY

Skills in ●●●●

Counselling & Psychotherapy

Series Editor
Francesca Inskipp

Series editor: Francesca Inskipp

Skills in Counselling and Psychotherapy is a series of practical guides for trainees and practitioners. Each book takes one of the main approaches to therapeutic work or key client groups, and describes the relevant core skills and techniques.

Topics covered include:

- How to establish and develop the therapeutic relationship
- How to help the client change
- How to assess the suitability of an approach or technique for the client.

This is the first series of books to look at skills specific to the different theoretical approaches and is now developed to include skills specific to particular client groups. It is an ideal series for use on a range of courses which prepare the trainees to work directly with the clients.

Books in the series:

Skills in Counselling and Psychotherapy with Children and Young People
Lorraine Sherman

Skills in Gestalt Counselling and Psychotherapy, Third Edition
Phil Joyce and Charlotte Sills

Skills in Person-Centred Counselling and Psychotherapy, Second Edition
Janet Tolan

Skills in Psychodynamic Counselling and Psychotherapy
Susan Howard

Skills in Existential Counselling and Psychotherapy
Emmy van Deurzen and Martin Adams

Skills in Rational Emotive Behaviour Counselling and Psychotherapy
Windy Dryden

Skills in Transactional Analysis Counselling and Psychotherapy
Christine Lister-Ford

Skills in Solution Focused Brief Counselling and Psychotherapy
Paul Hanton

Second Edition

Skills *in* COGNITIVE BEHAVIOUR THERAPY

Frank Wills

Los Angeles | London | New Delhi
Singapore | Washington DC

Los Angeles | London | New Delhi
Singapore | Washington DC

SAGE Publications Ltd
1 Oliver's Yard
55 City Road
London EC1Y 1SP

SAGE Publications Inc.
2455 Teller Road
Thousand Oaks, California 91320

SAGE Publications India Pvt Ltd
B 1/I 1 Mohan Cooperative Industrial Area
Mathura Road
New Delhi 110 044

SAGE Publications Asia-Pacific Pte Ltd
3 Church Street
#10-04 Samsung Hub
Singapore 049483

Editor: Susannah Trefgarne
Assistant editor: Laura Walmsley
Production editor: Rachel Burrows
Marketing manager: Camille Richmond
Cover design: Shaun Mercier
Typeset by: C&M Digitals (P) Ltd, Chennai, India
Printed in Great Britain by Henry Ling Limited at
The Dorset Press, Dorchester, DT1 1HD

Library of Congress Control Number: 2014940144

British Library Cataloguing in Publication data

A catalogue record for this book is available from
the British Library

ISBN 978-1-4462-7483-5
ISBN 978-1-4462-7484-2 (pbk)

At SAGE we take sustainability seriously. Most of our products are printed in the UK using FSC papers and boards.
When we print overseas we ensure sustainable papers are used as measured by the Egmont grading system.
We undertake an annual audit to monitor our sustainability.

CONTENTS

LIST OF FIGURES AND TABLES

LIST OF FIGURES

LIST OF TABLES

ABOUT THE AUTHOR

Frank comes from a working class family on the Wirral and takes any opportunity to mention his beloved local football team, Tranmere Rovers FC. He has worked as a psychological therapist over four decades and feels that he may now be getting the hang of it. Working in a variety of roles and settings, he qualified as a counsellor in 1984, and as a cognitive therapist in 1994. After a brief 'CBT evangelical' period, he saw the error of his ways and now firmly opposes Schoolism, believing that the therapy profession should unite around the idea that we can all learn from one another. He has learnt much from the psychodynamic and the humanistic approaches. In his recent publication, *Cognitive Behaviour Therapy: Foundations for Practice* (SAGE, 2013) and in this volume, he illustrates how such learning can result in more inter-personally sensitive and satisfying practice of CBT.

ACKNOWLEDGEMENTS

This book has evolved slowly and from interaction with many colleagues, students and friends. I would like to thank them all because each discussion has added to the strength and subtlety of my understanding of this work. I would like to name you all but most will have to 'know who you are'. A few, however, deserve special mention on this occasion: my live-in style consultant, Annie, and the members of my CBT skills development group – Christine Board, Liz Ford, Pamela Iles and Sarah Summers. It is great to be part of the Sage family and particular thanks are due to the team who managed me and this book: Susannah Trefgarne, Laura Walmsley, Rachel Burrows and Sophie Richmond.

COMPANION WEBSITE

Skills in Cognitive Behaviour Therapy, Second Edition, is accompanied by a companion website with free online resources for students and lecturers.

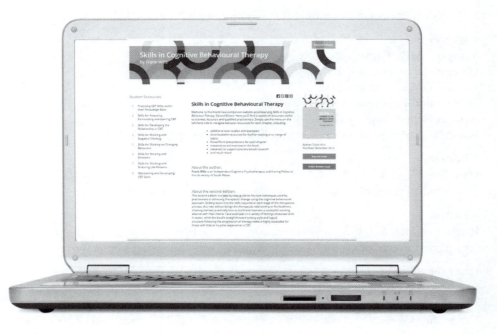

Visit **https://study.sagepub.com/wills** to access the following resources:

Chapter 1
A Guide to the Basic Concepts of CBT
Teaching and Learning Exercise on Rationale Giving
PowerPoint Presentation on Practising CBT Skills within their Knowledge Base

Chapter 2
Different Formats for Formulation
- ◆ Sample Case Formulation – Bron
- ◆ Sample Case Formulation – Bes

PowerPoint Presentation on Skills for Assessing, Formulating and Starting CBT

Chapter 3
PowerPoint Presentation on Skills for Developing the Relationship in CBT

Chapter 4
GD/SD Form
Thought Record Form
Clients' Guide to Using Thought Records
Additional Material on Forceful Cognitive Methods, Cognitive Distortions and Defusion
◆ Case Study – Blood Phobia

PowerPoint Presentation on Skills for Working with Negative Thinking

Chapter 5
Template ABC Form
Case Studies – Jana and Karen
Clients' Guide to Relaxation
Behavioural Experiments Diary Form
Activity Scheduling Form
PowerPoint Presentation on Skills for Working on Changing Behaviour

Chapter 6
Case Study – Bes
PowerPoint Presentation on Skills for Working with Emotions

Chapter 7
Review of Hall & Iqbal, *The Problem with CBT* (2010)
PowerPoint Presentation on Skills for Working with Enduring Life Patterns

Chapter 8
Practice Based Research Materials
Discussion of Training and Supervision
Extract from Wills, *The Acquisition of Competence during CBT Training*. PhD Thesis (2008).
PowerPoint Presentation on Maintaining and Developing CBT Skills

INTRODUCTION

Come, come whoever you are – wonderer, worshipper, lover of leaving, it doesn't matter. Ours is not a caravan of despair. (Rumi)

I have written a series of publications about cognitive behavioural therapy (CBT) over a period stretching from the mid-1990s until now. Each publication has made me think about how CBT, therapy and myself have changed in the intervening time. New editions in particular perhaps accentuate this process. Looking back at the first edition of this book, I can see one change that sets the tone for this new edition. For reasons that I explain in detail throughout this book, I am now concerned that CBT should try to reach a wider audience of people working in the helping professions, partly by being less precious about the role and methods of the CB therapist and partly by recognising more of CBT's similarities to other ways of helping clients. CBT was the 'new thing' when I began my therapeutic career in the 1970s but is now much more of a mainstream model of therapy. 'New things' understandably tend to stress how different they are from what has gone before, but as they establish themselves they can afford to relax more, open up previously closed borders and encourage commerce across those frontiers. I therefore would now like to see CBT develop as a set of concepts and methods capable of being adapted for use with a much wider set of practitioners than it currently is. This book will therefore offer a wider set of case examples than those most usually associated with practising CBT, and will describe the model being adapted to the clients of social workers, counsellors, youth workers, those who work with voluntary agencies and many others. For these reasons I have made frequent use of the terms 'psychological therapy' and 'psychological therapy skills'. 'Psychological therapy' is used as a generic term for both counselling and psychotherapy. 'Psychological therapy skills' is used to denote the use of skills by those who may not have the formal role of CB therapist.[1] This emphasis is not meant to disrespect the skills of anyone but to build on the idea that these skills are so useful that they could be relevant to more contexts than they generally are now.

Early models of CBT practice tended to emphasise techniques, outcomes and protocols and somewhat ignored the importance attributed to the therapeutic relationship

---

[1] This follows similar definitions to those adopted by the British Association for Counselling in the 1980s.

ocess in other types of therapy. Such an emphasis in CBT could be
.he need to describe and test techniques, but this is much less justifi-
oook therefore tries to sketch out how interpersonal and emotional
ially associated with other models of therapy can be used in CBT. CBT
a set of ideas and methods that may be practised with creativity to fit the
ations in which practitioners in the helping professions and their clients
find   selves. Nor does CBT have to be practised in fixed and rigid ways. The final
chapter suggests some ways of developing CBT skills on an on-going basis by using
ideas from therapy process research and reflective practice (McLeod, 2010, 2013a).

At the end of the introduction to the first edition of this book, I offered an equiv-
alent of the *Guardian's* 'digested read': for that edition it was *CBT once more – but this
time with more feeling!* For this edition I might allow myself the luxury of adding a few
more words: *Sometimes we get hooked into 'being a CB therapist' – we might do better to
focus on using CBT skills therapeutically.*

In our books on CBT, Diana Sanders and I have repeatedly used a Paul Gilbert
entreaty from 25 years ago that CB therapists should 'take time out from their technique oriented approaches and consider what it is to be a human being' (Dryden &
Trower, 1988, p. 66). It is as true today as it was then.

CBT practitioners are sometimes nervous about adopting methods not backed by
research findings. Many of the ideas here have mainly come from the evidence of
extensive practice over many years. Sadly there has been very little research of specific
skill usage in CBT, and this remains in my view a crucial gap that hampers practice
development. I do however make some suggestions, especially in Chapter 8, on how
this gap could be bridged.

I identified with James Lovelock's (2014, p. 19) recent description of his practice of
being a 'lone scientist' and his relationship with the world of establishment science:

> I do not scorn the captains and colonels of science who lead successful teams but
> we need the loners too.

One colleague recently produced a list of the 'Masters of the Universe in CBT' (note
the male noun) and I was at first chagrined, then pleased, not to be on the list.
Reflecting on this I realised that the title I aspire to is *the Les Dawson of CBT* – and
that has of course to include his piano playing.

1

PRACTISING CBT SKILLS WITHIN THEIR KNOWLEDGE BASE

On matters of style, swim with the current, on matters of principle, stand like a rock. (Thomas Jefferson)

All people offering psychological help to their clients aim to do so in as skilful a way as possible. This book proceeds from the assumption that the concepts and methods of CBT can greatly help in achieving this aim, and its final chapter will suggest ways that practitioners can develop a self-efficacious approach to CBT on an on-going basis.

Skills of course need to be underpinned by knowledge – without it we can be good at engaging clients in the journey but the direction of travel may remain obscure. This chapter will take up the challenge of the quotation from Thomas Jefferson above, first by giving a brief account of the development of CBT and then by describing a set of simple CBT principles that emerged during this evolution.

THE NATURE AND EVOLUTION OF CBT

CBT is a family of models of psychological therapy based on the fundamental idea that psychological problems, such as anxiety and depression, are influenced and maintained by patterns of unhelpful ways of thinking, feeling and acting. Psychological problems often have specific types of thoughts that link naturally to specific patterns of unhelpful feelings and behaviours. Therapists formulate a model of client symptoms and their underlying patterns and then therapist and client collaborate to plan and implement a series of interventions designed to produce change for the better.

It is now commonly held that CBT has developed in three 'waves'. The *first wave*, behaviour therapy, emerged between the 1950s and the 1970s. Behaviour therapists, partly reacting against psychoanalysis, have been wary of speculating about inner thoughts and motives. They like to formulate difficulties and solutions in terms of explicit behaviours. They have an honourable history in formulating the first major alternatives to 'medical model' treatments in the field of psychiatry (Bruch and Bond, 1998).

The refusal to speculate about the inner life, however, probably limited the range of issues that the behavioural approach could deal with and so this gap was bridged nicely by the development of the *second wave*, cognitive therapy, and the subsequent integration of behavioural and cognitive approaches into CBT[1] between the 1970s and 1990s. Beck's cognitive therapy for example shared the desire evident in behaviour therapy to develop what came later to be known as evidence-based practice, and both Beck and Ellis laid emphasis on behavioural change (Wills, 2009). Additionally cognitive approaches obviously had great interest in internal mental processes so that, as Rachman (1997, p. 17) puts it, 'cognitive therapy is supplying content to behaviour therapy'. Weishaar (1993) notes the great enthusiasm with which the therapy field greeted the research showing the effectiveness of cognitive therapy for depression, and similar results became increasingly evident in other, diverse problem areas.

Eventually, however, the limitations of CBT became clearer and this has been a significant factor in the emergence of the *third wave*, which I would term 'the mindfulness and acceptance wave', from the end of the 1990s up to the present day. Mindfulness-based cognitive therapy (MBCT) was developed by Segal, Williams and Teasdale (2002) as an effective way of countering depressive rumination and hence is now a major factor in relapse prevention. The need for new interventions to deal more effectively with rumination showed some of the limitations of standard cognitive interventions to restructure negative thoughts. MBCT developed ways of helping clients to 'view thoughts from another place' and this has been echoed in other third wave models: acceptance and commitment therapy (ACT) shows that negative thoughts can be 'defused' rather than restructured, and compassion-focused therapy (CFT) has suggested that negative thoughts are best viewed from a stance of self-compassion. In light of these considerable changes, it can seem that there is a danger of CBT becoming fragmented. Wills with Sanders (2013) review the challenges of third wave developments and argue for integrating insights from them in a way that retains the simplicity and parsimony of the paradigm as a whole, and this book also shares this view.

THE PRINCIPLES OF CBT

The principles underpinning the CBT skills, methods and strategies described throughout this book uses the template of CBT principles, first described by Aaron Beck (1976; Beck & Emery with Greenberg, 1985) and further developed by his daughter, Judith Beck (1995) – see Figure 1.1.

---

[1]The first use of the term 'cognitive-behavioural' seems to have been in 1972.

> **A base from which to help clients:**
> *CBT requires a sound therapeutic relationship.*
> *CBT is collaborative.*
>
> **A way of understanding clients and their problems:**
> *CBT is based on a cognitive behavioural formulation.*
>
> **A strategic posture for our helping efforts:**
> *CBT is relatively short-term.*
> *CBT is problem-focused and goal-oriented.*
> *CBT is initially focused on present-time issues.*
> *CBT is structured and directional.*
> *CBT is educational.*
>
> **A skills base for implementing such strategies:**
> *CBT methods are inductive and Socratic.*
> *CBT makes regular use of homework tasks.*
> *CBT uses a variety of techniques to help clients to develop more flexible and adaptive ways of thinking, feeling and behaving.*

Figure 1.1 The principles of CBT (adapted from Beck, 1976; Beck et al., 1985; J. Beck, 1995)

The basic but evolving principles offer practitioners ways of developing clarity on:

◆ therapeutic relationships with clients

◆ concepts for understanding clients and their problems

◆ strategic postures for therapeutic interventions

◆ skills to implement strategies.

CBT works from a therapeutic relationship based on collaboration

I have sought to convince therapists from other traditions that CBT therapists really do believe that building a therapeutic relationship is an essential part of what they do. My argument has been based on three main propositions:

◆ The therapeutic relationship in CBT has significant heritage and continuity from other approaches to therapeutic work. This point is further explained under the heading, 'Empathy, warmth and genuineness'.

◆ CBT has, however, its own particular take on the therapeutic relationship – see the section 'A collaborative working alliance, empirical in nature and pragmatic in spirit'.

◆ Although the relationship in CBT aspires towards simplicity, in the right hands it can be practised with interpersonal sensitivity and can embrace skilled use of transference and counter-transference – see 'Interpersonaly sensitive CBT'.

Readers may find it helpful to regard the above as steps to guide their development in CBT. Newcomers to using CBT skills should concentrate on establishing empathy, warmth and genuineness and then add CBT collaboration to them. Finally as they become more aware of the subtleties of therapeutic work, they can begin to add in a more relational dimension to their work.

Empathy, warmth and genuineness

Beck, Rush, Shaw and Emery's (1979) description of the therapeutic relationship in their seminal work on cognitive therapy clearly owes a debt to the ideas of Carl Rogers:

> As described by Rogers (1961) the therapeutic relationship in cognitive therapy is characterised by genuineness, respect and, within reason, warmth. (Beck et al., 1979, p. 21)

Cognitive theory, however, suggests that the way that clients see the therapist's empathy will be influenced by their belief system: helpers seen as empathic by some may seem patronising to others. Warmth in CBT is often accompanied by a degree of optimism; practitioners may sometimes choose to be a little 'upbeat' with the client, especially the depressed client. Judicious use of humour, not overdone, can help to reframe certain ways of thinking.

Empathy can be extended by the reflection of meaning as well as by reflection of feeling (Ivey, D'Andrea & Ivey, 2012). Cooper (2003) shows that exploring meaning is also a central concern of existentially based helping. A form of cognitive empathy develops as the understanding of feelings is enhanced by the expression of what those emotions mean. The CBT practitioner can make this link explicit by saying something like: 'Anyone who is thinking *I have lost everything* might well feel low, as you do now.' Blending reflections and Socratic questions extends empathy, rather as is done in motivational interviewing (Miller & Rollnick, 2002), and this is illustrated in the discussion of Guided Discovery through Socratic Dialogue (GD/SD) in Chapter 4. Empathy can be further enhanced by exploring how *emotion* drives – *motivates* – behaviour.[2] Empathic dialogue can also challenge clients, though there then may be a need for a degree of genuine tact: genuineness is a quality as important to CBT therapists as to others.

Helpers using CBT aim to bring these qualities together to form the basic therapeutic relationship and also to initiate 'collaborative empiricism' (see next section). A study by Arnow et al. (2013) showed that outcome in CBT is strongly linked to the quality of the relationship.[3] The presence or absence of this relationship is often evident at a

---

[2]'Emotion' and 'motive' derive from the same Latin root word meaning to 'move' or 'excite' – i.e. emotions and motives both move us and cause us to act.

[3]It should however be noted that the form of CBT used in the Arnow et al. study is cognitive behavioural analysis system of psychotherapy (CBASP: McCullough, 2000, 2006). McCullough has put considerable effort into developing the therapeutic alliance for the specific client group – with chronic depression. There are dangers in assuming that all variants of CBT have the same efficacy status (Gilbert, 2009b).

very early stage of CBT. Furthermore, Keijsers, Schaap and Hoogduin (2000), in a major review of therapeutic qualities in CBT, show that CBT practitioners seem to be just as good at enacting these qualities as therapists in other traditions.

A collaborative working alliance, empirical in nature and pragmatic in spirit

CBT practitioners have gone out of their way to stress that the operation of the model does not depend on a clever expert being 'in charge': though CBT can be subtle it aspires to lack pretension and to be 'down to earth' (Wills, 2006a). This is why such emphasis is placed on forging a collaborative working alliance between practitioner and client. Collaboration, however, simply means working together: the client's work and the therapist's work are different but must dovetail with each other. CB therapists work to help clients to identify and, sometimes, challenge their thinking. Clients report as honestly as possible on ways they react to trigger situations. If they see that these reactions do not work for them, they can be helped to commit to developing alternative ways of thinking that work better for them. They may however experience challenges of their thinking as attacks on themselves. It can therefore be helpful to use analogies in which client and therapist form a 'team' against the problem. Client and practitioner share responsibility for work and progress. The collaborative structuring devices of agenda setting and collecting feedback (see Chapter 2) can bolster this process. Early in therapy, practitioners will probably take more responsibility and will be more active but responsibility and control can gradually be handed over to clients. The initial stance may be one of tutor-coach but, as time goes by, this may evolve more towards a consultative mode (Neenan & Dryden, 2013). The basic working alliance is a joint venture to collect, analyse and review information about the client's life and use it to discern new positive directions for the future.

Interpersonally sensitive CBT

Therapy is an inherently interpersonal process, and CBT is therefore subject to the same kind of interpersonal and relational processes as have been identified and used more explicitly in other models of therapy. Becoming more aware of interpersonal processes allows CBT practitioners to make more flexible use of structure (Chapter 2). Without some such flexibility there is danger that CBT can become stilted and lifeless. The way clients react to CBT methods varies enormously and therefore the real art and skill of practitioners is to find the particular way that interventions may work best for the individual client before them. Learning how to do CBT in a way that is sensitively attuned to individual clients must therefore be a life-long process (see Chapter 8). It seems natural to me for practitioners from different appro-aches to learn what they can from each other, and CB therapists are now showing more willingness to do so. A good example is the way that we have opened our con-structs to an understanding of interpersonal processes (Gilbert & Leahy, 2007; Wills with Sanders, 2013). The discussion of interpersonal processes is further developed in Chapter 3.

CB therapists understand clients by making a cognitive behavioural road map

At the heart of the CBT paradigm there is a simple yet effective working model: the way people think about their situations influences how they feel and behave. It can be helpful to see if a client can work with this notion by using a dialogue such as the following to give a rationale for CBT:[4]

Practitioner (P1):	I sometimes explain how CBT can work by telling a story about two people I knew. They both worked in the same factory and were of a similar age and family set-up. Sadly, one day they heard that they were both to be made redundant. One of them thought to himself, 'I am such a failure. My wife might well leave me.' Thinking like that, how do you think he felt?
Client (C1):	Desperate, I should think. You know, really low and depressed.
P2:	Yes, that's right, he did. Now the other guy thought, 'This is bad. It's scary. On the other hand, I'm not really happy there: maybe this is a chance to try out other things I'm interested in.' How do you think he felt?
C2:	Well, better. He'd still be worried but he seems to have more hope.
P3:	And if a job did come up, who would be most likely to go for it?
C3:	The second bloke. The first one might give up: maybe not even apply?
P4:	That's right and that's exactly what did happen.

Giving a story that seeks to explain the main conceptual thrust of CBT – as the example above illustrates, the idea that how one thinks about something influences how one may feel and behave in relation to it – can work because it shows two people reacting differently to much the same situation. This stresses the importance of the way the event is appraised. It is often helpful to fit examples to the client's interests or background and to reinforce the central idea by drawing diagrams (see Figure 1.2).

Some important points emerge from this example. First, bad things do happen in people's lives – their reactions are not all about their inner psychology. Second, the person who shows a more adaptive response is still 'concerned' about his or her situation: they are certainly not happy or blasé. Concern is appropriate in this context and would be more likely to motivate a person to actively engage in surmounting the crisis of redundancy, though sometimes allowing oneself a period of feeling the loss is helpful. More discussion on the positive use of negative emotions can be found in Chapter 6. Third, the diagrams constitute examples of 'cycles' – one 'vicious' and dysfunctional, the other more functional. In the 'vicious' cycle example, the emotional and behavioural

---

[4]A teaching and learning exercise based on this rationale can be found on the companion website for this book: https://study.sagepub.com/wills

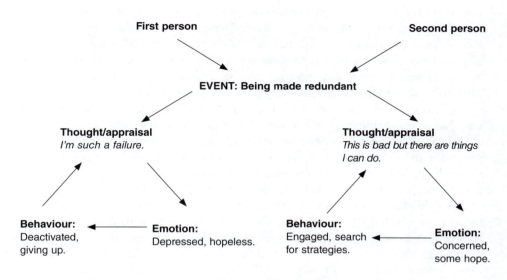

First person

Second person

EVENT: Being made redundant

Thought/appraisal
I'm such a failure.

Thought/appraisal
This is bad but there are things I can do.

Behaviour:
Deactivated, giving up.

Emotion:
Depressed, hopeless.

Behaviour:
Engaged, search for strategies.

Emotion:
Concerned, some hope.

Figure 1.2   The 'vicious cycle' concept – two cycles compared

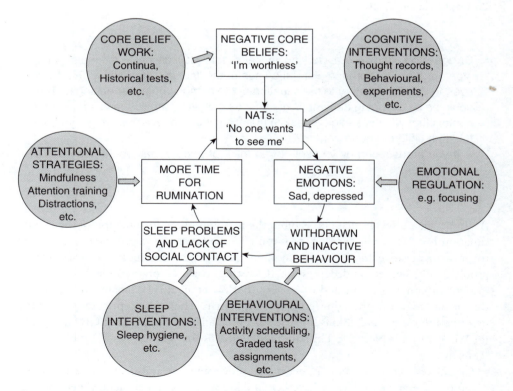

CORE BELIEF WORK: Continua, Historical tests, etc.

NEGATIVE CORE BELIEFS: 'I'm worthless'

COGNITIVE INTERVENTIONS: Thought records, Behavioural, experiments, etc.

NATs: 'No one wants to see me'

ATTENTIONAL STRATEGIES: Mindfulness Attention training Distractions, etc.

MORE TIME FOR RUMINATION

NEGATIVE EMOTIONS: Sad, depressed

EMOTIONAL REGULATION: e.g. focusing

SLEEP PROBLEMS AND LACK OF SOCIAL CONTACT

WITHDRAWN AND INACTIVE BEHAVIOUR

SLEEP INTERVENTIONS: Sleep hygiene, etc.

BEHAVIOURAL INTERVENTIONS: Activity scheduling, Graded task assignments, etc.

Figure 1.3   Vicious cycle with therapy targets

responses may well unwittingly confirm the prediction in the negative thought – what can also be termed a 'self-fulfilling prophecy'. In contrast, the functional cycle offers more hope for resolving the problem. Finally, the separate elements of the 'vicious cycle' diagram can each be regarded as potential targets for a series of change strategies: triggers can be changed; beliefs and thoughts can be modified; emotions can be 'worked through'; and 'behavioural experiments' can be tried (see Figure 1.3).

'Vicious cycle' diagrams are used frequently in CBT practice – sometimes drawn on a pad or on a whiteboard. They should be regarded as provisional, not set in stone: clients can draw them in their client notebooks and take them home to think about, play with and customise (see Chapter 2). It can be a powerful moment in therapy when clients first become aware of their own negative thoughts. 'Seeing' them written up on a whiteboard or in a client notebook can further enhance these moments.

The redundancy situation in the rationale–giving story above is one that can speak to many people, but the context may also be adapted to their own experiences, that is, situations in offices, schools and other places. Despite the modern setting of the example, it also carries an echo of the wisdom of the Socratic and Stoic traditions, most famously stated by Epictetus (1995), who said, 'People are disturbed not by events *alone* but by the view they take of them' (*Enchiridion, V*). Once again we note that 'stuff happens' – but we can have some control about how we react to events. Systematic consideration of 'triggers' also requires sensitivity to social, economic, political, ethnic and cultural factors that impinge on the well-being of us all (Gilbert, 2009a; Levinson, 2010).

Suggestion If you are working in pairs, role-play giving a rationale-giving story for therapy: perhaps along the lines of the 'factory' story above. Try, however, to amend the story to the situation of the person you are speaking to. This could be by changing the employment focus or shifting the scene to some other context that you think might speak to them: e.g. how, for example, might you put this to a child or young person?

If you are working by yourself, try to think of a story that would appeal to a recent client.

A simple 'vicious cycle' diagram is often the first step in the formulation of the client's situation in CBT terms. Further steps can take the form of recognising cognitive distortions in negative thoughts and looking for thoughts commonly associated with problems like anxiety and depression. 'Catastrophisation', for example, is often very evident in thinking connected to anxiety (Barlow et al., 2011). Finally, adding beliefs that relate to these thoughts completes the map. These concepts are more fully described in Chapters 2 (Skills for Assessing, Formulating and Starting CBT), 4 (Skills for Working with Negative Thinking) and 7 (Skills for Working with Enduring Life Patterns).

Cognitive factors include information processing, attention and interpretation. Cognitive therapy could easily have become known as 'appraisal therapy' because it is the cognitive processes of appraisal that are really the most important to successful CBT work. Most automatic thoughts are about trivial matters. The negative thoughts of clients that most often turn out to be relevant in CBT are almost always linked to appraisals of meaning connected to who clients think they are, what they think they should be doing, and with whom they think they should be doing it. The development of mindfulness in therapy also shows us the importance of the way clients may be paying attention to their negative thoughts. Mindfulness suggests that we can both think and be aware of thinking. Helping clients to relate to thoughts by thinking 'I am having the thought that …' can help them step a little outside negative thoughts and, in a sense, learn to not take them so seriously. Readers should bear this in mind as we shift through different layers of thinking, attention, appraisal and meaning.

Suggestion Think back over the last few weeks and search for an incident where you felt a strong emotional reaction. For the purpose of this exercise, it is usually best to think of a negative emotion that you *half know* is a little problematic (for example, where you reflect that something got to you more than it *should* have done). See if you can trace out your reaction in terms of the pattern of trigger–thinking(appraisal)–emotion–behaviour. If possible, draw out as shown above.
   Is there any element of a 'vicious cycle' in the reaction chain you have identified? If such a situation arose again, how else might you choose to react? What did/does this situation MEAN to you?

CBT has characteristic ways (strategies) of approaching helping clients

Short-term therapy

CBT is often associated with shorter-term work, perhaps in contexts such as the NHS, which are necessarily resource-conscious and have stressed the need for shorter-term methods. The usual range of formal CBT – between 10 and 20 sessions – would once have seemed impossibly short to some, but now I am frequently told it seems luxurious compared to the framework of 6–8 sessions[5] that many have to work in. The range of between 10 to 20 sessions emerged from research on CBT with depressed clients that suggested that the most parsimonious results came from a mean of 17 sessions (Beck et al., 1979). A theoretical justification for shorter-term work, however, stresses the fact that the collaborative alliance between practitioners and clients rarely solves all client problems and should therefore be focused on facilitating clients to solve their own

---

[5]A number of sessions now frequently specified in employee counselling and in the Health Service (Reeves, 2012).

problems by becoming their own therapists. This would help clients avoid future relapse and this seems to be one of CBT's main strengths – a review by DeRubeis, Siegle and Hollon (2008) shows that cognitive therapy is as efficacious as anti-depressant medications in long-term outcomes in the treatment of depression, supported by neuro-scientific evidence. Short-term work is, in my experience, popular with clients, especially if they can request extensions if they so wish. As CBT has expanded to address more complex problems, however, longer-term versions of it have developed (see Chapter 7).

Problem and goal focus

CBT has initial preference for short-term work and this is important because it influ-ences other aspects of working style. When a CBT approach is offered as a brief intervention, it is helpful for practitioners both to use educative materials and to use limited time with clients well. It is good therefore to be focused, and one – but not always the only – focus is the problem and/or symptoms that the client brings. A clear problem focus leads naturally to agreed goals. As Egan (2013) has pointed out, goals are the flip side of problems.

Present-time focus

As problems are assessed and a formulation of them is built up, it is often apparent that although there is a problem in current functioning, this problem has a 'history' and may be reflected in early development. CBT often begins with an inclination to work with the current, present-time problem and has placed somewhat less emphasis on historical and developmental factors. This aspect of CBT developed because much of its theory and practice came from focusing on clear syndromes with relatively discrete symptoms, such as unipolar depression (Beck et al., 1979) and panic disorder (Clark, 1996). As CBT has expanded into wider areas, however, it has become noticeably more flexible in terms of both length of contact and in attitudes towards working with more his-torical and developmental issues (Wills with Sanders, 2013). If we maintain that CBT is essentially a set of principles and methods that can be applied quite flexibly then we can also take a more flexible stance on length of therapy. Longer-term versions of CBT have emerged in the form of dialectical behaviour therapy (Linehan, 1993, 2004) and schema-focused therapy (Young, Klosko & Weishaar, 2003). This new flexibility means that CBT interventions may develop in a variety of different ways. They may centre on 'standard' work with current symptoms within the traditional short-term framework. If this work is relatively successful, yet underlying issues are evident and the client wants to work with them, work can refocus on those underlying issues, perhaps even within the range of short-term interventions. It is not always necessary to completely 'work through' all these issues so that therapy may still be completed within a short-term time frame. Alternatively, there are criteria[6] that can inform a judgement on whether 'stand-ard CBT' would not be a suitable approach for this particular client (Young et al., 2003), and therefore therapists may then use a longer-term, schema-focused model, perhaps

---

[6]These criteria are reviewed in Chapter 7.

going up to and beyond 40 sessions or lasting for longer than one year. Carefully researched work by Cummings and Sayama (1995) suggest that most caseloads will carry around 10% of clients who will need longer-term help and 5% who may even need to keep coming back for periods of therapy over many years. The title of a paper by McGinn, Young and Sanderson (1995) nicely captures a growing mood in CBT: 'When and how to do longer-term therapy and not feel guilty'. It is interesting that short-term versions of psychodynamic therapy are now based on the fact that many clients do not stay that long in therapy (Levenson, 1995) and one version has produced good efficacy results for the treatment of panic (Busch, Milrod, Singer & Aronson, 2012). This treatment is, however, longer than the usual CBT treatments, though it may be especially useful when panic is associated with interpersonal difficulties.

Structured and directional

As clients may be experiencing some chaos in their lives, therapy structure can be helpful to them. Structured steps should however be used with a 'light touch' and fitted to the needs of the client – see Practice tip on p. 16. Most clients expect some direction but this should be supplied in a 'directional' rather than a 'directive' way (see Wills with Sanders, 2013, p. 30).

Educational focus

Another factor that emerges from these short-term and problem-solving strategic postures is that CB practitioners have traditionally taken a consciously educational role. This role may be relatively didactic, exemplified when the therapist gives a depressed client 'normalising' information about the condition. A client, for example, may become overly self-critical because of poor concentration and motivation, and it is often helpful for them to realise that these traits may well be 'the depression speaking', and are not the client's inherent personal qualities. This kind of normalisation also carries a meta-message typical of CBT: *This is something we can learn to manage.* There is a more subtle aspect to the educational role, one that is closer to the 'tutor-coach' role. In this mode, the therapist's role is to help clients to 'learn to learn'. This begins by trying to foster the quality of reflective curiosity in the client: *What is happening to me?* Gradually reflection may become more active as the client learns to 'think about thinking' and to regard their behaviours in more detached and mindful ways so that new responses can become more possible.

A skills methods base for implementing strategies

Inductive and Socratic Guided Discovery

CBT practitioners use their methods based on the aim of encouraging clients to develop realistic views of the predicaments in which they find themselves. They do this but not without first helping clients to test their current negative views of their lives. This is referred to as an inductive process because it starts with observations and then tests the implications of these observations for current theory. The aim of this reality testing is to create cognitive dissonance that in turn promotes changes of mind. The use of Socratic questions is central to CBT (Wills, 2012), and I call this process Guided Discovery through Socratic Dialogue (GD/SD). Mindfulness theory suggests to me that the effectiveness of GD/SD is likely to come from, not as we first thought, changing the content of thought but from *changing the relationship clients have to the way they think*. This perspective on cognitive work is described in Chapter 4.

Homework

Homework completion is associated with greater gains in CBT practice (Kazantzis, Deane, Ronan & L'Abate, 2005) and may be increasingly regarded as a 'common factor'[7] (Kazantzis & Ronan, 2006) in all kinds of helping. Using the time between sessions for these activities also helps to compensate for having less time when working within time limits with some clients. All in all, time limits can have positive as well as negative effects.

A variety of techniques and methods

CBT skills and techniques will be described more fully in the rest of this book. Here the focus is on showing the relationship between skill use and principles of CBT that influence why and how client problems are addressed in the way they are in CBT.

We can for example see the GD/SD process at work in the rationale-giving stories presented earlier. Then we discussed the role of these stories in building up the client's understanding of what therapy is aiming to achieve. Another rationale-giving story uses a common experience that will be known to many: greeting someone on the street who apparently 'blanks' them. Many people, when asked their thoughts on this scenario, report thinking either 'He doesn't like me' (sad external appraisal) or 'What a bastard' (angry external appraisal), or 'I must have done something wrong' (internal appraisal). If we encounter this situation when feeling confident, we might stop the person and ask, 'Didn't you see me?', and might then get some information about what happened. More likely, though, we will review the situation and perhaps reflect, 'Have I done anything that might have offended him? I can't think of anything. Perhaps he was just distracted.' We are essentially 'reviewing the evidence' – a normal everyday cognitive activity. If we were feeling low when we were 'blanked', however, we'd probably be more upset and would be much less likely to act assertively. Even later, we may still find it hard to 'review the evidence' and come to a more positive view. It should be acknowledged too that we may never know the absolute truth of the situation but can usually be sure enough to put the experience behind us.

An upsetting but isolated incident is not usually the main cause of mental health problems. Once psychological problems start to develop, however, these incidents may

---

[7]A 'common factor' may be defined as something that is helpful to therapy and occurs across all or most models of practice.

tend to increase and take their toll. Once a tipping point is reached, symptoms may occur in a syndromal way and then kick-start 'vicious cycles' of yet further symptoms.

Breaking into these vicious cycles with therapeutic interventions may well begin with behavioural work. In depression, for example, the effects on concentration may make any kind of higher-order cognitive work too difficult, at least for a while. As we will see in Chapter 5, however, 'activation' – increasing levels of behavioural activity and encouraging more proactive behaviours – can result in steady improvements in mood that in turn make cognitive work and cognitive shifts more possible. Sometimes a behavioural change alone can shift thinking. I might, for example, hold the negative and depressing belief 'I can't make myself heard at work', but if I do find a way of making myself heard and see for myself that I have done so, my belief systems, faced with dissonant cognitive information, may shift to take in this new information.

Cognitive change takes place at different levels. Negative automatic thoughts (NATs) are everyday processing events which may be modified by techniques such as 'reviewing the evidence' and thought records (see Chapter 4). These techniques essentially help the mind to process information as it does when functioning well. Sometimes evidence is written down in a client notebook or on a whiteboard, and this helps clients to be more aware of their thinking processes. Having completed this task in the session, the client might be encouraged to keep it up as a homework task.

Getting clients to write down things for themselves supports their responsibility for, and control of, change. It can be easy for a persuasive practitioner to think up good challenges to NATs. The change that comes from practitioner challenges, however, may be short-lived and may not get the client into the habit of being her or his own therapist. This emphasis on getting the client to do work may be one of the reasons why CBT therapists report fewer problems with client dependency than other types of therapy. Recent approaches to CBT have stressed the fact that traditional cognitive restructuring can be overdone, and clients may at times be better encouraged to 'defuse' negative thinking by regarding it more mindfully.

As well as working on NATs, CBT practitioners are likely to build up experiences of working with deeper levels of cognition in the forms of assumptions, rules of living, core beliefs and schemas. These interventions are typically more complex and long-term and involve using more interpersonal, emotionally and mindfulness-based, and relationship-based, factors (see also Chapters 3, 6, 7).

It can be seen that CBT uses a variety of techniques to change thinking, mood and behaviour. The book concludes by discussing both how to integrate all these skills into an overall model and how to establish a process of on-going skills development.

CONCLUSION

CBT is a skill-oriented form of practice that combines general therapy skills with CBT-specific skills.[8] CBT-specific skills are located within a set of principles governing how to understand client problems and how to help in the collaborative planning with clients on the way to jointly implement interventions to ameliorate such problems.

---

[8]Further references on the mix of general and specific skills are given in Chapter 8.

The principles are adaptable but serve as navigational devices to keep the CBT ship on course and to steer clear of the shallow waters of banality and the stormy waters of chaotic therapy.

Follow-up suggestion Looking back at the principles in Figure 1.1, which of them are you in ready agreement with? Are there principles that are more difficult to accept? If you had to 'sign up' or 'take the oath' for this set of principles and could amend one or two, which ones would they be and how would you amend them?

PRACTICE TIP: TITRATING CBT STRUCTURE

Learning to use therapy structure in a way that is comfortable to each individual client is very much one of the main skills of the art of CBT. We probably begin with the assumption that the therapy will be quite structured while at the same time retaining an exquisite sensitivity (Beck et al., 1979: 65) to individual client needs in this and other areas. Beck et al. (1979) refer to 'titrating' the degree of structure. Structure, for example, is often helpful to depressed clients because it helps them concentrate and remember. Many clients come from other therapists complaining of being subjected to over-long silences, during which they felt worse. Interestingly, they have often interpreted these silences as meaning that the therapist did not care about their problems. While I am sure that they were mostly wrong in this assertion, it does remind us of the cardinal cognitive principle that people will understand what is happening to them in terms of their current thoughts and feelings. As in the previous tip, words are very important here too. Many therapists working in other models seem to think that it is very bad for the therapist to be 'directive', but what about a therapy that 'lacks direction' or a therapist who is not able to communicate 'directly'? All these words and phrases are related to each other. Therapists should be aware of the client's language and meaning: they may frequently find that they are not derived from reading therapy books.

FURTHER READING

Rachman, S. (1997) The evolution of cognitive behaviour therapy. In D.M. Clark & C.G. Fairburn (Eds.), *Science and practice of cognitive behaviour therapy* (pp. 3–26). Oxford: Oxford Medical Publications.

Wills, F., with Sanders, D. (2013) *Cognitive behaviour therapy: foundations for practice*. London: Sage. (Especially Chapter 1)

2

SKILLS FOR ASSESSING, FORMULATING AND STARTING CBT

In displaying the psychology of our characters, minute particulars are essential, God save us from vague generalisations. (Anton Chekov in a letter of 1886)

As human beings tend to do, client and practitioner are getting a sense of each other from the first moments of contact. Can I trust this other person? Can I help here? In a sense, therapeutic 'assessment' is only a formalisation of these natural appraisal processes but it is vital because it will lead to our initial formulation and that in turn will act as a route map for our efforts to help.

This chapter will begin by describing some ways of using the initial appraisal exchanges to maximum advantage, followed by some thoughts about how well CBT might suit different types of client. It will then concentrate on the essential features of assessment, first on the skills of gathering the detail of *current functioning*. The chapter will then describe some of the skills needed to develop a satisfactory formulation of the client's problems, especially focusing on the client's *developmental history*. Finally, it will describe ways to structure sessions and to help clients to implement plans to facilitate change in the problems jointly identified in assessment and formulation.

FIRST CONTACTS WITH CLIENTS

First contacts with clients are influenced by the context in which work occurs. Where a service is located in a large organisation, the initial session may be the first time that clients speak to the people who will help them. In independent practice, therapists may handle initial inquiries via telephone or email and arrange appointment times. These are important moments that may set the tone of further contact. It sometimes seems as if it just gets harder to get quality time from providers of modern services. Email can allow clients to start contact in a low-risk way but there are also downsides to technological advances: for example, websites can sometimes serve to insulate providers from service users and give access to services in the ways most convenient to the website designer. People wishing to refer themselves are often nervous and unsure, and usually put high value on responses that are friendly, relaxed and open. Helpers should also note the questions people ask and the way they ask them: in them we may be getting glimpses into clients' ways of seeing the world. Sometimes understanding emerges from difficulties in making contact. One client left a message for a voluntary counsellor to call him back but then always seemed to be at work, even late into the evening. This felt significant and indeed emerged as being so: the client was going through a stressful period at work and faced the possibility of redundancy. He was working long hours to keep on the right side of his bosses but was thereby pushing himself inexorably towards stress-related illness. The initial contact call may also prove to be a moment when hopefulness, sometimes referred to as 're-moralisation', begins. Clients will often ask directly, 'Do you think you can help me with my problem?' They are probably appraising whether help is likely to be worth the expenditure of effort and resources that may be required. They have every right to ask about this: How long might the process take? What are the approximate costs in time and/or money of seeking help? Even at this stage, practitioners equally have a duty to ensure that CBT is a reasonable investment for clients. Discussing how CBT may work for different clients may even include ruling out a 'poor bet' situation. Practitioners can follow this discussion with clients by sending them information sheets and leaflets. Sometimes, however, it may be in clients' best interests to redirect them to another service or practitioner.

The suitability of CBT for different clients

In the first edition of this book, I followed the orthodox approach of asking which clients were suitable for CBT. Generally I reached the conclusion that there was only limited benefit in using most available criteria in the so-called 'inclusion' and 'exclusion' of clients because it is hard to know how a person may react to help until it is under way. Then one can see how clients *actually* respond to the therapy. Criteria for 'inclusion' and 'exclusion' in many therapy books are those used in university or research settings so that the approach described is the one frequently and correctly used in research trials. This may not be so appropriate for everyday practice. Concepts of inclusion and exclusion seem also to assume that CBT is an invariant product that does not change much between different practitioners. I prefer to think of CBT as a set of concepts and methods that may be adapted to diverse settings.

When I look at the criteria for clients who do best in psychotherapy, I sometimes think that you have to be in good shape to do well in therapy. How helpful, for example, is it to know that the clients most suitable for CBT should have good access to their thoughts? First, it would probably improve prospects for any type of help. Second, if we make the judgement that a client cannot access their thoughts easily, what do we do then? Suggest some other form of psychological therapy or medication? Is it not possible to help clients to recognise their automatic thoughts? Indeed capacity to access thoughts is probably not an *either/or* ability but is more likely arranged on a continuum from good to poor access. In the absence of any research findings on this matter perhaps the most we can draw from such considerations is that we should know when CBT might be a longer-term venture. It is interesting that writers developing time-limited dynamic therapy have reached similar conclusions (Levenson, 1995).

Making critical use of diagnostic guides

We need to acknowledge that psychiatry has influenced the use of language and conceptual thinking in CBT. Probably because much of the developmental work for CBT was completed within the psychiatric sector, CB therapists do tend to make some critical use of guides such as the *Diagnostic and statistical manual* (*DSM*) of the American Psychiatric Association classification. They work slightly differently with panic disorder than they would with panic disorder *with* agoraphobia, for example (Hackmann, 1998). Some CBT practitioners *are* diagnosticians, though probably most are not. Some therapists have understandable reservations about 'labelling' clients, and we certainly should never mistake a diagnosis for the whole person. We do however owe it to clients to 'know our stuff' about these patterns of symptoms inside out – I have encountered many clients with obvious problems that their previous helpers had completely missed. Using the *DSM* is not exactly 'rocket science' and it is possible to make critical use of the criteria as guidance to the sorts of symptoms clients might be experiencing, without forcing 'labels' on clients. The use of these criteria is, in any case, rarely as clean-cut as is sometimes implied; clients often seem to meet the criteria for several different categories[1] and it can be hard to know which of them marks the best starting point. The trickiest labels are those linked to the controversial term *personality disorder* (PD). This particular area has been so muddied with misunderstanding – especially provoked by the word 'disorder' and the widely but wrongly assumed link with anti-social and criminal behaviour (Wills with Sanders, 2013) – that some therapists miss out on understanding their more helpful aspects: for example, how they can help us to see how certain quite puzzling symptom factors may be connected in something like 'borderline personality'. 'Personality' mainly refers to the fact that patterns of negative functioning are so pervasive and enduring that they suggest influence across the client's whole character – in fact PDs are sometimes called *characterological disorders*. The idea that clients may have pervasive patterns, perhaps dating back to childhood experience, is a familiar concept in the field of psychological help. The *DSM* criteria can guide us in organising our understanding of more complex clients – though we can do so alongside critical observations based on our own judgements.

---

[1]The technical term for this is 'co-morbidity'.

Assessing how clients react to CBT

Thinking about how different clients react to CBT helps us to anticipate certain avoidable problems. We might ask ourselves, and then test for, whether the client will be able to:

◆ accept responsibility for change

◆ undertake out-of-session tasks ('homework')

◆ accept a structured approach

◆ settle into a CBT therapeutic relationship.

Responsibility for change: Hayes, Strohsal and Wilson (2004) suggest that CBT practitioners have tended to take an overly rational approach to client motivation: at times naively believing that because clients feel bad, they will *of course* want to work at feeling better. This ignores a tradition in therapy that recognises that at least some clients may need to go through some complicated twists and turns to get to this point. As Hayes et al. (2004) have pointed out, clients often begin therapy with highly mixed motivations towards change. Psychodynamic therapists may think of Freud's observations about the 'compulsion to repeat' negative patterns. The motivational interviewing perspective suggests that motivation and commitment for change normally rises and falls through several cycles over time. A careful combination of empathy, probing and Socratic questioning has been shown to be an effective way of enhancing motivation and responsibility taking (Miller & Rollnick, 2002). Questions to facilitate 'I statements' may help here: especially when clients show the tendency to externalise their feelings by continually blaming others. Clients can get fixated on what others are *doing to them*. When this comes up it can be helpful to ask a 'you question', such as 'So when he/she does that, what do *you* do?', that encourages an 'I statement' response from the client – 'I get so mad I just storm out.' Focus is thereby brought back to the client in a way that can empower a more proactive response if this one is not working too well. 'Storming out does not seem to get you what you really want – that is, to be heard. Might it be helpful to work on how you can get to be heard?'

Approach to homework and structure: The way clients might take to CBT can also be appraised by suggesting that CBT will be more likely to help them if they can do homework on a reasonably regular basis. While writing this book I had the fascinating experience of finding a forgotten notebook that I kept as a client 20 years ago. I now keep a small supply of notebooks to give to clients as 'therapy notebooks' to use for making notes on sessions and for doing homework exercises in. There is something nice about this giving gesture and I have noticed that it seems to make clients more inclined to do tasks between sessions. At the same time, therapists also need to be aware that the ability of clients to do things like homework may be adversely influenced by the stress of lives affected by illness, poverty or any number of other pressures. The harder the completion of a homework task is, however, the more rewarding it can be. The degree of preparation needed for clients to engage in CBT may also be ascertained by observing how a client reacts to a story that presents a conceptual rationale for CBT and by initial reactions to its structure. Some clients are resistant to structuring because it carries some meaning of being controlled: practitioners should show the ability to vary structure and the therapeutic relationship accordingly. Therapists should respond flexibly to these different client needs, aiming to make CBT as accessible as possible to each individual client.

These concerns also relate to the nature of the *therapeutic relationship* and this will be discussed in detail in the next chapter.

Matching CBT to different clients

Figure 2.1 contains questions that practitioners can ask themselves three or four contacts into CBT to assess how suitable CBT is proving for the client. If some answers are negative, we need to think how we can amend the style of therapy to sort them out.

> 1. Does the client seem more or less hopeful now?
>
> 2. Is there collaboration?
>
> 3. Are clear and realistic goals emerging?
>
> 4. What is the balance of work and responsibility between client and therapist?

Figure 2.1 Questions to assess how therapy is going three to four sessions in

> **Suggestion** Think of a recent client and apply the questions in Figure 2.1 to your work with him or her so far. Do any of your answers point towards any technical or relationship problems in the therapy so far? If so, how can the work and/or relationship be amended in order to try to ameliorate them? If you are still waiting to start with clients you can think of how you might react to what you have read so far if you were a client.

Getting the detail: assessment of current functioning

Getting detail – 'the complex of tiny occurrences' of our opening quotation – about the client's current functioning is important because we need to know which areas of functioning are likely to prove the most fruitful for therapeutic work. Detailed information is also important because initial improvement might be slight and can be easily overlooked. To some extent, this part of assessment involves having the right kind of information-gathering format and then going straight ahead and using it. The format presented in Figure 2.2 is one devised by Diana Sanders and me, from various sources, and tried and tested over a number of years.

1. Current problem:
What is the problem? Give a recent, detailed example, collecting information on:
Triggers to problem (external or internal)
Thoughts/ Feelings/ Physical factors/Behaviours
Environment – family/ social/ work

2. What keeps the problem going now?
What makes things better? What makes it worse?
Safety behaviours and unhelpful coping strategies: Avoidance/ Checking of symptoms or danger
Seeking reassurance from others/ Rituals/ Suppressing thoughts or feelings
Worrying away at the problem continuously/ Hopeless and lack of belief in change
Other people's negative behaviour/ Lack of social support or/ Too much support and dependency
Continuing life events and stresses

3. How did the problem develop?
History of the problem: What started in the first place/ What was going on in the person's life at the time?
Is it lifelong or recurring?/ Main life events and stresses/ Key themes in the individual's or family's life
Ideas about underlying assumptions and rules

4. Developmental history:
Early life history/ Family and relationships/ Themes within the family
Significant life events/ Medical and psychiatric history
Occupational and educational background
Previous experience of therapy

5. General health issues:
Medication/ Prescribed or non-prescription drugs/ Alcohol, smoking
History of dependency

6. Expectations of therapy and goals:
Hopes for and fears about therapy
Problem list/ Identify main goals for therapy

Figure 2.2 Assessment information, to be adapted to client need (adapted from Wills with Sanders, 2013)

Such a list can look daunting and may also raise the image of CBT practitioners with clipboards doggedly ticking boxes regardless of the time and pain endured by the client! We have all known assessments conducted in this way. One client described such an experience as 'death by clipboard'. It seems a world away from what I have called 'interpersonally sensitive' therapy. If we drew a continuum between the inter-personally sensitive and the clipboard modes, we can profitably aim for a position near the mid-point of the continuum during the assessment phase but can then move towards the interpersonal as the actual therapy phase proceeds. A nice interpersonal and collaborative tone can be set by asking clients to write their own referral letter.

This is interesting and can save session time. Therapists may also decide to keep a list like that in Figure 2.2 in front of them and make selective reference to it. Some practitioners are now under pressure to use particular formats and forms – these sometimes make sense to clinical management but may take up time on things that may not be of much interest to client or practitioner. We all have to 'toe the party line' at times but if practitioners think that heavy-handed styles of assessment interfere with the interpersonal sensitivity then they owe it to themselves and their clients to at least argue against them in team meetings.

Another argument against the clipboard approach is that we tend to assess and formulate from the word go. The more experienced we are, the more accurate and therapeutically useable our initial impressions are likely to be. We tend to form hypotheses about the client's problems quite early and refine them on a continuous basis – indeed often we only truly understand the problem when we try to change it (Binder, 2004). Therapists can avoid entanglement in 'clipboard mode' by regarding lists of assessment items such as that shown in Figure 2.2 as a checklist to consult *after* assessment – noting what ground *has been* covered and what else *still needs* attention. We need of course to stay open to the fact that initial hunches may prove wrong or incomplete – so all assessments should be provisional. This is especially true in the CBT model, whose theoretical ideas require us to keep modifying constructs as new information comes in. One reason why we sometimes hang on to using tick boxes is that we may not trust ourselves to remember what to cover. A major function of assessment at any stage, however, is to remind us of what we don't *yet* know, as well as to formulate what we do know. It is only rarely that omissions cannot be retrieved at subsequent meetings.

Suggestion Think of a current difficulty you have, and without rehearsing it at all, talk about it for 5 to 10 minutes. If you are working with another person, she/he should note down what you have said. Alternatively you could speak into audio recorder and then make brief notes. As you go over these notes, try to slot them into the various categories in Figure 2.2. Check which headings have information and which do not. You can then repeat the exercise over several cycles. You may find that you automatically turn to areas neglected before. If so, what might be happening is a developing and iterative (repetition and deepening) process as the unstructured 'conversation' interacts with the structured format.

It is usually good to start with assessment items that make the least demands on memory. This helps to 'warm up' the client's memory. We have stressed the ubiquity of the 'vicious cycle' concept in CBT, and the client is helped to be more reflective by 'working back from today': sifting through recent experience and searching for occasions when negative functioning was triggered. Here a young, stressed client is presenting concerns to a voluntary sector counsellor for a young peoples' agency about feeling depressed but has indicated that things at work are 'okay':

Practitioner (P1): Okay, so what sort of day are you having today so far?

Client (C1): Oh today – not too bad. But I'm on leave at present so I've been feeling a bit more relaxed. I mooched round the shops this morning actually.

P2: Right, so although your problem is not directly about work, when you are at work you are more likely to feel down.

C2: Yeah, I quite like my job actually but it is stressful and then that can come on top of all my worries about other stuff.

P3: How was the weekend?

C3: Funnily enough – good: I guess because I knew I'd be on leave this week.

P4: Funnily enough?

C4: Yeah, because weekends are usually the worst times because I am by myself. I can't decide out what to do and I dread being on my own.

P5: Right. So how was the weekend before that one?

C5: That was bad. I had a crap email from Louise on the Saturday morning and then I wasn't picked for 5-a-side in the afternoon. I was a wreck by the evening and didn't sleep well.

P6: Okay, they sound like good examples to put under our microscope. Let's go over what you were thinking and feeling firstly about Louise and then about 5-a-side. (*C*: Okay) Things like this come up regularly in life so it would be good to work on handling them better.

P2 links the client's present mood to his problems and then the practitioner follows the 'working back from today' strategy with P3. P4 and P5 pick up on some new client material and P6 weaves the gathered material into an agenda item.

Making a current example really work

It can be helpful to use the analogy of a 'chain reaction' when trying to trace out client reactions to troublesome triggers. This is because chain reactions work by one manoeuvre touching off several more and these cascade out yet more. Our brains often seem to work in this way so that it can be hard to get hold of these reactions because they are so fast and so complex. This can make us feel as though we are out of control of events, adding yet more negativity to our reactions. The first thing that practitioners may do is to help clients to view the reaction in slow motion. Slowing down and reflecting on what happened helps clients to establish a better relationship with the pattern of their reactions. Working on these vicious cycles may, however, misfire if they are not discussed in an emotionally engaged way. If CBT does not engage clients' emotions, the results of cognitive work can be mere 'logic chopping' and will not usually inspire change. Both emotional *and* cognitive change are necessary, but by themselves they will only partially facilitate therapeutic processing of problematic material such as, for example, the 'fear network' (Rothbaum & Mellman, 2001). Using communication based on present-tense and personalised language to 'describe the triggering event as if it were happening now' can enhance emotional engagement in this work and is demonstrated in the following dialogue:

P1: So let's go over what happened when Louise emailed you. I'd like you to try to speak in the present tense, sort of like, 'So I'm in my front room and I notice that an email has come in.' Can you do that?

C1: Yeah, will it help?

P2: It seems to but let's see. So what time is it?

C2: It's late, you know. Louise is in America so her emails come when I'm just going to bed. I told her to pick better times …

P3: Just try to stay with what is happening in the present tense. How are you feeling?

C3: Oh, right … Hot, you know, queasy. Oh … I'm feeling churned up, you know, things between us are fraught. I sometimes feel that she has gone off deliberately to get away from me. And now an email has arrived.

P4: What is going through your mind?

C4: This is it. The email will say it's all over.

P5: And what would that mean?

C5: I have driven her away. I'll never find another one like her.

P6: So now you're reading the email, what does it actually say?

C6: It's not what I feared but it is ambiguous …

The practitioner supports the rationale for the methods laid out in P1 by a 'present-tense' question in P2 and a guiding instruction in P3. The cognitive underpinning of the technique is brought in by the questions asked at P4 and P5. The client's responses at C4 and C5 give his 'felt sense' of what this event meant at the time and in the current moment.

Clients often report that when the story is told in this way, they feel some of the actual emotion that they felt at the time. This usually gives a greater sense of 'felt meaning' to the account and thus gets us closer to the real cognitive-emotional-behavioural whole experience that was triggered in the real situation. The feeling, however, should not be so strong as to overwhelm the client's capacity to process the event. This is similar to guidance for dealing with emotions in post-traumatic stress disorder (PTSD) and suggests that clients benefit from cultivating the ability to modulate emotions. First, it can be helpful to remind clients that they are in control of the process and can ask to come out of it at any time. They can be helped to learn to modulate emotion – one of the skills of 'emotional regulation' described in Chapter 6 – by the practitioner inviting them to rehearse a 'safe place' procedure before engaging in exploring traumatic emotions. Clients are invited to imagine a 'safe place', in some detail, where they would feel secure and then encouraged to imagine that place if they should start to feel overwhelmed during an exercise where traumatic emotions start running. Another method used to intensify emotions to the optimal level for processing meaning is the 'focusing' intervention (Cornell, 2013), described further in Chapter 6.

Discussion of the intensity of feelings reminds us that intensity (how *strong* are the feelings?) is part of establishing a 'baseline' of symptoms that the therapist is aiming to help ameliorate. This should also include the frequency (how *often*) and duration (how *long*) of symptoms – again because variations in all these qualities of symptoms need to be assessed so that changes for better or worse can be measured. CBT practitioners tend to use validated symptom measures such as the Beck Anxiety and Depression Inventories (BAI and BDI) and others to obtain a fuller picture of what is troubling the client (a list of measure sources is included in the Appendix). CB therapists have slightly different ways of using these measures but tend towards regular weekly use, and this allows monitoring and graphing of inventory scores: the visual impact of a pattern of reducing symptoms can raise clients' morale. I often remark to clients that even small changes with ups and downs can engender confidence in the view that the outlook remains promising.

Caveats about measures

Certain cautions need to be observed around measures: they are sometimes biased by the way people seek to describe themselves. For example, some clients so want to 'reward' the therapist by seeming to be cured that they may fool themselves into under-reporting their symptoms. For this and other reasons, inventory scores should not be taken completely at face value and should always be discussed with the client (Wills with Sanders, 2013). Discussion can be opened with remarks such as 'Well, that is what the scores say; what do *you* say?'

Making a formulation: adding in development information

As information builds up, there is a need to order it in useful ways. Therapists are motivated to make a formulation by the need to link up the various aspects of information on the client and give it shape and meaning. This linking and shaping, however, is most effective when it contains the seeds of a psychological explanation of the patterns evident within them. There has sometimes been a tension between psychological approaches that, for example, emphasise the way depressed *clients* may think and feel, and those that put more stress on the way this *individual client* thinks and feels. In making a formulation in CBT one seeks to bridge these two tendencies by developing an individualised explanation based on general principles: the general style comes 'off the peg' but the suit is tailored to the contours of the individual.

In essence, as practitioners formulate they bring together descriptions and explanations of the origins, development and maintenance of the client's problems. They develop answers to the client's questions: 'Why me? Why now? Why doesn't the problem just go away? How can I get better?' An organising map of the contributing factors to formulation is shown in Figure 2.3.

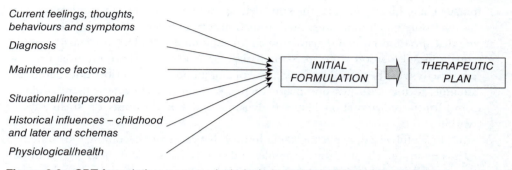

Figure 2.3   CBT formulation: parts and whole (adapted from Wright et al., 2006)

Working on formulation helps therapists in many ways: to understand the client, to make clinical decisions, and to understand why some clients 'press our buttons' (Kuyken, Padesky & Dudley, 2009; Persons, 2008). It helps therapists to feel more empathy for clients, and clients to feel more empathy for themselves. What helps therapists can usually also help clients in the same areas – giving them more understanding of themselves, of therapy and its glitches.

The following examples discuss two clients for whom somewhat similar and somewhat different factors showed up in assessment; they were then constructed into different individual formulations. Together, the two examples show how general and individual factors interact with each other, and how adding in the more historical elements in clients' material helps to individualise their stories. *Dan* was a young man who had severe social anxiety. Highly informative research on social anxiety has produced detailed descriptions of how people with social anxiety generally think, feel and behave when they are socially anxious (Butler, 2009). The research describes a general cognitive theme centred on self-conscious fear of negative evaluation by other people. Dan suffered from this in the extreme, especially when those feared other people were in authority. He was so in awe of authority figures that he had to ask a colleague to lurk around when his boss gave him work directions so that his friend could tell Dan the instructions that Dan himself had been too over-awed to take in.

Not long after meeting Dan I met another socially anxious client called *David*. He was also suffering severe social anxiety after taking on a new job so I hazarded that he felt this with his boss. 'Oh no,' he replied, 'with my boss, I know exactly what to say and do. It is in informal situations with my peers that I feel anxious. I literally have no idea what to say. The Christmas party is next week – I am terrified. I'll have to be off sick that day.' This shows perhaps that general theory only takes us so far – in order to get a formulation with a good enough fit to our individual client we have to dig out the individual details of the client's thoughts and feelings. From a developmental perspective, Dan had highly disapproving and voluble parents, feeding a tendency for him to form beliefs such as 'I am useless so high-status people will have no time for me.' David's parents were quiet people, 'laissez-faire' to the point of not ever really giving him even a little help or advice about how to live his life. The experience of this hands-off parenting style may have influenced some of David's core beliefs, such as 'I think I'm quite good but other people do not seem to notice' and 'No one is going to help me so I have to work things out for myself.' Although CB therapists do not pursue client history in quite the same detailed way as psychodynamic therapists, they have become much more interested in such history in recent years. It is interesting to me that the time-limited dynamic psychotherapy model (TLDP) has reached similar conclusions: Levenson (1995, p. 37) remarks that in TLDP 'it is not important to find out exactly what happened at every phase of childhood', and describes how her model attempts to focus on just one major theme. As I remark elsewhere, there could be some fruitful collaboration between dynamic and CB therapists on such ways of working.

One helpful way of exploring client history that can avoid becoming too enmeshed in it is to ask the client to give examples and stories that seem to them to capture the flavour of their childhood experience. Dan told me, for example, about how his father had a school report-day ritual in which it was assumed that his report would be bad. His father had the slipper ready for ritual corporal punishment before he had even read the report. Dan believed himself to be a 'bad person'. David told me of several occasions when he had difficult choices to make at school and had asked his parents for advice only to be, as he described it, 'fobbed off with dusty answers'. Further discussion of these and other methods to elicit core beliefs follows in Chapter 7.

Later on, Dan revealed what turned out to be an obsessional side to his anxiety when he turned up later and later for appointments, finally not coming at all. I was trying to work out whether to accept this as 'voting with his feet' or whether to pursue him by writing a letter. I looked at his formulation and was struck by the core belief that 'No one has time for me.' Actively writing to him seemed more likely to disconfirm that belief because writing showed that I was not indifferent to him. Letting his disappearance go may have risked conveying that I didn't really care if he came to therapy or not. Had his core belief been 'People do not trust me to decide for myself', I would have chosen otherwise. He responded well to my letter and came back to complete therapy and eventually told me that his lateness was caused, paradoxically, by being early. The sessions were at my home so that when he came obsessionally early, he couldn't come in. He then would go off to look at some shops, forget the time and suddenly come charging over for his therapy late and in the end so late that he dared not show his face. This was a highly idiosyncratic pattern and I do not think many therapists would have guessed it just on the basis of what had happened before.

If we laid Dan and David's formulations alongside each other, we would be likely to see striking similarities in the way they reacted to problematic situations and yet striking differences in the underlying beliefs arising from their histories and then of course a highly individual reaction of unknown origin.

The most comprehensive formulations have historical dimensions; a common shortened format is shown in Figure 2.4, followed by a shortened version of Dan's formulation in Figure 2. 5. There are, however, a variety of formats for formulation – including simpler and less diagrammatic ones (Wills with Sanders, 2013). Simpler formats can be

EARLY EXPERIENCE:
'Dan came from a poor family that lived in an isolated rural location. His father was a "strange tormented man". He subjected Dan to ritual beatings and then burst into tears. Dan's father felt that he himself had not achieved but was determined that Dan should be 'something in life'. Dan felt he was a constant disappointment to his father. His mother was depressed. She seemed to regret not being able to protect Dan from the father's harsh treatment. Dan also found teachers to be remote and aloof and not inter ested to protect him from the regular bullying he received from other pupils.'

CORE BELIEFS/SCHEMAS:
I am useless
I seem to get things wrong
People will criticise me if they can
No one would be bothered enough to help me
The world is a strange (unreliable) place

ASSUMPTIONS:
If I keep my head down, I may get through unnoticed
I don't know how to find someone to love or care for me

TRIGGERS:
Authority figures/boss
Public situations where I could be seen as making a mistake

NEGATIVE THOUGHTS:
I will be humiliated
This guy wants to make me look stupid
Everyone will laugh at me

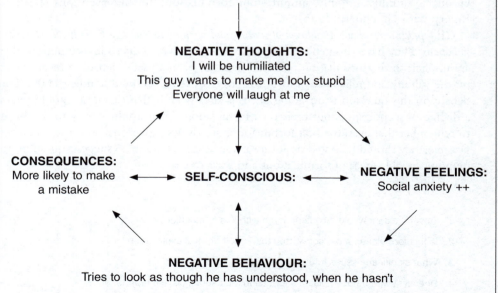

CONSEQUENCES:
More likely to make a mistake

SELF-CONSCIOUS:

NEGATIVE FEELINGS:
Social anxiety ++

NEGATIVE BEHAVIOUR:
Tries to look as though he has understood, when he hasn't

Figure 2.4 Longitudinal formulation map: Dan

more useful because the key psychological mechanisms are the most important things to clarify. Practitioners are therefore free to use whatever works best for them and their clients (see the companion website materials accompanying this book at: https://study. sagepub.com/wills).

Dan's father pushed him to achieve and sometimes reacted very badly when Dan seemed not to do well. Dan's mother was dominated by the father and suffered from depression. She could not offer Dan much help or support. These experiences have resulted in Dan having a profound lack of self-confidence. This now shows itself in public situations where Dan is expected to 'perform'. He gets the uneasy feeling that people will criticise or undermine him and this makes him unable to perform at his best. This feeling seems to have increased over the years so that now he often feels like giving up before he even starts.

Figure 2.5 Brief written formulation: Dan

General theory offers practitioners good starting points for teasing out key cognitive content when they make formulations. As we will see in more detail in Chapter 4, recent research for problems such as worry and intrusive thoughts points towards *thinking processes* (especially how we pay attention to events in our environments), rather than *thought content*, as being the most relevant foci (Harvey, Watkins, Mansell & Shafran, 2004; Wells, 2009). Socio-cultural factors may have been neglected in previous theory, and new work is proceeding on how to include them (Hays & Iwamasa, 2006; Levinson, 2010). There is perhaps a tension between having fully inclusive formulation models that may become rather bloated, and Beck's exhortation to 'simplify, simplify, simplify' our formulations and interventions (Beck & Emery with Greenberg, 1985).

CBT practitioners have a tradition of sharing and working collaboratively with clients on formulations. They have also generally been keen to review and question assumptions that are implicit to the formulation process. There has been a useful debate in recent years on the validity and reliability of formulations (Kuyken, Padesky & Dudley, 2009). The debate on this question is on-going but it is already clear that therapists should retain a degree of scepticism about their own formulations. The healthiest way to do this is to remember that even the best formulations are always provisional and that, wherever possible, they should be tested or at least made testable. Figure 2.6 suggests questions to pinpoint testable areas of formulations and ways to test them.

1. To what extent would the client agree with this formulation?

2. Is this formulation more convincing than another, rival explanation?

3. What significant issues in the situation does it not explain?

4. Does it fit with other available information: measures, clinical reports, etc.?

Figure 2.6 Questions to test a formulation (adapted from Kuyken, 2006)

Suggestion *Group discussion exercise*: earlier in the chapter we discussed two clients – Dan and David – with both similarities and differences on items that would be put into their formulations. Using the diagrammatic form shown in Figure 2.4, lay out formulations for Dan and David alongside each other and clarify what is the same and what is different. Then read the brief written formulation for Dan given in Figure 2.5 and construct a similar written formulation for David.

Other formulations are available on this book's companion website. With those and the above exercise in mind, what style of making a formulation do you think would be most useful to you?

Beginning CBT: from assessment and formulation to structuring the therapy

Wills (2006b) found that trainees' attitude towards using structure in therapy is one of the key determinants of how well they adapt to learning CBT. It is helpful to distinguish two key aspects to therapy structure. 'Surface structure' is the structure an observer may see by watching what steps the therapist takes: she may for example begin by asking a client to fill out a BDI, ask for a brief account of his week and then set an agenda, for example. Certain approaches to helping clients are quite hostile to such structuring and this can work against people trained in these traditions achieving clarity and efficiency in the way they practise CBT. This can delay the achievement of assessed competence in CBT.

There is, however, also 'deep structure' that may not be so obviously present in practice but is arguably more relevant to skilled practice. This kind of structure is not so visible because it operates in the processes of practitioners' minds whereby they identify the nature of the client's problem and the likely ways of helping with that problem. Earlier in this chapter I tried to indicate some 'structuring thoughts' in the practitioner's mind as he followed the steps of 'working back from today' (p. 23) and 'stimulating an emotionally grounded account' (p. 24). This kind of 'structure' guides practitioners' therapeutic behaviours rather than dictating them. Padesky (2004) tells

1. Brief update and mood check
(including use of measures)
2. Bridge from previous session
3. Collaborative setting of agenda
4. Review of homework
5. Main agenda items and periodic summaries
6. Setting new homework
7. Summary and feedback

Figure 2.7 CBT session structure – post-assessment session onwards

she saw Aaron Beck doing CBT: she initially thought that his work
.re and wandered aimlessly. It was only later when she studied a tran-
.e interview in more depth that she realised the 'deep structure' that Beck
.. following. His laidback manner had distracted her from seeing this.
.p structure is only learnt through training and continuing professional develop-
.. (CPD). At this point we deal with the overt structure. A session structure has
been described for the CBT session and is shown in Figure 2.7.

The structure shown in Figure 2.7 is for sessions following the assessment session.
The assessment session itself has the additional items of identifying problems, setting
goals and socialising the client into the CBT model. Practitioners give helpful educational information on typical client problems and discuss clients' expectations of how
CBT might help with those problems. Some socially anxious clients for example
become depressed through the sheer fatigue that comes from constantly having to
manage oneself in social situations. Understanding that many of the things that worry
them are slightly exaggerated but quite common social reactions, and that this causes
tiredness and deep sadness, can be empowering for them, especially when twinned
with the idea that healthier social strategies can be successfully learnt.

It is important to note that not all practitioners will use CBT in the formal steps
shown in Figure 2.7. Nonetheless, it may be worth practising and mastering a sequence
like this until it becomes second nature. Having got on top of this you can then try different ways of applying it and so find a way that is comfortable for you. Trainees should
not be surprised that this can feel awkward at first, but be reassured that it usually
becomes second nature relatively quickly. Such a structure can help practitioners organise
the conduct of the session and may also give a sense of reassuring familiarity to clients.

Update and mood check

This section is best kept quite brief. It is useful to remember that clients may have been
thinking about what they are going to say for some time before they arrive. Sometimes
the therapist might be greeted by a long account of recent stresses or a painfully detailed
story. At the other end of the continuum, especially when they are starting to improve,
people sometimes say, 'I don't really know what I am going to talk about today.'
Sometimes clients will have experienced other types of help based on getting things off
their chest so may even think that they are required to do just that. If clients keep
'offloading' in this way, it may eventually be rather disruptive of other therapeutic tasks.
It is important in this situation to be mindful of the fact that the practitioner may be the
only person who is actually really listening to the client. Practitioners may however need
to use immediate but tactfully put statements such as 'I feel like we may be wandering
off track here, what do you think?' to help to re-establish structure. This is not about
preventing clients from expressing themselves but about helping them to use CBT well
and keep on the track of problem solving – though working with the fact that they
communicate in this way may become a therapeutic intervention in more interpersonally focused work; this is described in the context of CBT in the next chapter.
Practitioners must be sensitive and able to negotiate such issues collaboratively with
clients. Clients can be quite robust in taking such feedback – some may have a shrewd

suspicion that they 'dump on people' at times, and may not be really sure what was required of them in the CBT context. Keeping on track is an important part of any therapy and it is probably worth being open to the fact that one will not always get it right. Equally, sometimes when it feels as if one has got it wrong this may look different in the longer term – i.e. what seemed like an irrelevance may later turn out to be a core issue. It is good to keep checking this when one takes client feedback – 'I steered you away from talking about X earlier; how does that seem now?'

Bridge

The practitioner creates a bridge to the previous session by simply asking if the client has anything 'left over' from the previous meeting. This should usually be quite a brief item. Occasionally, however, clients will have been brooding on some point and until that is cleared, it may bubble away below the surface.

Agenda setting

The update, mood check and bridge lead up to setting a relevant agenda. They tease out what may be on the client's mind and give therapist and client the chance to think through which topics would be most helpful to discuss in the session. If possible, agenda items should build on what has already been learnt about target problems in previous sessions. For example, a recent client came in still feeling upset about an incident with her daughter just before she left the house to come to the session. This incident tapped right into previous work on her poor relationship with her own mother, raising the disturbing possibility that she – like she thought of her own mother, was also a 'bad mother'. This incident therefore had high relevance value and went straight to the top of the agenda. If these underlying links had not been evident then it could still have been a valuable agenda item but equally may not have been. Such questions can be decided during agenda setting. It goes without saying, however, that agenda setting should usually be completed relatively early in the session. Practitioners used to less-structured methods may find it hard to keep these early items on track and so may be left setting an agenda when half the session has already gone. Unless some exceptional item has caused this, it clearly doesn't make sense to take so long to complete this step. The skill of agenda setting implies the desirability of using time well and requires an ability to keep to it – within reason. It can help to set rough time boundaries and the priority of specific agenda items. Previous homework is reviewed at this point but discussion of this is combined with the task of setting future homework in the section after next.

Main agenda items: focusing on issues

The overt structuring principle is very evident here and could sound 'controlling' to some readers. We should acknowledge that structure could indeed be experienced in this way. All approaches to helping people have their characteristic problems: being inflexibly over-structured is one of the main problems of CBT. What stops CBT from becoming too controlling is its commitment to collaborate with clients. For example, if you feel a client is straying from an important focus, you can say, 'Mary: before, we were talking about how you find it difficult to work with certain people at work and how that gets you down. I wonder if we may now have strayed a bit into details of the work itself. It may be important to discuss this but it may also be important to try to get back to the previous topic. What do you think?' Padesky (2006) notes that therapists can sometimes feel nervous about saying something like this because they hold 'therapist beliefs' such as 'If I structure clients, they will resent it.' This may be true for some clients, especially those who are ambivalent about being structured, but my experience is that most react well to agenda setting, provided they understand and respect the therapist's motives for doing it. Finally, it is possible to 'wear the structure lightly' as Aaron Beck seems to do. Some trainees have said to me that they are aware that they adopt non-directive values in helping people to counterbalance a tendency towards over-direction in their work. This may also work in the reverse direction: if you have ambivalent attitudes about structure, then structure may be the very way for you to go.

Homework and feedback

Other principles of CBT are also evident in the session structure, especially the importance of feedback and its link with collaboration and using homework. It is good to ask about what clients have found helpful in sessions and if anything was awkward or unhelpful. Practitioners are probably just as prone to the problem of approval seeking as most people but getting genuine feedback is not about that. We can, of course, enjoy positive client reports but we also need to know about what is not working for them if we are to keep therapy collaborative and on track. I tend to seek feedback *during* sessions because it can help one sense the client's reaction to interventions. One client recently said to me, 'You are being a b----r, Frank.' He said this in a nice gentle way and we had a bit of a laugh about it but when I reflected on it, I had been pushing him just a bit too hard on one issue.[2] Ways of agreeing home-work tasks will be discussed again in later chapters covering methods but the structural principle to emphasise is that if clients go to the trouble of doing homework, it must be discussed, otherwise they may become demotivated. Given how busy many people are these days, practitioners may feel mildly surprised when clients do homework, but careful attention needs to be paid to working out realistic and do-able tasks with clients. It is obviously important that they both understand why homework helps and feel they can negotiate tasks that are meaningful to them, making it more likely that such tasks will be completed. Like many aspects of CBT structure, most clients adjust to doing homework well. When asked about structure they often report that they enjoy the sense of knowing how things will run in their sessions. We can also guard against becoming too predictable, and instead allow sessions to 'freewheel' at times.

---

[2]See later discussion of the concept of the 'zone of proximal development' (ZPD), pp. 61–2 onwards.

Suggestion How do *you* feel about implementing CBT structure? If you have reservations, you wouldn't be the first. This may be a bullet you have to bite though – and most trainees find that with a little persistence, what first seems 'strange' becomes second nature eventually. Look down the structuring skills and pick one to practise now. You should also include a 'rationale' in your own words: e.g. 'Charlie, I suggest that we set an agenda for our session today and maybe for every session: I'll ask what you want to cover today and sometimes make suggestions too. We do this because CBT is short-term and we try to use the time well and cover all the concerns you might have. Does that make sense? Any questions about it?'

Using deep structure in CBT

Using deep structure is a more strategic activity and involves developing ways of therapeutic thinking that constantly direct your attention towards three questions:

◆ Why did this problem start?

◆ What keeps it going?

◆ What will bring it to an end?

As CBT practitioners listen to clients, they may well find themselves thinking about these questions and the different ways of addressing them. For example, a client may berate herself as being 'useless' and the therapist may look for things she does that she may be able to recognise as 'useful'. CBT theory, and all its levels of thoughts, beliefs and schemas, is wonderfully helpful in suggesting possible areas for alternative ways of understanding things and of having new experiences. The idea that self-consciousness incubates social anxiety helps us to realise that anxious feelings experienced by clients are likely to result from paying too much attention to internal feelings and not enough attention to external reality (Wells, 2009). When they can have the new experience that relief can come from focusing outside themselves, they can also feel the benefit of another aspect of therapeutic change – a new understanding of themselves and of others. Knowledge of the growing CBT research literature also helps practitioners by giving them accurate estimates of what the characteristic thinking patterns are for people with various types of problem (see the chapter on anxiety disorders in Wells, 2006). Practitioners can glean knowledge from all these sources to understand clients and to build up a 'CBT sixth sense' to inform both clinical judgement and intuition. There may be an element that is creative and slightly 'left field' about the ability to sense alternative, more accurate and positive ways of thinking that may help the client. It is difficult to describe this skill in words and within an entirely logical framework. Mixing theory and intuition, however, can guide and direct cognitive and behavioural interventions.

CONCLUSION

This chapter has covered much terrain as we have moved from collecting glimpses of clients' mindsets in the first interactions with them, through to a more detailed information-seeking format to establish the level of their current problems. This kind of detail, together with more historical material, is built into a formulation map, driven by identifiable and testable psychological mechanisms. A collaborative therapeutic relationship is established and maintained during these exchanges. This relationship is then used to establish goals for therapy and use structured methods to attain progress with achieving those goals. CBT principles inform each step of the journey, though there is much to be said for using the principles and the structure with a light touch. The following chapters will provide more detailed description of the CBT skills needed for using technical interventions on the subsequent steps of the journey.

FURTHER READING AND RESOURCES

Grant, A. et al. (2008) *Assessment and case formulation in CBT*. London: Sage.

Kuyken, W., Padesky, C., & Dudley, R. (2009) *Collaborative case conceptualisation*. New York: Guilford.

Westbrook, D. et al. (2007) *Introduction to cognitive behaviour therapy: skills and applications*. London: Sage.

A useful resource on assessing the ability to make a collaborative formulation has been devised by Christine Padesky, Willem Kuyken and Robert Dudley: the Collaborative Case Conceptualization Measure Rating Scale (CCCRS) and Manual are available as a free download at: http://padesky.com/pdf_padesky/CCCRS_Coding_Manual_v5_web.pdf

---

3

SKILLS FOR
DEVELOPING THE
RELATIONSHIP IN CBT

At first sight, his address is certainly not striking; and his person can hardly be called handsome, till the expression of his eyes, which are uncommonly good, and the general sweetness of his countenance, is perceived. (Jane Austen, *Sense and Sensibility*)

INTRODUCTION

If we want really to understand formal organisational structures we often have to trace the influence of informal systems that are hidden below their surface. Similarly we cannot really understand therapy without realising that beneath the surface of the formal exchanges in its dialogue lie unspoken exchanges in the relation between practitioner and client. For example, a client may seem to agree to the therapist's intervention while secretly thinking that he will never go along with it. As we have seen in Chapter 1, the therapeutic relationship in CBT is based on collaboration, but we can sometimes be aware of a distinctly non-collaborative vein not far below the surface.

This chapter advances the idea that there is a flow of relationship exchanges that may be barely visible but which runs alongside formal therapy. It is helpful for therapists to understand this, to know how they can guard against confusions that may arise from it and finally to know how it can actually be used for therapeutic advantage. There is a good reason for paying attention to 'ruptures of the therapeutic relationship': when practitioners respond sensitively, therapeutic outcome improves; when they respond poorly, outcome suffers (Katzow & Safran, 2007).

Readers familiar with the history of psychological therapy will recognise echoes of the psychodynamic concept of *transference* in this discussion. Transference can sometimes sound like a rather complicated idea but we can find in it a wider and simpler meaning: *People sometimes misread one situation by reacting to it as if it were more similar to another situation than it actually is.* A person who had an authoritarian father for example may react to many older men as if they were authoritarian. CBT has not used this way of understanding clients as much as other models of therapy. The purpose of this chapter, however, is to describe an understanding of these types of relationship exchanges in therapy that can be used within a CBT approach. To describe all the types of interactions that could take place between clients and therapists in CBT would doubtless require several volumes. The aim of this chapter however is to give readers a good feel for what these interactions might look like and what options of response are available to CB practitioners. More technically, the chapter will consider what skills can enhance (a) therapist and client *awareness* of unspoken relationship exchanges relevant to on-going therapy, (b) the *understanding* and discussion of them with clients, and (c) *therapeutic behaviours that facilitate 'working through'* the issues that lie within such exchanges. We begin by exploring what the term 'working through' means in this context.

WORKING THINGS THROUGH

The term 'working through' goes back to Freud (1914/1991) and is a well-used if less well-defined concept. We can take the example of the 'older men' transference above and explore what it might look like to 'work it through' in therapy. When such instances arise outside a therapeutic context they may not be noticed and therefore would rarely be discussed. In therapy, there is more potential for finding 'new space' for reflection. There is a certain 'hot house' effect in therapy that amplifies these moments because a therapist is more likely to notice and 'dwell on' them. It is more likely that the moment can be 'held open' and therefore reflection on what has transpired can begin and proceed without interruption or embarrassment. The art of practitioners here is to put forward their perceptions in a way that allows clients to consider them in reflective mode. Thus there begins a cycle of reaction and counter-reaction and from these exchanges new meaning may emerge. New meaning becomes possible because a hitherto unspoken issue is now being 'worked through' in these cycles and may slowly transform into something new by repetition, elaboration and amplification. Fialkow and Muslin (1987) suggest an analogy with jigsaw pieces – new pieces are found that allow a new picture with new meaning to emerge. A dialogue below presents what this might look like in CBT. The reader should understand that, for reasons of time and space, it is presented in a very truncated form:

Practitioner (P1): Terry, I noticed that when I talked about trying a role-play you reacted rather strongly – sort of like, 'Don't foist that on *me*!'

Client (C1): Well yes, I hate role-plays.

P2: Okay, I can understand that – but I was still surprised by the strength of your reaction.

...

C2: Okay yeah – I *did* react, didn't I? ... Maybe it was the drama connection. My dad thought he was a 'grand old man of the theatre' and it seemed like sometimes that my brother and I were newly trained actors to be 'directed' by his brilliance ...

...

P3: Okay, and I found myself feeling like protesting that you are reacting to someone other than me, but then I too am an older man?

C3:   Oh, I am not sure about that … 'older man'?

          …

P4:   And I remember that your Uncle Jacob really gets to you …

C4:   Jewish families can be very patriarchal, you know, and Uncle Jacob is kind of like Moses himself …

          …

P5:   Okay, is it possible though that sometimes – just for a moment perhaps – I become one of these older men just by virtue of being older rather than by truly sharing the characteristics that you attribute to those particular older men in your family that get to you?

Here we can see that the practitioner showed awareness of a hidden transaction, surfaced it for discussion in P1 and P2, and – using a key skill that we will later define as 'immediacy' about his own emotional reaction in P3, and linking to previous material in P4 – steered the therapeutic dialogue towards working an underlying issue through with his summary at P5.

AWARENESS OF RELATIONSHIP EXCHANGES DURING SESSIONS

There are two main ways of becoming aware of hidden transactions that emerge in therapy: first, by noticing a client's 'dissonant (out of tune) note' and the feelings induced in the therapist by it; and second, by realising that a more obviously disruptive event has occurred, such as a client criticising a therapist or refusing to go along with a therapeutic suggestion (to be discussed later in the chapter) – again alongside the awareness of feelings raised in the therapist by such a 'critical incident'.

PRACTICE TIP: BRON'S 'DISSONANT NOTE'

It was a cold and snowy January day and I laid a fire in my therapy room at home. I liked the idea of greeting my client, Bron, with a warming log fire as she 'came in from the cold'. The wood, however, was a little damp and as I began our session I noticed that the fire was going out. As the session went on I became so distracted by the dying fire that I asked Bron if I could stop to revive it. As I crouched to do so, I heard her say, 'I'm sorry'. A few minutes later, with the fire now ablaze, I acknowledged her apology but asked her why. 'For causing you trouble. If I had not needed therapy, you would not have been on your hands and knees.' This led to an interesting dialogue about both her apology and *my* discomfort at taking my attention from her. Bron commented, 'I seem to have to apologise for being alive sometimes.' The week before, we had sketched out a preliminary formulation and we now consulted it:

(Continued)

> *(Continued)*
>
> Bron's mother had died when Bron was 12 leaving her living with her Aunt Gwen. Gwen was devoutly religious and could be difficult, because she both dutifully gave and yet subtly withheld. Bron was deeply grateful to her but sometimes wondered just how 'kindly' her aunt really was. One day she had overheard two neighbours talking; one had said, in a world-weary way, how sad the situation was but that Gwen had been 'a true Christian' and 'taken Bron in'. Bron understood from this that she was a 'burden', a 'charity case', and felt that she should be forever grateful that she had been 'taken in'.
>
> This history pressed some of my buttons. Brought up near the Anglo-Welsh borders I had known women like Gwen in my social network. In addition, the spluttering fire symbolised one of my patterns: trying to do too much had left me short of time to set the fire properly. This minor incident reflected core relational themes for us both, and 'working it through' led to therapeutic benefit. It did not threaten the relationship as such but catching hold of it deepened therapy. A major incident, as I will describe later, more often seems directly threatening to the progress of therapy and is often associated with greater client and/or therapist distress.

Another kind of discrepancy can arise when a feeling is expressed in an unusual way. One client for example might describe painful experiences with a smile. This can reflect emotional tension but may also indicate some kind of internal rule such as 'grin and bear it'. *The point is that the unusual event must be* understood *in terms of its meaning to that individual client.*

RELATIONAL EXCHANGES IN CBT

Medical models of 'psychopathology' have had a significant influence on the development of therapy, especially perhaps on CBT. In particular they have sometimes promoted the idea that clients come to therapy with 'broken parts' for the therapist to fix. Some recent developments in CBT have suggested that the model can be practised in a more relationship-focused way (Wills with Sanders, 2013) and it is the ambition of this chapter to push that idea yet further.

Let us consider for a moment what both clients and therapists 'bring' to therapy in relational terms. Key elements that the *client 'brings'*, along with personal strengths, challenges, gender, ethnicity and culture, include those of her[1] problems and their crucial links to social and relational contexts. For example, Bron had a partner who worried about her and, as a former teacher, a network of colleagues who 'missed' her. During a previous period of depression, her friends had urged her to contact them for support as early as possible but she had not done so at this time. Bron feared being a 'burden' to her family and friends and sometimes wondered if they would be better off without her. The idea of being a 'burden' showed a bias against the self – a way

---

[1]As we are using the example of Bron here, the client is female and therapist male.

of thinking that is common in depression (Beck, 1976). This way of thinking was deeply embedded in her history and is evident in the core beliefs of her formulation. *The point to emphasise here is that the client's problems have more significance and meaning when seen in the context of how the client relates to her wider world – so that solutions to those problems are also likely to include addressing how she relates to her wider world* (Hayes et al., 2004; Martell, Addis & Jacobson, 2001). *The relationship with the therapist is a key sample of her relationship with that wider world* (Tsai, Kohlenberg, Kanter, Kohlenberg, Follette & Callaghan, 2009).

The *therapist 'brings'*, along with personal strengths and challenges, gender, ethnicity and culture, his experience of working with the type of problem the client brings. I have always felt quite 'at home' when working with depression, linked perhaps with the 'homely' environment I seemed to want to make for Bron. This theme is also in my history. As a boy I spent much time talking – interestingly often before an open fire – with a family member who was troubled by negative feelings from time to time. In particular I learnt the limitations of directive advice and the need for patience in 'being with' the sufferer; I now think of this as my 'very early training in therapy'. Relative comfort with depressed clients should of course not lead to complacency: I have experienced enough 'immovable' depressions to avoid that. Problems have visited my own life from time to time and I carry significant memories of those who helped me and of those who did not. As I sat with Bron all these influences – from complex thoughts about theory and practice to visceral personal emotions – were touching me and influencing my responses to her and her depression. *If the therapy relationship is acting, as suggested above, as a key example of the client's wider world, then it is also pulling specific relational themes from the therapist and his wider world.*

Figure 3.1 presents these factors and the relationships between them, including the fact that the therapeutic relationship will exist within an organisational, social and cultural context. Therapists can use such a diagram as a map of how relationship factors might be playing out with a particular client, and we use it now as a format to structure our exploration of how to clarify and deepen a more relationally and interpersonally sensitive approach to practising CBT.

As we examine the different types of influence implied in Figure 3.1, we can explore relationships between them and the sources of influence implied by them. It is helpful for example to think about influences that exert push and pull. Critical clients can *push* practitioners into rather defensive modes of practice while clients who seek constant reassurance can *push* their helpers to give more advice than those helpers know is likely to be useful. When clients are sad, this may *pull* caring responses from therapists. Client behaviours may exert push and pull by design or unconsciously: they are normal and it is best not to think of them as 'manipulation'. Because they are – or should be – interpersonally skilled, practitioners may well be especially responsive in relationships and so may get 'hooked' into them more quickly. We should therefore not be critical of ourselves but learn to recognise what has happened. Relational responses can become automatic and may exert negative effects – offering too much advice and reassurance can, for example, inhibit clients' motivation to learn to reassure themselves. As we read through the various CBT interventions in upcoming chapters, we will see that it is frequently helpful for clients and practitioners to 'de-centre' (step back) from their automatic reactions because when they do, that offers more prospect of choosing to do

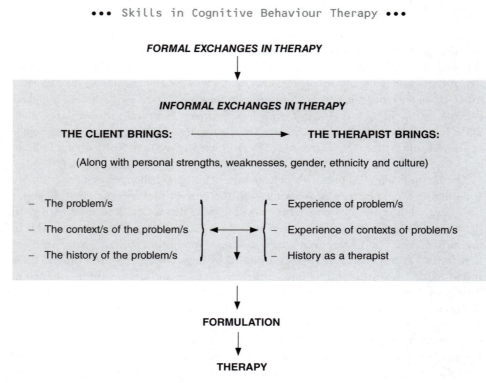

Figure 3.1 Relational elements within the therapeutic relationship

things differently – a key element in change.[2] As we examine the different domains of relationship influences in CBT we will pay particular attention to how *practitioners* can use skills to step back from automatic responses and choose to try different ways of being in the therapeutic relationship. These new ways should focus on facilitating help-ful new experiences for clients.

UNDERSTANDING RELATIONSHIP EXCHANGES IN CBT

The influence of clients' problems in context on the therapeutic relationship

Poor relationships may themselves be a cause of depression but, once established, depression has a profound effect on the relationships that surround the sufferer. This 'double whammy' effect has been well established by psychological researchers. In a recent major review, for example, Teo, Choi and Valenstein (2013, p. 3) assert that 'poor overall quality of relationships with one's partner ... and family members sig-nificantly and independently increased the risk of depression'.

---

[2]For more on helping clients to to step back from their thoughts by 'letting awareness do its work', see Chapter 4, pp. 68–79.

Most people who are close to depressed people probably begin by feeling quite sympathetic towards them. Some depressed people however may be unable to respond in a rewarding way to the help offered by those in their social networks so that even the most dedicated friends may eventually give up – increasing further isolation of the depressed person (Papageorgiou & Wells, 2003).

Anxious clients get short-term relief from being reassured by significant others but, in the longer term, the effect of reassurance quickly weakens so they feel compelled to ask for reassurance repetitively. This becomes wearisome for those closest to them and increases the risk that friends will give up and even start to avoid them.

Some people with a history of abusive relationships may understandably find it hard to trust people in general. This mistrust raises a conundrum for them because having been deprived of genuine love they may crave it badly, yet they can find it hard to trust potential partners and thus may not let them in close enough to give them the love they need. This can lead to an *approach-avoidance* dilemma that sometimes causes clients to move towards a potential lover or confidante only to pull back at the last moment. The oscillation in these behaviours is hard for others to both read and tolerate and so may lead to isolation of the client as those around them give up.

We might consider that if the above patterns are well-established aspects of clients' functioning, clients are likely to bring them to therapy. We should, however, note an important caveat: *while being sensitive to the possibility that client behaviours in therapy may be exhibiting the patterns described above, we should remain tentative and not assume that we know for certain that this **is** the case.* Interpersonally based models of therapy tend to assume that clients will bring samples of problematic patterns into the therapeutic relationship itself – practitioners can be drawn into the same negative reactions as those of significant others. Recognising these problems can, however, allow them to be 'worked through' in the therapeutic relationship. Most therapists have experienced at least some examples of this and yet the *extent* to which clients generalise these life patterns to other contexts, such as therapy, is not completely known. In fact even some psychodynamic therapists estimate that most clients do not present transference material in a useable form (Binder, 2004; Connolly, Crits-Christoph, Demorest, Azarian, Muenz & Chittams 1996). *It is important and respectful to clients not to assume that any one example of unusual behaviour in sessions is typical of a pattern of problematic interpersonal styles.*

These caveats are important to bear in mind because, while interpersonal interventions can lead to dramatic positive effects, they can also misfire – usually because they have been clumsily delivered or because the client was simply not ready to work in that way. As Egan (2013) notes, interpersonal work can be 'strong medicine', and the dose may need to be carefully measured. When a problematic pattern is correctly identified as occurring during therapy, however, relatively simple responses can be therapeutic. Some depressed clients, for example, may be unrewarding to their therapists and may test our acceptance and empathy to the full but can nonetheless be helped by learning to '*lighten up*' or to be *more playful*.[3] Practitioners sometimes express a fear of depression, almost as if it can be catching – perhaps because in an interpersonal sense it can be – that is, people close to a person in a low mood may find themselves feeling unaccountably low. It may be helpful to acknowledge this feeling with clients: quite often they are more

---

[3]See the story of *Mary*, pp. 48–9.

than half aware of how people see them anyway. A kind of grimness and over-seriousness can settle in with depression and this can estrange some clients from their former selves and then from their partners and friends. Therapeutic sessions can be a safe environment where new ways of behaving can be 'played with' – that is, tried out experimentally. The idea of lightening up could sound trite but I have found that many clients *have* benefited from thinking about how they might do this. *Lightening up* may perhaps sound less worrying than having to 'overcome depressogenic tendencies'. Trying out different interpersonal behaviours ties in with the principles of activation, reframing and behavioural experiments discussed earlier. Crucially, it can help the client to feel that it is possible to reclaim a former self that was not depressed. It is better however if this intervention emerges from within the client's frame of reference, otherwise it could be heard as criticism.

The effect of problems is often more pronounced in clients' close personal relationships but it may also influence clients' wider social relationships. As we will examine in more detail in Chapter 5, a crucial element in more recent approaches to the use of behavioural activation in the treatment of depression is to work on helping clients to increase both the quantity and *quality* of relationships in clients' wider social networks (Ekers, Richards, McMillan, Bland & Gilbody, 2011; Martell et al., 2001).

The ability to respond therapeutically to a client showing a problematic pattern during therapy – for example, refraining from acting angrily to a client who reacts angrily to something he supposes you have meant, and then trying to understand the anger during the session – is an advanced skill that will depend at least in part on your previous experiences of working with particular problems. Both new clients and practitioners are likely to experience such exchanges as being outside the usual cultural norm. New practitioners need to be patient and accept a gradual evolution of relational skills; more ideas on the evolution of skills are discussed in Chapter 8.

The influence of clients' and therapists' histories on the therapeutic relationship

As we saw in Chapter 2, the client's current problems may reflect distinctly familiar themes in their historical interpersonal functioning:

> *Don* was raised in a tough part of Newcastle. Both his parents had severe drinking problems and were highly inconsistent in their parenting. Don had joined the Army, learnt a good trade and had prospered after coming back to civilian life. Now, years later, he was struggling to establish a stable relationship with his partner. She, fed up with his behaviour, suggested a trial separation, during which he should 'sort himself out'. He was now depressed. While discussing his history I asked Don for a typical story from his childhood (see Chapters 2 and 7) and he told me the following story:
>
> *Often when I came home from school, I would find my parents lying drunk on the floor. There'd be no food for tea nor heat or light: power had been turned off due to debts. My disillusionment became total when I returned from a*

school trip to the Lakes. The coach got back to school at four on Friday. All the parents were there to meet the kids: all except mine obviously. The awful thing was I had to walk past all these 'happy families' to get my bag from the back of the coach – for me 'the walk of shame'. It was a historic moment for me: I said to myself, 'I'll never be humiliated again. I'll never rely on anyone again. From now on, I will look after me first.'

We can see that Don's recent experiences connect with his memories[4] of the more distant past. The strategy of 'looking after me first' worked well in the Army but was less useful in the context of an intimate relationship now. How can one fit a drive for independence into a situation usually characterised by a degree of mutual dependence? Don also showed a strong need for love yet struggled to trust enough to allow it to happen: hardly surprising given his earlier experiences. He had schemas that worked against each other – one driving a need to attach, the other driving a need to detach. This dilemma is a normal feature of development (Erikson, 1994) but clients with this kind of history experience it in a more intense form and with very strong, difficult emotions. We built a formulation (Figure 3.2) to understand his negative reaction when a friend failed a promise to get in touch.

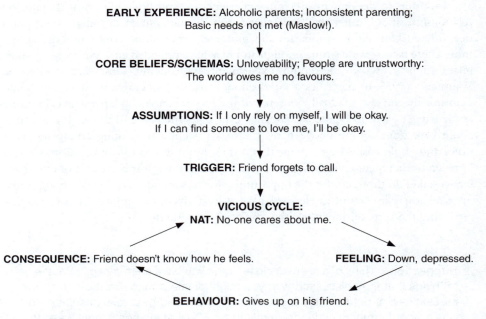

EARLY EXPERIENCE: Alcoholic parents; Inconsistent parenting; Basic needs not met (Maslow!).

CORE BELIEFS/SCHEMAS: Unloveability; People are untrustworthy: The world owes me no favours.

ASSUMPTIONS: If I only rely on myself, I will be okay. If I can find someone to love me, I'll be okay.

TRIGGER: Friend forgets to call.

VICIOUS CYCLE:
NAT: No-one cares about me.

CONSEQUENCE: Friend doesn't know how he feels.

FEELING: Down, depressed.

BEHAVIOUR: Gives up on his friend.

Figure 3.2 Don's CB formulation

Looking at the formulation in Figure 3.2, interpersonal material seems to come at us from every angle. Older and more recent trigger events are interpersonal in nature,

---

[4]We should always remember too that all memories are somewhat 'constructed'.

hinting at a long, relational learning history. The key cognitions are all interpersonal; even Don's self-concept is an appraisal of himself in relation to others. The planet on which he finds himself is anthropomorphised into a person with indifferent intentions towards him. The behaviour shows how he might move towards or away from others, and the negative feelings are reactions to aversive interpersonal events.

The formulation is usually understood as a relatively formal therapeutic step that moves between exploration during assessment and action of therapeutic interventions (Wills with Sanders, 2013). Here I am suggesting that it can also be a good moment to consider what has been flowing between therapist and client – what one might call an 'informal' or 'shadow' formulation.

Don and I worked well and effectively together.[5] The relationship was helped by the fact we shared a common northern working-class background. He reminded me of several of my relatives whose lives had been shaped by being conscripted into the armed forces and/or by going to sea. Therapists always need to establish that an old pattern is not only present but is indeed still 'active' in the current situation. It is interesting that, given the negative core beliefs about relationships evident in Figure 3.2, Don seemed able to enter into a 'good enough' relationship here quite quickly. It could be that his difficulty in relationships was different with men and women.

It is important to remember that therapy relationships are similar to but also different from other types of relationships – indeed, clients may be deliberately seeking out a relationship to disconfirm previous experiences – and hopefully most therapeutic relationships should offer that. This relationship, in the context of independent practice, offered Don clear boundaries and ultimately control: he could 'fire' me at any time. These factors were strong enough and may have provided an adequately 'holding' relationship in which he could experiment with being somewhat dependent. Winnicott (1955–6) describes a good-enough parent as being able to hold a child emotionally and also gradually loosen that hold to encourage independence. Looking at the trigger event in Figure 3.2 also, however, gives me pause to think of how things could have gone wrong between us. I have a weakness in making arrangements at times and could easily have arranged and then forgotten to call him, and this could have led to therapeutic breakdown – as we will describe towards the end of this chapter. Mistakes do though offer the opportunity for repair and I have wryly thought that my occasional displays of carelessness have at least given me opportunities to practise retrieving the sorts of difficulties that can arise from them!

Suggestion Think of a client or close friend you have seen recently. What sort of things that they discussed with you might fit into a map like the one shown for Don? What did he/she tell you about current and past relationships? How was/is your therapeutic/friendship relationship? What elements in all these factors seem to fit into common themes and what discrepancies are there?

---

[5] I described the outcome of this work in the first edition of this book, Wills (2008a, pp. 37–8), and in Wills with Sanders (2013, p. 23).

UNDERSTANDING ATTACHMENT IN RELATIONAL EXCHANGES

Bowlby's 'working model' of attachment (Holmes, 1993) has proved a powerful idea across different models of therapy. It can help clients and therapists understand and discuss how intimate relationships work. Human infants have particularly long periods of dependence so that secure attachment bonds have evolutionary survival value and appear to be wired in responses evident from the earliest moments of life. Anxiety and depression have elements of evolutionary responses – to danger and defeat respectively. From a relational perspective, these problems can arise from threats to or loss of a secure base. The lack of a secure base leaves humans less confident to explore and may lead to negative modes of attachment. Liotti (2007) suggests that if rational collaboration breaks down in a therapy relationship then clients may revert to and use previous modes of negative attachment in the way they relate to their therapists. If clients feel misunderstood on a basic level they may for example turn into a 'demanding baby' to get what they need. Therapists should therefore strive to develop containing relationships to promote good-enough security to allow clients to explore during therapy. We should also remember that detachment is an important stage of attachment (Guidano & Liotti, 1983). Secure attachment makes secure detachment possible. Similarly therapists should help clients to detach at the appropriate time.

Behavioural experiments can be designed with explicitly interpersonal aims (Flecknoe & Sanders, 2004) and can be seen as forms of client exploration from the secure base of the therapy relationship. The attachment concept gives us a language to talk about developing and ending patterns in relationships, including the therapeutic one. It is important to be aware of and to respond to different client needs in this respect.

Suggestion Draw a continuum line with 'attachment' on one end and 'detachment' or 'autonomy' on the other, and place various people on it. For example, some people have strong needs to be attached, whereas others seem happier with autonomy. Start with yourself and then add clients onto it. What are the implications of the various places assumed by these people and the relationships between them? For example, what happens when people with strong drives towards attachment have to link up with people who have strong needs for autonomy? Are there productive ways in which families and organisations can balance everyone's need in this respect? How have clients with attachment problems presented in therapy?

Understanding how complementary relational responses operate

Negative behaviour often seems to exert a pull that draws others into a 'complementary response' that in turn merely confirms the first person's worst fears (Safran & Muran, 2000). A complementary pattern of this type is evident among many clients suffering from social anxiety.[6] When they are scared, usually of being judged in social situations, they can take on a defensively detached state that others may see as 'superior'. This pattern draws unwanted attention and hostility from others, the very things the socially anxious clients most fear – instead of deflecting unwanted attention they attract more of it (Sanders & Wills, 2003) – resulting in a self-fulfilling prophecy that 'People do not like me and will criticise me.'

These self-fulfilling patterns in clients are so well established that they appear like the natural order of things but will, however, eventually become obvious to practitioners. Rather than react to them straight away, practitioners can mull the pattern over in supervision – a place where these insights can be tested and thought through. Even where there is an obvious pattern, it may not be clear how, or even whether, we should respond. Information to help us decide these questions may be in the formulation: i.e. in what we have already learnt about the client's interpersonal functioning in current and historical contexts. Interpersonal strategies will often be evident in beliefs about relationships as well as in our informal, relational formulation.

Two sources of interpersonally potentially significant information are: relationship signals – already referred to as 'dissonant notes' – and relationship breakdowns. *Relationship signals* ('interpersonal markers') are incidents that reveal underlying interpersonal patterns. They are samples of behaviour that are 'windows into understanding the whole cognitive-interpersonal style' of the client (Safran & Segal, 1990, p. 82). They often have an off-key feel to them and may occur to the therapist when she finds herself musing, 'What on earth was going on between us then?'

Mary came to her first session and immediately bombarded me with questions about myself. I started to feel irritated as, before saying a single word about herself, she asked me in great detail about my training, how I had got interested in the work, how I organised my practice, etc. A common therapeutic interpretation might be to wonder if such behaviour signalled anxiety or an issue of trust. Later on in the session, however, Mary gave me a rather different and more individual explanation for her questions. She had been an ill-favoured eldest child who was used as a 'skivvy' to care for her more indulged younger siblings. She came to believe: 'I just don't measure up – I am not as good as other people.' No matter what she achieved or how hard she tried, she expected to be judged negatively by people and thought they would never be interested in her. Years later, on a sales course, a tutor unwittingly gave her a strategy to overcome this problem. 'Ask about your customer: be interested in him and he will be interested in you,' she was instructed. By asking me lots of questions, she was saying to me, 'I am interested in you: please be interested in me.'

---

[6]For a royal example, see Juliet Nicholson's description of the supposedly 'haughty' Queen Mary in *The perfect summer* (2006).

It emerged that this very specific strategy was part of a more general 'people-pleasing' strategy that Mary followed zealously. Unintended and ironic consequences often result from such strategies: this behaviour really annoyed Mary's work colleagues, who then took her generosity for granted and were even more likely to treat her like a skivvy. In supervision, I role-played Mary's people-pleasing style and my then supervisor commented, 'Wouldn't it be great if she could lighten up and be a bit more playful.' I gave this feedback to Mary and she got it right away. She seemed almost relieved once she had identified this solution and moved forward rapidly from that point.[7] It is often helpful to capitalise on such a breakthrough by helping clients to brainstorm situations in which they can try out the new strategy – in this case, playfulness. Egan (2013) suggests a series of steps for giving forethought to how the various options that emerge from brainstorming may be tested in imagination for viability and effectiveness. One such step, for example, would be to try to work out who might be the best person with whom to practise 'playfulness' – perhaps the person most likely to respond positively. This kind of anticipation can help to ready the person for action. In this instance the new behaviour had the additional benefit of getting Mary some positive feedback – something she had previously striven for. It again seems nicer for Mary to have the problem of needing to 'be more playful' than to have a nasty-sounding 'disorder' called 'social phobia'.

In this case, the effect of Mary's 'relationship signal' was relatively benign and was identified and worked through at a relatively early stage. Other markers, for example, ones showing mistrust in the therapist, are more likely to cause problems in the relationship if left unhealed. *Relationship breakdowns* (alliance ruptures) occur when the relationship between client and therapist begins to falter. They are not necessarily always very dramatic events and may even seem to be about some apparently rather minor detail of the therapy, but what marks them out is an intensity of feeling on one or other or both sides. We discuss them in the context of the skills for handling them, identified in the next major section.

Suggestion Think of any incidents that may have happened between you and your clients over the years. One supervisee told me about a client who regularly brought a bag of chips into the session with her. Thinking back, do any of these incidents seem like they may have been 'interpersonal markers' for the client's underlying interpersonal patterns and/or the way they may have interacted with your underlying interpersonal patterns? If you are still waiting to start work with clients, you might be able to understand how to play these situations by thinking of a friend who displayed some unexpected behaviour – for example, someone who had always been very generous suddenly becoming mean over a specific issue? If you thought it was worth raising with him or her, how might you do that and how do you think they would react?

---

[7]For further description see Sanders & Wills (2013, pp. 15–16, 22, 232).

KEY SKILLS FOR WORKING THROUGH INTERPERSONAL PATTERNS AND RUPTURES IN THERAPY: IMMEDIACY AND META-COMMUNICATION

Defining immediacy and meta-communication

The best way to share impressions about how people come across in sessions is by using immediacy (Inskipp, 1996), also termed you/me talk (Egan, 1975). Egan (2013) distinguishes between relationship immediacy – the ability to reflect on the history of your relationship with the other person and how it might have developed in the way it has – and here-and-now immediacy – the ability to reflect on what is happening in the present moment with the client. It is helpful to think of using immediacy in both senses as a two-stage process. First, practitioners bring an observation about the relationship into the session, and then, second, allow a mutual process of reflection and counter-reflection to explore what is actually going on between them and clients. It is usually helpful to reflect first, in supervision, for example, and even wait until an incident has occurred several times, before moving into using immediacy. Egan (2013) offers useful steps in delivering the immediate statement:

◆ Say how the client affects you

◆ Explore your contribution to what is going on

◆ Describe the client's behaviour and offer 'reasonable hunches' about what is happening

◆ Invite the client to consider what is happening.

One factor that makes such 'immediacy' work well is when we are able to offer feedback that the other person can 'swallow' (i.e. accept): user-friendly feedback often stresses the deliverer's behaviour and emotions rather than the receiver's. It is also worth remembering that the use of immediacy is not part of usual social interaction and may seem puzzling to some clients.

Meta-communication

Meta-communication was initially developed in interpersonal therapy (Anchin & Kiesler, 1982) and brief psychodynamic therapy (Strupp & Binder, 1984) and has been applied to CBT by Safran (Katzow & Safran, 2007; Safran & Segal, 1990). Technically meta-communication simply means the facility to communicate about communication but it is used and defined by Safran in the context of dealing with ruptures in therapeutic relationships by recognising them as related to the respective *cognitive-interpersonal* styles of both client and therapist. It is useful to consider using this perspective when the practitioner notices feeling 'stuck' in the client's cognitive-interpersonal cycle. She can then break free from unhelpful aspects of what is going on between her and the client. Although both parties must participate in this effort, it is reasonable to expect therapists to be prime movers and to cultivate the necessary skills to do so: these skills are awareness, collaboration, empathy, negotiating and immediacy. In CBT meta-communication can help by applying immediacy skills to problems threatening therapeutic collaboration. A client may be feeling hurt but may take a 'carry on regardless' approach to this. A highly incongruent version of this situation can arise when the client may want the practitioner to understand that she is hurt but does not want the 'embarrassment' of this being acknowledged and dealt with. It would be hard for true collaboration to remain in place in this kind of double bind situation so the therapist may make a tentative stab at describing what she thinks is 'going on' in the hope of drawing the client back in by collaborative exploration and problem solving to 'set things right again'. The practitioner might for example say, 'I am just wondering if I may have hurt you when I described how your relationship with Ted came over to me. I know that conflict makes you feel uncomfortable and wonder if you feel inhibited about telling me about your hurt. You are entitled to feel fed up with other people at times so it could be a good step forward for us if we could put this on the table and sort it out. What do you think?'

Sometimes the interpersonal breakdown has started with something the practitioner did, and we should be ready to own appropriate responsibility. For this reason, we should regard the discomfort of possible breakdown as 'information about something' and try to be as honest as possible in our subsequent review – perhaps in supervision – of what that something is. A supervisor can frequently help to formulate the situation and our role in it and then form testable hypotheses about what the mechanism is. A hypothesis needs to be testable because it might be wrong and because client–therapist collaboration might find a more accurate one.

Jo was a final-year undergraduate who had been depressed and close to giving up on her degree. Therapy, however, had coincided with a remarkable recovery and this was evident well before the end of her academic year. Her student counsellor was a bit surprised that Jo kept adding extra sessions as they approached the end of each contracted period of therapy, because Jo had shown strong tendencies towards an autonomous streak throughout therapy. Discussion in supervision, however, revealed that on-going pressure of work caused the practitioner himself to feel pressured to finish up as much work as he could. In supervision, it was decided that the counsellor would discuss the whole situation with Jo in as open a way as possible, asking her to help her counsellor to resolve it in a way that met both of their needs and interests. Interestingly, Jo was amused at the thought that she might be seen as 'dependent' but also revealed that she wasn't really sure how therapy ended. The theme of 'not quite knowing how to end things' was evident in her formulation: she had spent long periods of her teenage years alternating between her mother and father after they divorced, and she found each and every transition difficult. Once this issue was talked through, she and the practitioner easily devised an appropriately tapered termination of therapy.

The message devised in supervision and conveyed to the client in the next session in this instance may be regarded as the type of communication that aims to identify a problematic interpersonal pattern between client and therapist and then initiate joint exploration. The starting point is often about helping clients understand the impact that they may have on others.

Practitioners can sometimes react badly to 'being dumped on' by clients and may then unwittingly hurt clients by seeming to suggest that they 'talked too much'. When faced with being given a torrent of information, they might however feel comfortable saying something like, 'Can we just hang on a moment? I am finding it a bit hard to keep up with you. It would help me if we could slow things down a bit and focus a bit more.' Clients may surprise us by giving such permission and often add, 'I'm glad you said that. A lot of people reckon I go on a bit. I'm never quite sure about what detail might be required so it would help me if you did focus me.' Notice that the response focuses on *the practitioner's* feeling of being overwhelmed and the need to 'slow down' to help the struggling *practitioner,* using the first two of the steps in immediacy described by Egan (2013): the starting point is *our* frailty – *we* can't keep up – and the proposed action is a joint one – that *we* slow down and focus a bit more. Trainees, however, often fear that saying something like this would be seen as rude or 'cutting across' the client, but that fear makes an assumption about what clients feel. Rather than make assumptions, it is often easier to ask them straight out. Getting a better handle on how we really come over to other people can give people an uncommon and priceless opportunity for personal insight.

We have already given several examples of how unusual relationship patterns may suddenly intrude into therapy sessions without any real disruption (*Bron*) or with only mildly disruptive effects (*Mary* and *Jo*). In these instances there is a minor problem for the therapy but the effect of surfacing them has added deeper understanding to a therapeutic process. Disruption, even termination of therapy, may occur when important client needs or wishes are missed. Clients may then be covertly demanding in the session or may try to articulate the need in an unclear way. Katzow and Safran (2007) remind us that the final stage of 'worked through' meta-communication is reached when clients come to a new experience – of their voices being truly heard:

Practitioner (P1): Pam, what I think you might be saying is that you think that I got that whole thing about you feeling 'powerless' wrong.

Client (C1): (*hesitates*) … Yes … (*embarrassed*) It's no big deal though.

P2: Are you softening the blow for me now?

C2: Yeah … no … yeah. It is hard to tell people when I think they get me wrong … so I often play a bit dumb … but it feels important to try to do it here …

P3: Yes, it is – I am glad you did. I mean it is not comfortable for me to hear it but it is important that I do – I can't really help you properly without that kind of feedback.

C3: Phew – it was so hard to say it … but it feels so good to be heard …

P4:   I was not 100% sure if that was what you meant … you were a bit embarrassed and went round the houses a bit, I reckon … might it be worth practising being more direct?

            … (Later) …

C5:   Phil, you have helped me a lot but you got that thing about powerlessness wrong … I don't see it that way and when you said it I felt hurt, like you were underestimating me … but it is great that we have gone over it …

In P1 and P2 the practitioner encourages the client to use an active behaviour – assertion – that is one of the goals for therapy and establishes its importance to the therapeutic process in P3 and P4; and the client acknowledges that she has had a new 'corrective emotional experience' in C5.

Repairing ruptures in therapy

Safran and Segal (1990) name seven types of common alliance ruptures in CBT:

1. The client is sceptical.
2. The client is sarcastic or otherwise negative.
3. The client alludes to problems in the therapy indirectly by reference to another relationship.
4. Client and therapist disagree on goals or tasks.
5. The client is over-compliant.
6. The client does not respond to an intervention.
7. The client activates 'therapy safety behaviours' – e.g. only revealing low-risk feelings.

Practitioners may first become aware of a rupture developing in sessions as a feeling of physical discomfort in themselves – in me often a shivery feeling in my neck. Ruptures can, however, offer great opportunities for therapy to move forward. They may involve the client withholding feelings, engagement or commitment from therapy. Practitioners should try not to feel too wrong-footed by them. Being calm is much harder for them during major breakdowns, when they must try to step back and avoid reacting too quickly. Responses 'on the rebound' may tend to be retaliatory, and may result in putting down the client or in too hasty reassurance or apology – though it is always good to bear in mind that the therapist may have made a mistake. Using empathy is invariably an integral part of healing breakdowns and may offer a chance to compensate for an earlier lack of empathy. Sometimes breakdowns occur because a client has experienced a sense of shame in a session (Gilbert, 2009a). Going over old wounds can easily trigger shame. Sometimes a therapist can unwittingly imply that a client is 'stupid' by artlessly challenging one of their negative automatic thoughts.

The important first move of the therapist is to become 'unhooked' from the client's interpersonal pattern. This demands the ability to use what Casement (1985) has called the 'internal supervisor' and feeling relatively comfortable with our own feelings. This is especially true of negative feelings that arise in therapy. Our ability to use such feelings is sometimes blocked by what Leahy (2001) has called 'therapist schemas', such as 'I shouldn't feel angry about clients', or 'It is unprofessional to feel bored by clients.' It is important to realise the pressure we sometimes put ourselves under by adhering, even unconsciously, to such beliefs. They may make us over-concerned to 'achieve something', 'be something' or 'do something', perhaps especially the latter in CBT. Therapists can work on developing a different type of attention: a kind of non-attached awareness (Safran & Reading, 2008), close to what is discussed as 'mindfulness' elsewhere in this book.

The most difficult situations are confrontational – for example when clients may be sarcastic, angry or get into 'complaint mode' about therapy or the therapist. These sorts of behaviours can be powerfully provocative to therapists. First, it is natural for therapists to feel threatened or scared about this and it can be okay, even helpful, to own this, provided it is not retaliatory and acting *out of* the fear. It is hard to be criticised by clients and it is natural to want to defend oneself. If we defend ourselves too readily, however, we would often miss a golden opportunity of finding out about something more therapeutic: the client's interpersonal patterns, one's own interpersonal patterns or the way both patterns interact with each other. Therapy often proceeds more quickly when clients can take responsibility for their own functioning so when therapists take such responsibility, it should help the client to do the same:

> *John* was a former health professional whose life took a difficult turn after he had behaved strangely towards clients during home visits. He attempted to convert clients to his religion. When they refused to let him in, he shouted into the letterboxes telling them that they could not hide from God. After recovery he became a quiet but difficult member of his therapy group in a day hospital. His nurse and key worker Vera offered him counselling and tried to introduce him to dialectical behaviour therapy (DBT) methods for self-soothing. John was scathing about this and told Vera to keep away with 'all that baby stuff'. Vera felt hurt by his rejection of her efforts and was provoked into a row with him. In supervision she was able to reflect that he had made her feel deskilled just as she had thought she was gaining some competence in psychological work. She was then able to swallow her pride and restart negotiations with John about the work they *could* do together. Once again he knocked her back with the unexpected remark that his wife said to him that, 'No therapist worth her salt would have argued with you like that.' It turned out that John's wife had completed a short course in counselling skills and had been influenced by Laingian 'anti-psychiatry'. Once again Vera reflected on the grain of truth in the wife's complaint. She could acknowledge this grain of truth with John but then patiently began to rebuild her working alliance with him. Vera wryly observed to her supervisor – 'The mills of collaboration can indeed grind slowly and exceeding small!'

If therapeutic incidents could lead to an official complaint then this of course puts things on an entirely different basis, and practitioners would be well advised to seek professional or even legal advice and support before taking responsibility for problems linked to specific official complaints (Bond, 2010).

Developing interpersonal responsiveness over time

Therapists develop their own styles of interpersonal responding – and at different paces. Of all the skills described in this book, readers may find this chapter seems the most oriented to skills identified with psychotherapy. Relational skills can, however, be practised at all levels of helping work. People new to the field should not be in a rush to practise them but rather let them mature over the years of their developing careers. They can start just by noticing clients' different relational styles and then by identifying their own reactions to those styles, and take these observations with them for further discussion in supervision. The question 'How is this client affecting me?' is rarely unproductive in supervision. As you gain confidence in spotting these factors in operation it may then be interesting to think whether you could make a response – for example by using immediacy or meta-communication – that might lead to therapeutic advantage by offering the client a new or uncommon experience. As we have underlined several times, this kind of feedback does not crop up much in everyday life so the fact that it can be discussed in counselling and psychotherapy adds massive value to that kind of helping endeavour.

As well as learning about different client patterns, practitioners can also learn much about their own patterns and how *they* respond to different client challenges. In addition to the forum of supervision, it may be helpful to review unusual incidents in therapy by writing reflectively on them for a time. This can be formalised into keeping a 'reflective journal' (Bolton, 2010; Wright & Bolton, 2012) and these often have a secondary value as records of practice that may be part of necessary continuing professional development (CPD) and accreditation processes. Once a therapist has made a few successful interpersonal interventions, such work can seem intoxicating. Practitioners should, however, be wary of analysing interpersonal breakdowns as if they emanate solely from the clients' 'stuff'. Kahn (1991) eloquently makes the case for considering how the therapist's own issues and behaviour, including errors, should also be examined as possible factors in therapeutic breakdown. In this way we can do intoxicating work and yet stay quite grounded.

Suggestion *Group exercise*: each member should present a client or colleague or friend with whom he/she had protracted difficulties. (Hint: it may be helpful to present a 'critical incident' in which these difficulties were encapsulated.) The other group members (one as 'client advocate' and one as observer) should try to help the presenter to map the underlying interpersonal patterns, including any contribution from the therapist. They may also try to formulate and deliver an alternative response.

CONCLUSION

Other models of therapy have been explicitly based on the interpersonal dimensions of the client's life and of the therapeutic relationship. Theorists and practitioners from these perspectives have added much to our understanding of the therapy process. Such a perspective was initially not a focus in CBT but has become used more often as practitioners engage with the necessarily messy processes of trying to help people. CBT has developed a richer understanding of interpersonal patterns in the lives of clients and how these may make themselves felt in therapy sessions. It has also developed more ideas to help its practitioners respond to clients' interpersonal needs in a more informed way. People in the early stages of developing therapeutic skills should be content to allow the particular skills of this chapter to develop slowly but surely as they become more experienced in the field.

PRACTICE TIP: ON USING IMMEDIACY

'Immediacy' can indeed be strong medicine (Egan, 2013) – so that frequent and large doses are rarely used. The interpersonal dimension is an intriguing one and can become quite heady stuff for people in the helping professions as they first learn about and then use interventions based on relational material. It is important, though, for practitioners to remember that they enter these exchanges with many advantages. Interventions are usually launched on their initiative and with theoretical and practical approaches to guide them. These interventions work by making clients become a little more self-conscious. It is, however, easy for clients to become much more self-conscious and uncomfortable. This can result in the therapist seeming to be a 'clever clogs' but clients may feel thrown and/or hurt. Such an impasse is usually quickly evident: the client looks puzzled, with uncomfortable facial expressions, body shuffling and verbalisations like 'I'm not sure what you are getting at here'. In a way, one can be in a new alliance rupture. Usually it is best to step back at this point. Further work on the focus in question may still be possible later. The issue can be picked up during feedback at the end of sessions.

See Egan (2002) for training exercises on immediacy.

Follow-up suggestion   *Small group exercise: Adapting Kagan's interpersonal process recall (IPR) to examine relationship issues in the therapy process*

Audio and video recordings of therapy sessions are excellent sources for detecting interpersonal processes in action and may be so used in supervision. IPR, first devised by Kagan (1975), is a procedure for tracking interpersonal processes in a learning or supervisory context. The basic method is for the person who is reflecting on the way they did the therapy to stop the recording at moments that strike them as containing learning. Other group members then use 'inquirer leads' to engender reflection on what was going on for the practitioner. Participants can pick up new awareness by paying attention to reactions in their own body and mind as they listen. They can think about whether there are any unspoken feelings evident in the session and what else might have been done or said.

For a detailed description and exercise, see Inskipp (1996, pp. 96–100).

FURTHER READING

Gilbert, P., & Leahy, R.L. (2007) *The therapeutic relationship in the cognitive behavioural psychotherapies*. London: Routledge. (Especially Chapters 5 and 7)

Wills, F., with Sanders, D. (2013) *Cognitive behaviour therapy: foundation for practice.* London: Sage (Chapter 2).

4

SKILLS FOR WORKING WITH NEGATIVE THINKING

People are generally better persuaded by the reasons that they themselves have discovered than those by which have come into the mind of others. (Paschal, 1670/1995: 10)

INTRODUCTION

It has been argued throughout the book that the way clients think about their lives influences how they live them. We now turn to the tricky matter of how unhelpful ways of thinking may shift and be modified or changed in the healing process. There have however been major paradigm[1] shifts in the way CB therapists themselves think about how they can most effectively help clients to modify their thinking; to adapt a Bob Dylan lyric, cognitive change methods themselves are a-changing. These paradigm shifts have emerged mainly from the challenges of new 'third wave' concepts in CBT − especially from those aspects that emphasise the role of mindfulness and acceptance in therapeutic change.

We therefore begin with a description of the challenges posed by third wave approaches to traditional CBT methods. As this book is focused on skills, the analysis will centre on the implications of these ideas for CBT practice. In particular I will review the current status of Guided Discovery through Socratic Dialogue (GD/SD), often regarded as a primary method in cognitive interventions. It will be argued that GD/SD is a generic and pervasive CBT skill that underpins many CBT methods, and that GD/SD can accommodate to third wave ideas and therefore so can many other traditional cognitive interventions used in CBT.

---

[1]A paradigm may be defined as a distinct system of ideas that can be laid alongside any other for the sake of comparison.

The chapter proposes a continuum of cognitive interventions ranging from those that are relatively non-directive to those which are more directional, deliberative and effortful. The motto of the former is 'Let awareness do its work' and that of the latter, 'Helping awareness do its work'. Implicit in this continuum is the notion that practitioners can choose techniques from it in a way that allows for skilful matching to individual clients – according to their preferences and skills, the issues being addressed and the practitioner's assessments of 'the proximal zone' of individual clients – that is, the degree to which they show readiness to learn from different styles of intervention. Decisions to match clients and methods along this continuum will be illustrated by case examples, including characteristic difficulties with different methods.

THE CHALLENGES OF THIRD WAVE CBT

Critiques of traditional CBT made by third wave practitioners have typically identified several problems arising from: (a) premises that are overly rational and optimistic regarding change, (b) the extent of client 'resistance' to change, and (c) the extent to which well-meaning yet ill-directed interventions may exacerbate psychological problems. A brief review is offered here but wider discussion of these points may be found in Wills with Sanders (2013), Hayes at al. (2004) and Ciarrochi and Bailey (2008). It is worth noting that sometimes these arguments can seem to allocate a 'straw man'[2] role to previous versions of CBT – though in my view they have enough of 'a kernel of truth' to make them well worth the attention of CBT practitioners.

Overly rational approaches to change

Let us start with an example – that of a situation of rejection followed by a negative thought commonly linked to depression: *Nobody cares about me*. We may start by thinking that this is unlikely to be literally true of many clients, and usually there would be at least some evidence to the contrary, including hopefully our own responses to the client. What may be lying behind this thought is that a relationship of special value has been lost and its like may never be found again – so that in some sense the person concludes that they are unlovable. There may also be a feeling of public shame from the sense of an audience watching one be rejected – perhaps the genesis of the idea that no one cares. These feelings may also be enhanced in those people who have not had the experience of good-enough parenting in their past. When we take these other factors into account it takes but little empathy to understand how some clients in desperately lonely situations may 'feel' these thoughts to be true. Humans are hard-wired to respond to rejection (Welford, 2012), and emotional response can be deep and disturbing. It is also easy to understand that clients can become frustrated if a therapist indicates 'not getting it' by appearing to glibly suggest that 'things are not all bad'.

---

[2] A 'straw man' acts as a convenient stereotype against which to form an opposing argument.

The original and standard CBT approach however does appear to offer some optimism at this point: if our thinking gets 'out of line' with reality as we get more depressed then it may be that we can begin to find some small pieces of evidence that there are people who *may* care about us and these small pieces of evidence could snowball into a critical mass that could start to change how we think, feel and relate to others. This kind of hope is indeed often held to be the crucial first stage of effective change processes (Ilardi & Craighead, 1994). It does not take much experience of practising CBT, however, to learn that the change rarely comes this easily. Clients may seem reluctant to accept that reality is any other way than their negative thoughts tell them or even that such thoughts could change – for others perhaps, they think, but not for them. Sometimes therapists conclude that clients do not really want to get better, and Beck began his long march towards contemporary CBT by demonstrating that clients did not have a 'need to suffer' (Beck et al., 1979). A better way to see this fear of change may be to realise that clients often have 'sunk costs' – i.e. have invested heavily – in the ways they have been trying to solve their problems prior to therapy (Leahy, 2001). Our hypothetical client may for instance be thinking that if he lost weight or dressed more snappily or told better jokes he could 'make' someone love him – why then would he hear a CB therapist's suggestion that he could try changing his thinking? Sometimes clients say that they would like CBT to 'zap their negative thoughts' or 'retrain their brains', and this makes me feel uneasy because it makes therapeutic change sound like an easy and impersonal mechanical process. In contrast to being technicians who will 'zap' negative thoughts, we increasingly think that negative thoughts and feelings need first to be accepted before they can be changed.

The extent of client resistance to change

The 'sunk costs' argument is only one of Leahy's suggestions about the type of 'resistance'[3] that may arise. Hayes (1999) has also stated a similar argument when he suggests that clients may initially seek to recruit practitioners to facilitate new versions of the strategies that have already failed them; in the case we have been developing this would involve the client asking the practitioner to teach him a new way to 'make' people love him. Another major theme in apparent resistance occurs when clients feel *invalidated* by the therapy or the therapist. Linehan (1993) first brought this concept to prominence in the development of her treatment approach – which she called dialectical behaviour therapy (DBT) – for borderline personality disorder (BPD). BPD clients are extremely sensitive to invalidation and can easily interpret attempts to change their thinking as invalidation of both their thinking and their very selves. We must acknowledge straight away that there may be more than a kernel of truth in the client's ideas on this. Practitioners may have to walk a narrow line between validating clients' worth as human beings and suggesting that, nonetheless, change might still be

---

[3]I use inverted commas because this is a term used mainly by therapists – clients rarely see things this way.

helpful to them, hence the use of the word 'dialectical' – i.e. systematically weighing contradictory ideas to resolve their apparent contradictions – in DBT. Although problems in feeling validated are particularly prominent in BPD clients, they also come up for many other clients. Gilbert (2009a) has made the intriguing suggestion that interventions in psychotherapy are unlikely to be effective unless they stimulate clients' abilities to view themselves compassionately. We will return to developing self-compassion in clients later in this chapter but will for now say: *Therapists may often need to work on helping clients to 'hear' alternative thoughts in a compassionate voice.*

Finally it is not useful for practitioners to regard 'resistance' as primarily a motivational factor in the sense of personal will: it is better to see it as part and parcel of psychological problems – and perhaps in Hayes' (1999) words – 'If you don't want it, you've got it'. Third wave approaches often put emphasis on the link between experiential avoidance and the maintenance of psychological problems; it is perhaps inevitable that when one is suffering one naturally wants to push that suffering away. Pushing it away, however, often seems to only make it rebound with greater force. It is therefore best, as advocated in ACT, to have 'psychological flexibility' as the main therapeutic aim rather than 'distress reduction', because distress reduction easily allies with experiential avoidance. There are likely to be no absolute rules, though, but rather rules of thumb in my exploration of criteria to assist in the pragmatic choice of cognitive intervention methods.

Exacerbating problems by interventions not targeted on the client's 'zone of proximal development' (ZPD)

The ZPD concept was originally developed by Vygotsky and has been widely used in educational research to understand how children learn. Greenberg (2011) has adapted the concept in the context of how clients learn in therapy. This has, in my view, facilitated advances in humanistic models and brought potential for skills integration with CBT (Wills with Sanders, 2013). ZPD in the therapeutic context is an area of potential learning that is accessible to a client with help from a practitioner. This area lies between those skills clients have already established and those just beyond them at present, even with help. Thus ZPD is an area where there is client potential for interactive learning. Interventions misfire if they are not close to the ZPD: if they fall within an established area then they have the feel of 'old news', and if they fall within an inaccessible area they may elicit a client response of incomprehension. Clients are often searching both consciously and non-consciously to reorganise their thinking in a trial-and-error process (Mansell, Carey & Tai, 2013). Most practitioners are also often feeling around for the appropriate area of intervention and it is natural for there to be a certain amount of 'hit and miss' in searching for it. I find it useful to remind myself of this concept when orthodox cognitive interventions seem to fall flat and clients respond with something like 'I know I am not really a failure but …' or say incredulously, 'You really think that I did not know that!' It may well be that clients have repeatedly avoided a negative thought by 'pushing it out' with such cognitive interventions. This impasse is usually a clear signal to switch focus, although there are sometimes reasons to persist or try again later. This reinforces the desirability of therapeutic goals related to psychological flexibility.

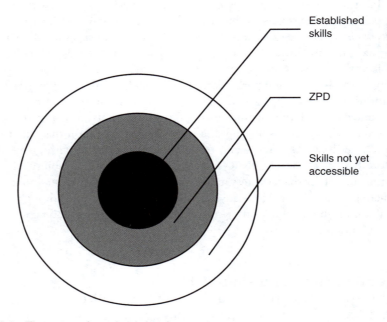

Figure 4.1 The zone of proximal development

USING A RANGE OF COGNITIVE METHODS

I have argued elsewhere (Wills, 2012; Wills with Sanders, 2013) that GD/SD remains a central skill in CBT because it is a higher-order skill that informs the use of other skills and methods in the model. GD/SD will therefore now be described in relation to the continuum of cognitive skills and interventions that forms the overall structure of this chapter. At the 'non-directive' end of the continuum are what we can think of as 'light-touch' skills that rely mainly on setting up a learning experience and encouraging the client's awareness to unfold during that experience – for example, exercises such as 'mindfulness of the breath' or simply getting clients to 'look at' a negative thought written on a whiteboard or in a therapy notebook. On the 'more directional' end the therapist proceeds by introducing more complex, deliberately designed methods such as using thought records to facilitate cognitive restructuring. Even when using a more directional *method,* however, practitioners are usually well advised to maintain a relatively light-touch and non-directional *style* (Mansell et al., 2013).

We begin the exploration of cognitive skills by defining and analysing examples of GD/SD and will then use the continuum framework to structure descriptions, case examples and analysis of its skills.

Non-directional interventions	More directional interventions
Awareness:Acceptance:Validation:Mindfulness:Compassion focus:Defusion:Metacognitive interventions:Cognitive restructuring:Challenge/confrontation	
'LET AWARENESS DO ITS WORK'	*'HELP AWARENESS DO ITS WORK'*

Figure 4.2 Continuum of cognitive interventions

This continuum allows practitioners to choose which interventions to fit clients' skill sets and ZPDs. Practitioners also benefit from thinking about how the range of skills is covered in their own current skill sets and method preferences.

GUIDED DISCOVERY THROUGH SOCRATIC DIALOGUE

Guided discovery can be regarded as an overarching strategy that underpins many uses of skills in CBT. It refers to the way CB therapists seek to facilitate clients' movement from less functional/flexible patterns of thinking, feeling and doing towards more functional/flexible ones. Practitioners use various types of questions and prompts in Socratic dialogue and these interact to facilitate an experimental frame of mind whereby clients consider new ways of thinking, feeling and behaving and 'try them on for size'. Guided discovery oscillates between the two poles of client self-discovery and practitioner guidance. The main interpersonal skill in using GD/SD lies in finding the best balance between guiding and facilitating clients to discover for themselves.

A series of questions and prompts in GD/SD helps clients to retrieve information that is relevant to their concerns but lies 'outside the box' of their currently biased negative processing style (Overholser, 1993). Certain types of question – analytic, evaluative and synthesising – effectively combine to stimulate higher-order cognitive processes associated with GD/SD. Analytic questions (AQs) typically encourage clients to 'unpack' problems by exploring relationships between their component parts. Evaluative questions (EQs) explore the meanings that clients give to various factors associated with their problems – often leading to a 'repacking' of the issues under new definitions. Therapists can then use synthesising questions (SQs) and summaries (Ss) to gather and link emerging material so that clients can draw new conclusions and insights. Some therapists would argue that these moves are all part of a larger movement towards building a new internal narrative – for example, *When my partner finished with me I felt that no one would ever love me again and that no one around me cared about me. Now I am learning that people around do care about me and that I have just as much chance of finding a soul mate as most other people.*

GD/SD may proceed in different ways but there follows a commonly used and helpful sequence (Overholser, 1993) in which practitioners:

1. Ask analytic and evaluative questions to uncover relevant information that may be currently outside the client's awareness, and then

2. Use accurate listening and reflection, and then

3. Summarise the information gathered, and finally

4. Ask synthesising questions inviting clients to apply the new information to their original beliefs or patterns.

The dual nature of GD/SD arises from the fact that typical questions are both open yet directional: open-ended questions invite clients to expand on their views, while directional questions probe below the surface of them. GD/SD is illustrated in a linked series of therapy dialogues with a client, *Bruce*, dealing with being rejected by his partner:

Client (C1):	(*Despondent*) I have no real friends.
Practitioner (P1):	(*Surprised*) Really? So, for you, a real friend is what? (AQ)
C2:	… someone you can have fun with … and … you can say what you both really feel.
P2:	You said you went to cricket with friends … how do they measure on these things? (EQ)
C3:	You know blokes … fun but it was all piss taking!
P3:	Do you mean they all took the piss, all the time? (AQ)
C4:	No … in fact, Terry told me about his break-up with Mo – said he felt devastated … like me … actually it isn't that I don't have real friends … I just don't have a girlfriend.
P4:	And that's one of our goals: to increase your chances of meeting someone; but we shouldn't forget what you do have – some good mates by the sound of it.

In response to the analytic question –what is a 'real friend?' – (AQ) at P1, the client's answer in C2 defines two criteria (fun and sharing feelings) that allow the practitioner to ask an evaluative question – was there fun with those friends? (EQ) – at P2 and a further AQ – did they just take the piss? – at P3. The questions combined to clarify the goal restated at P4: to move from a cold life with 'having no real friends' to a warmer one of 'some good mates but no girlfriend'. It is not yet clear where this will lead but by looking at actual friends, the dialogue is now about more specific and concrete matters and these can be more easily explored and their implicit evaluations reflected upon. The way a client evaluates things is a fertile area in therapy because evaluation often degenerates into the ultimately limited categories of 'good' and 'bad', whereas important life issues are rarely this black and white. Black–and–white thinking is also a frequently encountered cognitive distortion (Burns, 1999) – a variant of the over-generalisation that is often targeted in GD/SD. Themes of the first dialogue were developed in a later session:

C1:	(*Discussing drinking*) I think alcohol doesn't really agree with me. My mates can knock it back … but I can't keep up – and it messes with my sleep … Why do I get drawn into it?
P1:	So what do you think it is that draws you in? (AQ)
C2:	… the fear of standing out. I'd be called a wimp – only piss taking but hard to take.
P2:	So that makes it hard to take the healthy option? (EQ)
C3:	I sound like a wimp – not standing up to my mates and not being my own person!
P3:	Being your own person … sounds important. What would that be like? (EQ)

C4: This reminds me of when I was going out with Brenda. She liked the theatre – which I do. We went to a play and the boys were like – *His bird's making him go to the theatre*. I could hide behind that – I didn't have to say *I* liked the theatre.

P4: You're a bit trapped between your mates, your more intellectual interests and having a girlfriend (S). How does all that fit together? (SQ)

C5: I end up not getting what I want. (*P*: Which is?) I want a girlfriend, a cultural life and some time with my mates (*P*: Sounds reasonable).

The practitioner's analytic and evaluative questions at P1 (what is?), P2 (what effect?) and P3 (what would?) stimulate thoughts that lead to new ground. The summary and synthesis in P4 encourage the client to take the important step of clearly articulating what he really does want. We notice that the client is racing on under his own impetus now so that some of his linking thoughts – for example, those going from 'being one's own person' to how that played out with Brenda – are unreported. As we move to our final vignette, it is important to note that frequent summaries help to conserve and organise what is unfolding in the developing dialogue. Padesky (1993) suggests that a lack of summaries is often what most inhibits successful GD/SD. A final dialogue shows how further GD/SD both develops new directions and links with previous material:

C1: (*Talking in a later session about a new woman in his office*) … she seemed keen to speak … because she's less posh than the others … I think she sees me as like her … probably feels sorry for me.

P1: What tells you that? (AQ)

C2: You know my luck!

P2: Okay – so that's how it feels. Is there any other evidence? (AQ)

C3: She has asked me to go on a bike rally for the environment … but I'm supposed to go to football with the lads. Imagine telling them I was doing that!

P3: Okay, let's gather that in: There's a woman who might be interested in you. She might not meet your mates' criteria but you said you want to be your own person – so what about your criteria? First of all, bikes? (EQ)

C4: Well … I used to be keen on bikes when I was younger … went off to youth hostels and all that. (*P*: The environment?) No involvement before but I'm interested in politics … she seems lovely … so yes, it meets my criteria. (*Laughs*) I'd be my own person, I reckon!

Therapists' and clients' tasks run parallel in skills work. In GD/SD the therapist's questions are often matched by the client's internal questions (e.g. C3 shows the client scanning his mind for the 'evidence' requested by P2), and the client's summary at C4 matches the therapist's at P3 (linking the role of bikes in the client's past and present life).

These dialogues are from separate sessions spaced over several weeks, which emphasises the fact that GD/SD often takes time to develop. We can also see the client's development issues running through them – passing through the 'identity' of the peer group stage and on to the 'intimacy' in young adult stage (Erikson, 1994 [1959]). Practitioners need to practise GD/SD patiently so they refrain from being overly persuasive at any one moment in time; not trying to force a 'Damascus' moment, we rather seek to 'catch the prevailing wind' of the client's mind.

Sometimes it is helpful to reinforce GD/SD with written methods. These range from merely writing a negative thought on a whiteboard and contemplating it with the client, to the more formal steps of a thought record (Padesky & Greenberger, 1995). A thought record can strengthen the structuring of GD/SD, especially when GD/SD questions are included in its format. A thought record also seems to mimic the steps of normal and healthy problem solving (Wills, 2009). An important therapeutic rationale for modifying negative thoughts is to achieve more harmony in the functioning of the emotional and cognitive tracks in the brain (Epstein, 1998; LeDoux, 1996). As Dryden and Neenan (2004) observe, cognitive change needs to be both intellectually and emotionally convincing. CB therapists therefore need to be just as comfortable on the client's emotional and interpersonal terrain as any other type of therapist.

GD/SD and interpersonal attunement: How guided? How discovery-based?

In my view, GD/SD itself occupies several notches on my posited continuum. We might expect to find versions by Padesky (1993) and Teasdale (1996) at the lighter-touch end and Ellis's version (1973) at the more directional. Padesky (1993) argues that GD/SD should not seek to change minds and should proceed without any pre-conceived direction. Teasdale (1996) argues that directional cognitive interventions are likely to focus on propositional and 'rational' meanings rather than the more implicational and emotional meanings that are associated with more profound therapeutic change. It seems unlikely however that, given the diverse needs of clients, there is only one way of implementing GD/SD. Wells (1997) takes a more pragmatic view, suggesting that non-directive exploration is likely to involve more time than is usually available in everyday clinical work. We might also expect that more directional GD/SD may be appropriate in some cases. Ellis (Dryden, 1991) has argued that psychopathology is not 'polite' and will not merely go away when nicely invited to. In my practice, I have found that clients troubled by strong hostility and anger can be locked into righteous anger and may not respond to light-touch GD/SD. Some CB theorists have stressed the influence of Epictetus, and it is interesting that the meagre records we have of Epictetus' dialogues are mainly in the form of exhortations – though they may not have been actually conducted in this way. Sherman (2005) also points out that Epictetus' discussion of grief shows a less austere philosophy than is sometimes imagined. In summary, it may be better to conceive of a continuum of GD/SD styles adaptable to the needs of individual clients.

Beck (1976) describes how his discovery of automatic thoughts came when a client reported negative thoughts about him and the therapy process. As discussed in Chapter 3, such thoughts lurk beneath the formal content of therapy. They may focus on issues like feeling pushed around by therapists or by the structure of therapy (Beutler & Harwood, 2000) – thus adding to the desirability of the case for light-touch work. There are also, however, situations when clients have reported thinking, *I wish this therapist would be more direct with me.* The client's formulation is a good guide to what client thoughts and beliefs are played out in the therapeutic relationship, but therapists still need skill and courage to explore what is going on between them and clients in the here-and-now by using immediacy (Wills, 2008a). Such an approach to CBT can ensure that it is delivered in a flexible and interpersonally sensitive way.

Suggestion   Developing a fluent GD/SD style is an absolutely key skill in CBT. Like many forms of skill learning it is helpful to drill oneself by working at 'imprinting' a template of simple GD/SD steps in your CB therapist DNA. At first this will feel mechanical but it will eventually fuse naturally with your own individual working style. The more you master the steps so that they are automatic, the more you will feel 'freed up' for more subtle and interpersonally attuned use of the skill. The basic steps of GD/SD are shown in Figure 4.3. If you are following this suggested exercise alone, think of a recent client who reported a negative automatic thought (NAT) and then go through the steps of boxes A, B1, B2, C1, C2, D1, D2 and E by developing a dialogue from how you imagine it would have unfolded. If you are following the exercise in a group, allocate the roles of practitioner, client and observer/s and try out the dialogue reporting the actual exchanges in the boxes A to E. (You will find an unfilled version of Figure 4.3 on the book's companion website: https://study.sagepub.com/wills, and may print it off to use for the exercise.)

NON-DIRECTIVE COGNITIVE SKILLS AND INTERVENTIONS

The integration of behaviour therapy and cognitive therapy into CBT is a fascinating story in itself (Rachman, 1997). One helpful step along the way came when Bandura (1997) developed his social learning theory. Previously a behavioural straitjacket had restricted learning theory, whereas Bandura showed, most vividly through his 'Bobo dolls' experiment, that much learning could also occur through observation. Although this work was mainly oriented towards modelling effects from the observation of the behaviour of others, it also raises the question of how people learn from just looking at and observing the world around them. Everyone is familiar with the experience of having an 'aha moment' when you look at or hear something you have seen or heard many times before but now you suddenly 'get it'. For me the significant trigger often is auditory – just a few words of the sound of a voice are enough to open my mind to what is being said. Bandura (1997) specifies attention and memory as being key steps in observational learning; there needs to be enough quality of attention and then some retention in memory of the experience to initiate a significant track of learning and development – perhaps because they allow for the

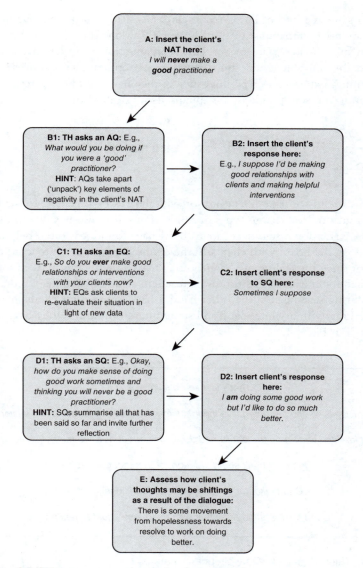

Figure 4.3 GD/SD – process and exercise for suggestion

natural movement of mind that seems frequently to follow the experience of cognitive dissonance. Cognitive dissonance occurs when the mind has to grapple with several contradictory ideas. The mind finds it difficult not to try to bring contradictions into some kind of coherence – so that cognitive dissonance often sets off a natural change process. This discussion heralds my intention here to explore some ideas of how these processes may follow the experience of merely encouraging clients to 'observe' their negative thoughts, first by writing them on a whiteboard or therapy notepad and then via exercises used in mindfulness and acceptance. This may promote a client's ability to 'hold that thought' as a precursor to a shift in mind as described in the 'method of levels' (Mansell et al., 2013) – a perspective increasingly seen as a potential contributor to third wave CBT. Mansell et al. (2013) propose that the human mind is in a state of constant reorganisation in order that it can better understand the multiplicity of signals in the environment. This process intensifies when the mind experiences a conflict such as dissonance, and often results in a shift of approach in the way problems are appraised and dealt with.

Using a whiteboard or therapy notebook

CB therapists tend to make liberal use of whiteboards or flipcharts to write up and display formulations of various types during sessions. It is also possible to use therapy notepads to write down significant items but I have found it is often helpful to 'look at' thoughts on the board with clients. Some counsellors find a whiteboard difficult as it carries for them the feeling of a 'classroom'. This is a useful sensitivity as some clients will have bad memories of classrooms or teachers, which may indeed influence their reactions during sessions. On the other hand, I have found most clients react favourably to working with a whiteboard, and some interesting things they have said about it are quoted in Fig. 4.4.

That's just so ridiculous, isn't it?

Sometimes when I say a negative thought I imagine you/us writing it on the whiteboard.

I imagine writing on the board and then think about how we might talk about it.

Oh no – I can't stand the sight of that thought – rub it off?

Can I take the pen and write an additional comment?

Can I take a photo of all that with my phone – just to remind me?

Figure 4.4 Clients' reactions to whiteboard material

My clients' most common reaction of those shown in Figure 4.4 is to take a photograph of the whiteboard with their mobile phone. This is an interesting reaction because it relates to the idea that one of CBT's great strengths is its capacity to serve as a 'take away therapy' – adding to therapy 'generalisation' – the transfer of therapeutic effects from sessions to everyday life. Generalisation is quite hard to achieve and it is known that many of the insights raised in sessions may be lost by 'washout' (Ivey et al., 2012). The phone photograph allows clients to literally take away insights from sessions but the other points in Figure 4.4 also signal an extra psychological dimension too – by imagining themselves and the therapist using the whiteboard, clients are also taking away some of the 'feeling' of the support they may be experiencing in sessions and with it an efficacious sense that 'these problems can be managed and ameliorated'. The quotations in Figure 4.4 suggest that whiteboards have considerable potential to enhance learning in CBT and this is illustrated in the following example:

Mei was a socially anxious 6th-former. One of her A-level subjects was psychology and this helped her to have a good understanding of the principles of CBT. Her social anxiety was in part related to the fact that her father pushed her very hard to achieve, and in part to the experience of racist bullying in a previous school. She felt strongly driven to be 'top of the class', not just academically but also socially. She had to be witty, knowledgeable and impress whatever company she was in. She felt constant anxiety when anticipating social situations and worse when she was in them, and developed depression in addition to her social anxiety. She had read in one of her texts that CBT was the 'best treatment' for social anxiety and depression but frequently found that cognitive restructuring made her feel worse because, although she could see that her NATs were not strictly correct, she still felt bad. This plunged her into yet deeper depression as she regarded CBT as 'her last hope'. Her school counsellor now therefore adopted a form of cognitive intervention described by Barlow et al. (2011) in which alternative thoughts are written alongside the NAT, and the client is encouraged to regard all thoughts as being potentially plausible.

The CBT-trained school counsellor used the cognitive methods of Barlow et al. (2011) in combination with a whiteboard during the following dialogue, and the final whiteboard presentation is shown in Figure 4.5.

P1:   You felt really bad after the class discussion about the government's education policy (*CL*: Yes) – what was it that resulted in you feeling so bad?

C1:   Well I hadn't understood what a 'free school' is. I thought it meant that you didn't have to pay so I asked, what was so bad about that? They all laughed at me and I felt so stupid.

P2:   Just going back to cognitive therapy for a moment – what thought went round your head?

C2:   I am boring.

P3:   Okay (*Writing 'I am boring' in red on the board*). So you are boring because you missed the point of this conversation? What about in other situations, what are you?

C3:   (*After some thought*) I am challenging.

P4:   (*A little surprised by the jump in tone and content, and writing 'I am challenging' in green on the board.*) Tell me some more about that.

C4: Well, I don't like to see people getting away with lazy clichés – like jokes about old people and stuff like that … (*The dialogue went on to establish three other self statements:* 'I am well-organised', 'I am stubborn', *and* 'I'm feisty').

P5: Interesting – it is looking like a more varied picture; how does it feel to look at it?

C5: Amazing actually – because I am all those things too … It just feels so much more okay to be me … quite peaceful actually! … I am going to take a phone photo of that!

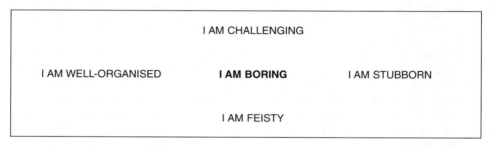

Figure 4.5 Mei's whiteboard

Previous cognitive interventions with Mei had focused on asking her to review the evidence about whether she was, for example, 'boring' but had frequently developed into arguments, with Mei seemingly grimly hanging on to her negative thoughts. This lighter-touch intervention bypassed argument and found the desired destination by a different but easier route. Also appearing on Mei's whiteboard is a diagram based on that used in Dryden and Yankura (1992) which shows that, like everyone, Mei had a *Big I* – an overall personality description – made up of lots of *little I's* – multiple personality traits. This can be a particularly good way of illustrating to clients how inflexible self-concepts nearly always sell the whole person short. Here Mei's thought/belief *I am boring* is weakened because it becomes just another 'little I' rather than being the whole 'Big I' of who she is. Figure 4.5 shows in a highly visible way the sense we have been exploring here of facilitating experiences in which clients can 'play with' seeing things in new ways.

Allowing different ways of seeing things to coexist

Barlow and fellow researchers at the Center for Anxiety and Related Disorders (CARD) in Boston developed a protocol for the trans-diagnostic treatment of emotional disorders, describing the approach as both 'emotion-focused' and 'cognitive-behavioural' (Barlow et al., 2011, p. 17). The protocol is trans-diagnostic because it targets key areas that underpin different types of emotional disorder – in particular, maladaptive emotional regulation strategies. As in older types of cognitive therapy and CBT, cognitive appraisals – 'thinking traps' – are addressed but in a significantly different way:

> Unlike some other cognitive therapies, [our] emphasis … is not on eliminating or suppressing negative thoughts and replacing them with more adaptive or realistic appraisals, but rather on increasing cognitive flexibility as an adaptive emotion regulation strategy. (Barlow et al., 2011, p. 18)

We too can bring this strategy into our work by encouraging clients to see that, in any given situation, there are a large number of different aspects of that situation that can be focused on and given meaning to. Flexibility in thinking is likely to be a better aim for many clients because, as noted earlier, they have often been using problematic ways of 'fixing' their thinking anyway and there is a danger that overly directive cognitive work may collude with that aim. Another – probably allied – problem can arise when clients become overly self-critical and blame themselves for their problems. Any suggestion that their thinking is 'wrong' or 'irrational' or 'distorted' may sound like blame and risk further raising negative emotions so they may block active problem-solving behaviours.

In at least some client situations therefore, rather than 'interrogating' negative thinking by looking for evidence about a targeted thought, practitioners can focus on showing links between negative thoughts, trigger situations and emotional reactions. The first step shows the role that negative appraisal plays and this is followed by showing what thinking traps may be operating, and then a final step generates alternative thoughts or ways of seeing the situation. This effectively aims to show clients that alternative views can coexist alongside each other. They can regard them just as different ways of seeing things – in fact this seems to be a normal state of mind for many. These alternatives may contain bigger and smaller grains of truth and have different effects on the client's life. Because the appraisal is not 'under attack', it does not have to be defended, and cognitive dissonance may then develop naturally to do its healing work. A worksheet incorporating these ideas is shown in Figure 4.6.

INSTRUCTIONS: *Enter your negative automatic thought (NAT) in any of the above boxes and then add in as many other possible ways of seeing the situation to the other boxes. Use brainstorming to come up with as many other 'thoughts' – even if they seem a bit ridiculous. You can also try starting by placing the NAT in a different box, and may also find it interesting to experiment with using different colours (see Mai's thoughts in Figure 4.4).*

Figure 4.6 Coexisting thoughts worksheet

Paying mindful attention to negative thoughts

A new approach to negative thinking has been evolving in CBT and a key point arises with the change of goal from cognitive modification to cognitive flexibility – similar to a key goal in ACT – psychological flexibility. This is a 'third wave' development because it attempts to avoid suppression and avoidance that have in recent decades been placed more squarely 'in the dock' for their role in causing and maintaining psychological problems. Avoidance and suppression are most usually 'busy activities' that cause more problems than they solve. The approach described above may be better described as 'letting the negative thought be and seeing what it will do' – again perhaps hoping that cognitive dissonance will naturally come to 'do its work'. This may strike readers as being a 'mindful' perspective and we know of course that mindfulness has developed strongly in CBT and psychological therapy in recent times. Mindfulness is seen as a key element of most of the third wave models of CBT (Hayes et al., 2004).

A full consideration of mindfulness is beyond my purpose here but CBT practitioners are increasingly faced with having to put some thought into how their conduct of individual therapy might link with their experience of MBCT in groups. There are as yet few authoritative guidelines[4] as to how this may be done and yet many CBT practitioners do now admit that this is precisely what they are doing. While acknowledging that most of the really convincing evidence of the effectiveness of therapeutic mindfulness does come from studies of group MBCT, I describe below aspects of my own and others' practice in which mindfulness interventions have been used with individual clients – they include three main sources: practices from MBCT, compassion-focused therapy (CFT) and approaches to client validation (Leahy, 2001; Linehan, 1993).[5] Fennell (2004, p. 1062) suggests that it is possible to import 'a shift of emphasis, taking direction from the central message of mindfulness' into individual CBT. This can include practices of MBCT, especially perhaps when some strong negative affect is experienced in the session:

> *Farouk* was a young man who had experienced strong feelings of panic during an Alpine holiday some years before and had frequent recurrences of these feelings, seemingly at random moments – including during therapy sessions. He never identified any specific negative thoughts or triggers that could be examined in orthodox CBT fashion. He did identify a more generic negative thought that encapsulated how he felt at these times: 'The worst has already happened.' He was interested in spiritual practices and asked about trying mindfulness exercises. During one session at the practitioner's home he suddenly went into one of his panics and, as agreed, the practitioner focused him

---

[4]One promising-looking one is Burdick (2013).
[5]I do also wish to acknowledge that there are completely different traditions of mindfulness in therapy in models other than CBT (see Hick & Bien, 2008).

on his breath and on regarding his thoughts as floating like clouds across his mind. This helped him to 'surf' the waves of his panic. Just as this exercise was ending, the practitioner's daughter returned unexpectedly from school and, not realising her mother 'had a client', shouted a series of irreverent comments into the therapy room. The therapist went out to inform her daughter of the situation and returned to find the client in stitches of laughter. This unexpected 'switch of attentional focus' proved grist to the mill of the ensuing discussion of how changes in attention can enhance psychological well-being!

It is helpful when therapists can back up mindful interventions with individual clients by advising them that they can also join a mindfulness group – now frequently available in many localities. Clients can also choose to use self-help books on mindfulness (Kabat-Zinn, 2012; Williams, Teasdale, Segal & Kabat-Zinn, 2007; Williams & Penman, 2011).

Work with individuals using mindfulness can transfer principles from group-based MBCT – for example, that it is best to start with an experience of mindfulness and to put aside the usual CBT tactic of introducing it without giving a rationale first – because this may pre-shape the experience, the very mechanism we are trying to get away from. As in group-based MBCT a considerable amount of time may be devoted to reviewing the experience – a process well illustrated in Zindel Segal's DVD showing a mindfulness group in action (Segal, 2009). Williams and Penman (2011) suggest that activities using mindful contemplation of thoughts link well to mindfulness of sounds because, in a sense, a thought is like a sound in one's mind, and this can be a starting point when dialoguing with clients after exercises promoting mindful attention to thoughts. An example of paying mindful attention to depressive rumination follows:

Bishan suffered from depression linked to rumination. He felt stuck between two relationships, feeling he could not be true to either one. His practitioner introduced some basic mindfulness practices to see if he could deal with his rumination over this situation in a different way. He began the exercise well but suddenly reported having an intrusive thought – *I'm a shit bloke.*

C1:   This happens when I am by myself at home, I just keep getting this thought, *I'm a shit bloke, I'm a shit bloke* – it is like a dirge going round and round my head.

P1:   Is it possible to say to yourself, I am just having the thought that I am a shit bloke, it's just a thought, not a fact? *(Writes the thought on the whiteboard.)*

C2:   *(After a period of quiet)* For a while but then it comes back …

(Continued)

(Continued)

P2:   Okay – that is what brains do … they wander back and forth but we can learn to let a thought come and go and to come back to the breath …

C3:   (*After a period of silence, he suddenly laughs*) It is such a crap thought, isn't it!

P3:   (*Also laughing*) Yes, having the thought that you are shit is crap!

C4:   (*After more quiet*) Okay, it has come back again … but I can let it go … again … (*More silence*) … there's something else – those words and the voice I hear saying them reminds me of someone I hate … an actual someone I played cricket with … he was a real bully … he just needled the whole team but we were all too scared to say anything …

Here the mindfulness practices seemed helpful to Bishan by offering a different way to work with his tendency to ruminate. It was also interesting that when he let the thought go, other more reflective cognitive activity was released and in fact this material kept developing. Having realised that the ruminative self-criticism was like a bully, Bishan could entertain the idea that he might be able to learn to be kinder and more compassionate to himself.

Developing self-compassion

Paul Gilbert (2009a, 2010) has made a striking suggestion that therapy in general and cognitive interventions in particular are unlikely to work well unless clients can apply 'compassionate thinking' to their situation. This may explain why cognitive interventions, even those of such seeming merit to CB therapists, may miss the mark completely with some clients; even when feelingly delivered by the practitioner, inside the client's mind they are heard in flatly rational or even unkind ways. Gilbert (2010, pp. 6–7) describes how he gradually came to this perspective:

> Over 20 years ago I explored why 'alternative thoughts' were not experienced as helpful. This revealed that the emotional tone, and the way that such clients 'heard' alternative thoughts in their head, was often analytical, cold, detached or even aggressive. Alternative thoughts to feeling a failure like: 'Come on, the evidence does not support this negative view: remember how much you achieved last week!' will have a very different impact if said to oneself (experienced) aggressively and with irritation than if said slowly and with kindness and warmth … it seemed clear that we needed to focus more on the feelings of alternatives not just on content – indeed, an over-focus on content often was not helpful.

Arguing for compassion can seem like stating the obvious and it would indeed be hard to argue that compassion was irrelevant, but it is obviously more complex to figure out how we can put this insight to work in therapy. Seeing compassion as a technical matter would surely do scant justice to the concept and yet we do at some stage have to think of how it may be replicated in terms of a therapist skill – probably broadly conceived as a form of words to put to clients, a way of putting those words, and a way of working on our own inner processes to run alongside these 'interventions'. After analysing the exercises of CFT (Gilbert, 2009a, 2010) it seems to me that most of them are remarkably similar to those of the standard cognitive therapy, perhaps though reproduced in warmer and kinder language. Imagine, for example, Ellis (1973, p. 113) saying his trope about 'disputing *musturbatory* thinking' to a client:

> Everyone in this goddamn world should be real nice to me and make sure to remember to call me …

Gilbert (2009a, p. 296) seems to be trying to hit the same cognitive theme with the unsurprisingly kinder and warmer words, to be addressed to clients for self-help:

> Have rules like 'People should never let me down' or 'People should never forget about me' become background rules of my life? Have I ever explained my rules to others? If I haven't, would they accept them? Well, probably not, actually, because they are not very reasonable rules to force people to abide by if I am honest.

It is interesting to me that Kristin Neff, on the cover of one of Gilbert's books (2009a), endorses his work by noting that his ideas are down to earth so that one feels one is 'having a chat in his living room with a warm cup of tea'. This may remind the reader of the image of the 'fireside chat' mode of therapy that I discussed in Chapter 3 – and also perhaps of Hobson's (1985) description of 'conversational therapy'. We should of course acknowledge that there will never be just one mode of doing therapy and that 'different strokes' are required for 'different folks', but warmth, empathy and kindness may certainly go a long way for many clients. We conclude this consideration of mobilising compassion in our work with a therapist–client dialogue with some reflections on how the dialogue unfolded:

C1:   … (*Describing how he set off a smoke alarm in a holiday let apartment*) I just ended up thinking *I'm just so fecking useless.*

P1:   Does your dad come into this?

C2:   Yes, he was a top-rate mechanic and could fix anything … he'd show me but I could never do it as well as he did … I felt a disappointment to him … He never said anything but I just felt he was thinking I was useless …

P2:   These sound like powerful experiences … could they be influencing you now?

C3:   I did a thought record on this and when I looked at the negative thoughts, I thought to myself that those thoughts really give me a good kicking … in the positive evidence columns I could write that I am good at it and all that … I did feel better but something still gives a feeling of being kicked in the guts by situations like these.

P3:   It seems important to hear these alternative thoughts in a compassionate voice …

C4:   That's an interesting idea … my wife is interested in Buddhism and she's been telling me about loving kindness … you know, 'Let loving kindness come into my heart …'

At this point, practitioner and client decided to conduct an experiment to see if they could bring these two approaches to working with negative thoughts together. First, they sat together contemplating the problem of not being recognised as useful to a significant other. Then they meditated upon the idea of bringing loving kindness into their hearts before returning to further contemplation of uselessness. The client now reported a sense that his 'heart softened towards himself'. He looked again at his thought record and at the relationship between his original NAT ('I am so fecking useless') and his alternative thoughts ('I am not so good at some manual tasks – fixing cars – but good at others – keyboard skills – and really good at others – computer coding'):

C1:   When I look at those two thoughts I see that the NAT is harsh, name-calling but striking whereas the alternative thought is accurate but – I hate to say this – dull and boring …

P1:   So the NAT grabs your attention (C: Yeah) … but it's a bit like a tabloid headline … simplified – simplistic even …

C2:   (*Laughing and going into tabloid mode*) USELESS MARK – Will he *NEVER* learn?

P2:   Yeah – and they pay those headline writers big bucks because …

C3:   They sell the papers to the punters … in far greater numbers than the 'quality' papers …

This dialogue occurred during a final CBT session and was part of a review of what had been helpful to the client and how he could keep on track in future. This client made fluid use of the CBT model, and the positivity of his client experience is evident in the fact that he helped his practitioner – an experienced therapist – see some aspects of the work of CBT that he had not fully appreciated before. This new insight turned round the fact that there can be something compelling, even 'sexy', about NATs that is rarely matched in their opposing alternative thoughts. The practitioner had been giving much thought to the role of cognitive restructuring in CBT in light of developments in the third wave of the model. He was therefore immediately interested in this new insight into why cognitive restructuring works sometimes but not at others. So he picked up on the client's idea quickly and adds in a metaphor ('the tabloid headline') at P1 and P2 – which the client then runs with to produce an ironical tabloid headline about himself – 'USELESS MARK – Will he *NEVER* learn?' This metaphor is a rather more worldly version perhaps of Paul Gilbert's compassion metaphor, but in some senses a NAT is like a tabloid headline: it makes only small sense (if that!) but it is forceful and can 'seal the deal' with the unwary reader. As has been said, the Devil often has the best tunes.

There appears to be a growing trend towards 'light-touch' cognitive interventions; see Mansell et al.'s (2013) interesting ideas about 'method of levels' interventions. But if 'forcefulness' does play a role in the way NATs produce their negative effects, then we need also look at the more directional and deliberative methods, and how their forcefulness may play a role in cognitive change. This will be a shorter section of the chapter because such methods were well covered in the first edition of this book, and key elements of that coverage can be found on the companion website for this edition: https://study.sagepub.com/wills.

HELPING AWARENESS DO ITS WORK: DIRECTIONAL AND DELIBERATIVE COGNITIVE CHANGE

In some senses the methods in this section 'confront' negative thinking, and it is valuable to pause for a moment and think what this really means. In discussing the more non-directive end of the spectrum we have made much of the value of not being overly confrontational with negative thoughts because this can sometimes seem to entrench such thinking yet deeper. The actual meaning of the word 'confront' means 'come face to face with' and one might add to this 'without necessarily having received an invitation to do so'. The circumstances that might justify such a manoeuvre would presumably be where an issue is being avoided or where thinking is so stuck on some old track that the client may need to be forcibly pointed towards the possibility of other tracks. Negative thinking can seem like a less-than-popular relative who keeps turning up and 'banging on' about something that one does not necessarily want to hear about. Sometimes the only way to deal with this is to forcibly point out how you are experiencing the other person – and this will not always be greeted with a welcome. I find that clients with excessive anger can sometimes come over in this way and we may have to consider whether going over and over the same angry ground is a good use of therapy time; in fact there is evidence that it mostly reinforces dysfunctional anger (Lilienfield, 2007). When there appears to be a need to 'cut across' a sequence of negative thinking this can be a marker to consider using a *directional* (my preferred term for 'directive' in relation to CBT: see Wills with Sanders, 2013, pp. 30–1) cognitive method. Another marker is when we have used some of the more awareness- and acceptance-oriented methods without success. Finally, in an argument also developed in Chapter 6 on emotions in CBT, clients often need to re-establish a better balance between their emotional self and cognitive self (Epstein, 1998). Under stress clients may become 'flooded' by negative emotions and may need to use more deliberative steps to help their disoriented cognitive 'balancers' function again. Techniques that involve helping clients to write things down may be particularly helpful in this respect. These general considerations need also to be weighed against experience of the individual style of the client we are working with. If we follow the strategy of beginning at the non-directive end of the spectrum and moving to the more directional end as necessary, then we would always have some such knowledge to base the use of more directional work on. I personally would assess the fact that I now most usually follow the strategy of initially working in a non-directive style for cognitive interventions, and only move to a more directional style later as necessary, as the main way my working style has been influenced by third wave approaches, to my and my clients' benefit.

Using deliberative cognitive strategies: thought records and 'defusion' techniques

Many CB therapists seem to have become more reserved about the use of cognitive restructuring over the years – mainly I think because experiences of its counterproductive use make a larger impression than many more benign experiences of positive use – itself perhaps leading to a form of cognitive distortion. It may be, however, that many of these negative experiences of using cognitive restructuring arise primarily from its *premature* use. It is important to remember that cognitive restructuring consists of three steps: identifying thoughts, evaluating them and *then* finally responding to them (Beck, 2011). It is unfortunately quite easy to move through these steps too quickly. Being overly persuasive is perhaps a characteristic problem for CB therapists, because it is easy to forget that what is a familiar pattern of discussion for them is not so familiar to clients. CB therapists have been powerfully armed with precious knowledge that allows us often to have a shrewd idea of what, for example, a socially anxious client is likely to be think-ing and sometimes we can get trapped in a desire to launch a 'clever' intervention based on such a formulation. As I put it in the first edition of this book, 'Whilst recognising the utility of generic formulations, therapists also need to listen very carefully for the actual individual and idiosyncratic thoughts that each client will report as variations on generic themes' (Wills, 2008a, p. 56). Careful listening and good use of counselling skills (Inskipp, 1996) can be part of an altogether gentler way of working up to coming face to face with NATs. The ubiquitous whiteboard can again be pressed into action to draw up vicious cycle patterns of thoughts, feelings and behaviours that seem to go together. Clients can be encouraged to keep simple records of thoughts and feelings in their therapy workbooks and, as the Suggestion below notes, record examples of hearing the NATs of others – sometimes easier to hear initially than one's own!

Suggestion: *Fieldwork assignment*   Many clients have told me that once they become aware of the concept of negative thoughts, they often experience hear-ing other people say them: especially people close to them in their families and workplaces. It may be easier to hear such thoughts in others than in oneself at first. Hearing one's own is a new insight that may come a little later. For some people, this extremely valuable extra insight is hastened by writing down NATs overheard during the passage of everyday life. Clients can then periodically ask themselves, 'Do *I* ever have a thought like that?' You may wish to try this as a fieldwork assignment.

Another way of finding both the right area and time to challenge cognitions is to ensure that we are targeting an emotionally significant area. People have many negative thoughts but not all of them are significant. The following dialogue between a young client and CBT-oriented youth worker shows how giving a client permission to 'speak from the emotion', and the use of belief ratings, can help us to achieve emotionally significant change:

Practitioner and a distraught teenager discuss her reaction to a difficult phone call from her estranged father.

P1:   You felt upset after your dad's phone call. What was said?

C1:   Basically he called to remind me not to forget to get a birthday card for Gran.

P2:   So how did you feel about that?

C2:   I felt pretty angry: you know, like that he thought *I* might forget. I never forget! Why did he seem to think that I might forget this time?

P3:   What is your theory on that? Why did he seem to think that?

C3:   He doesn't trust me … or help me properly any more (*looks very upset*).

P4:   What's the feeling now? Speak from there (*indicating the gut*).

C4:   Sad, sad … a bit lost, you know: the nice him has gone forever.

      (*A little later*)

P5:   So there seemed to be two feelings just now: anger and sadness. Can we take them one by one and look at them and see what's behind them? The angry bit first: if 100% were the angriest you have ever been; how would you rate how you felt then?

C5:   Not too bad; 40% maybe, I am used to it with him, you know.

P6:   The thought seemed to be, 'He thinks I will forget Gran's birthday'; is that right?

C6:   Yes but I don't really believe that: it is just his interfering ways really.

P7:   So how much out of 100 do you believe that thought?

C7:   Not so much – about 30% I suppose.

Practitioner and client went on to identify that the sadness rating was much higher at 80%, twinned with a belief rating of 90% for the thought 'He does not trust or

Thought:	Emotion:
He thinks I'll forget Gran's birthday (30%)	ANGRY (40%)
He does not trust or help me anymore – I miss the nice him (90%)	SAD (80%)

Figure 4.7   Thoughts/feelings ratings

help any more – I miss that part of him.' This establishes that the sad thought and feeling are more meaningful to the client and probably should be tackled first.

Practitioners should not expect the identification of negative thoughts always to go smoothly. A variety of problems can occur and these require therapist patience and creativity. If clients struggle to link thoughts and feelings, practitioners may need to proceed more slowly and adopt a more educational style. This problem, other problems, and frequently used solutions are shown in Table 4.1.

Table 4.1   Problems and solutions for identifying negative thoughts

Problems working with negative thoughts	Possible solutions
The client confuses feeling with thinking: e.g. 'I just feel like I'm going to fail the exam.'	*Reflect back to the client with the correct terms: 'So you think you'll fail the exam, I guess then you feel anxious?' Refer back to the terminological difficulty when the client has put it the right way round.*
The client cannot identify a clear thought associated with distress: e.g. 'I was on my own, I just started feeling anxious. I didn't seem to have a thought.'	*Work back to a set of theoretical explanations and ask the client which one seems closest to his experience. 'When people are anxious they often fear something bad will happen. Does that ring any bells?'*
The client's negative thought is a 'megaphone statement': 'When my car failed, I thought, "typical".'	*Reflect back and add a probe: 'So you thought typical … of your luck? Like fate is against you?'*
The client's negative thought is in the form of a question: 'Why was it me that was left out?'	*Point out that the question could mask a negative thought and ask, if so, what would the 'negative answer' to the question be.*
The client's negative thought is hidden in other material: 'I was thinking about how my work had been going' (in relation to feeling low).	*Make the thought/feeling link by asking, 'Does the fact that you were feeling low imply that you fear that your work hasn't been going well?'*
The client cannot identify the negative feeling associated with the negative thought: 'I just felt yewk.'	*Go with the client's vocabulary in the belief that a more precise feeling is likely to emerge as therapy progresses.*
The client cannot rate the emotion experienced.	*Use an analogue scale.*

Three useful ways of evaluating negative thoughts are: first, using GD/SD to explore them (see earlier dialogues on pp. 64–8), testing for cognitive distortions (see Chapter 4 items on companion website) and testing the validity and utility of NATs (see companion website). Identification and evaluation of thoughts, along with restructuring them, are all incorporated into the thought record methodology – see later section.

Using cognitive defusion

Hayes et al. (2004) have added a significant new conceptual tool for working with negative thoughts – cognitive defusion.[6] Rather than targeting the language content of negative thoughts as is done in more orthodox CBT, or exploring the way that clients attend to such content as might be done in CBT influenced by the strategies of mindfulness or attentional methods, cognitive defusion is based on undermining the unhelpful aspects of the structure of language itself. This follows Hayes' long-term interest in the behavioural analysis of language as first described by B.F. Skinner (1957), although it also has some forerunners perhaps in some of Ellis's speculation about the nature of language and his exploration of the concept of 'e-prime' (Ellis, 2000). At its simplest, cognitive defusion works on changing the context of language; for example, clients may be encouraged to try singing the words of heavy negative thoughts to a light-hearted tune. One elderly client with OCD (obsessive compulsive disorder) felt that he had to write down all the names of the players when he was watching football on TV. Unfortunately it did not just stop at that – the list habitually expanded to all the games he had seen the players play in before, the results of those games, the commentators … ad infinitum … He was eventually persuaded to sing, 'I've got to write all the players' names down … da-dum, da-dum, da-dumpty dumpty dum' to the tune of 'Always look on the bright side of life'. This made him laugh and also seemed to help him to put these negative thoughts aside. Further discussion of defusion and examples in practice are offered on the companion website. Illustrating defusion via an example of helping with OCD is apposite because the limitations of cognitive restructuring when working with OCD have been acknowledged since the very earliest CBT models. This is probably because clients with OCD tend to 'over-think' things, and some types of cognitive intervention amplify that tendency. There is an increasing range of cognitive interventions with OCD (Wells, 2009) – testament to the growing sophistication of methods in CBT.

Using metacognitive interventions

Adrian Wells' (2009) metacognitive model works on the idea that 'positive' metacognitive beliefs, such as 'If I don't check everything I do I will make an unacceptable number of mistakes', often play a key role in maintaining OCD symptoms. In this model the starting point is usually an identified NAT such as 'I might have caused harm', but instead of exploring this thought to either evaluate it or challenge it directly, Wells offers templates to formulate the problem in such a way that the maintaining role of the underlying metacognitive belief is made clear to the client. Change techniques are then applied to the metacognitive belief rather than to the original NAT. A worked example is shown on the book's companion website.

---

[6]It should be acknowledged that some ACT therapists have argued that methods such as cognitive defusion should largely replace methods of cognitive restructuring.

Cognitive restructuring with thought records

There are in fact a variety of thought records that are used in CBT practice (Wills, 2008a). Table 4.2 shows a generic thought record that can act as a culminating step, enabling practitioners to gather material from many of the methods already described. The thought record in the figure shows a worked example of a client whose first attempt at using it did not prove effective. The first attempt is shown in the first row (in italics). The second row (not italics) represents a more successful attempt. Discussion of the work involved in both of these attempts is presented in an in-depth discussion posted on the companion website to this book, and this represents a set of guidelines for working with thought records in general.

Readers should note that the first three columns of the thought record essentially offer a format for writing down client material containing the key negative thoughts and feelings in the context in which they occurred. The other four columns are used to gather material from the evaluation of, responding to and challenging of the negative thoughts identified in the first three. Characteristic problems encountered in evaluating, responding and challenging are summarised in Table 4.2, and further commentary on these difficulties is also lodged on the book's companion website.

CONCLUSION

I began this chapter by acknowledging the fact of times changing in CBT – and this theme is particularly evident in the changing nature of approaches to modifying negative thoughts in the model. It has become clearer that the range of methods shows distinctions in the extent to which clients are encouraged to focus mainly on awareness of such thoughts – in the hope that awareness itself will stimulate cognitive change – and in the extent to which clients are offered direction to achieve such change. I have made the case for the utility to practitioners of a continuum of methods from the less to the more directional ones, and suggested that practitioners begin at the less direct end and proceed towards the more directive end as they should find necessary. I hope that the utility of such a continuum can be tested by methods and process research on CBT – a part of a practitioner's essential knowledge that has been lacking in CBT research, dominated as it has been by outcome research. My own experience as a practitioner and supervisor suggests, however, that new practitioners are best advised to make an initial strong focus on developing good listening skills (Inskipp, 1996) and building up methods on the less directive end of the cognitive intervention skills continuum, and then turn to developing skills at the more directive end as they become more experienced. Practitioners with more experience can use the continuum to make an inventory assessing their competences at different points on the continuum – with a view to consolidating those skills they feel confident in and undertaking some development on skills they feel less confident in.

It has been a challenge to incorporate in one chapter all the main skill elements that can now be involved in developing CBT practice. I am comforted, however, by the fact that modern publishing technology allows for back-up materials to be lodged

Table 4.2 Seven-column thought record: worked example

Trigger	Emotion	NAT	Evidence for NAT	Evidence against NAT	Alternative adaptive thought	Outcome
Blood on money from cash point	Anxious 80%	I have to wash my hands. I have to change my clothes.	Not hygienic.	No infections transmitted this easily. Probably very common.	I should rationalise that the risk is negligible.	Anxiety 60%
Blood on money from cash point	Anxious 80%	I have got dangerous germs on my hands. I could kill my son and husband.	Germs are everywhere.	Germs are only very rarely dangerous. Blood infections aren't that hardy.	I may have germs on my hands but they are almost certainly harmless.	Anxiety 30% Resist washing hands and/or changing clothes.

Table 4.3 Problems and solutions in evaluating and responding to negative thoughts

Problems	Solutions
Problems with evidence (columns 4 & 5)	
Strongly adverse life events.	*Focus on empathic listening. Identify ways of thinking that may be making the problem even worse. Suggest that it may be useful to review how helpful these thoughts are.*
The quantity of the evidence favours the negative. The quality of the evidence favours the negative.	*Discuss the balance of the evidence. Where either the quantity or the quality of the evidence balances towards the negative, suggest an 'open verdict'.*
The client finds it difficult to evaluate a negative thought as anything but true (negative evidence is more compelling or credible).	*Use belief ratings: anything less than 100% indicates a degree of doubt that can be built on.*
Problems with the alternative thought (column 6)	
The client describes the alternative thought as having intellectual but not emotional conviction (head but not heart).	*Go back over the whole sequence. Check the exact wording of the NAT and the alternative. Recheck the quality of the evidence. Also suggest that emotional conviction does take longer and may take some time to 'bed in'.*
Clients say things like 'Yes (I know I'm not really a failure) but ...'.	*Draw out the 'but' – often it is underlain by some unspoken fears or even by a metacognitive rule such as 'If I don't worry about this, I'll get complacent'.*
Problems with the end result (column 7)	
Client reports no change in negative feeling.	*Discuss the need to use the method over time. Write in a comment on how it could be different next time. If persistent, review focus and consider shifting focus to cognitive processes rather than content.*

on a book's companion website; and I hope that readers can be reassured by the fact that a continuum model of skill development suggests that they do not have to learn everything all at once but can plot a course of learning that is both rationally sound and emotionally intelligent.

FURTHER READING

Beck, J. (2011) *Cognitive behavior therapy: basics and beyond*. New York: Guilford.

Ciarocchi, J.V., & Bailey, A. (2009) *A CBT practitioner's guide to ACT*. Oakland, CA: New Harbinger.

Leahy, R.L. (2003) *Cognitive therapy techniques: a practitioner's guide*. New York: Guilford.

Wells, A. (2009) *Metacognitive therapy for anxiety and depression*. Chichester: Wiley.

5

SKILLS FOR WORKING ON CHANGING BEHAVIOUR

Success nourished them: they seemed able so they were able. (Virgil's Aeneid, V, 231)

INTRODUCTION

When we say that people 'talk the talk' but do not 'walk the walk' we suggest that they are not matching their fine words with fine actions – that talk without action is cheap. We suggest they are not matching their fine words with fine actions – that talk without action may be cheap. While many fine and insightful words are spoken in therapy, we also have a duty to help our clients think how they can reinforce changes of attitude in action. Behaviourally oriented therapy has been developing for nearly a hundred years now so it would be surprising if it did not offer us some useful skills for changing problematic behaviours.

This chapter focuses on two key skills for helping clients change key behaviours: first, helping depressed clients to become behaviourally active, and, second, helping clients with anxiety problems face up to feared situations. It will argue that it is possible to achieve changes in thinking in parallel with behaviour change, and I also echo the theme developed throughout this book, namely that most therapeutic activities offer opportunities for interpersonal and emotional change. Changes in interpersonal behaviours – such as increased assertiveness – can also be directly targeted. We begin by considering how we can adopt a behavioural perspective to understand clients and their situations, and help them develop more awareness of their own behaviours. As in the other methods chapter, I advocate a continuum beginning with the relatively non-directive activity of raising awareness of behaviours, and ranging to the more active methods to help clients convert behavioural awareness into establishing specific new behaviours.

HELPING CLIENTS TO DEVELOP BEHAVIOURAL AWARENESS

We begin this section by considering two clients who needed help to change behaviours that are problematic to them:

> *Matthew* suffered from long-term depression, sometimes with manic episodes. He had been in a good job but eventually had to give it up. He spent his days reading and going for long solitary walks. He became increasingly cut off from his wife and children and friends.
>
> *Claudette* was anxious in social situations. She had started a new job and the stress of fitting in at her new office had pushed her to the edge of coping. Before going to an office party, she had hidden in the loo for almost an hour. She then walked across the room slowly (so that people would notice that she had come) but returned to the toilet before grabbing her coat and going home.

People suffering from emotional or physical pain sometimes behave in ways that reinforce their problems. Matthew lost the ability to carry out many of his active social behaviours and this led to a vicious cycle of isolation, rumination and more depression. A good way to break this cycle was for him to behave in more socially engaged ways. Claudette's tactic of avoiding situations only made her more anxious. Ironically, it probably ensured that her self-conscious behaviour became more evident to others. She too needed to behave in more confident and proactive ways to break this cycle.

Suggestion Can you think of clients or people you know who are like Matthew and Claudette? Try to define their specific concrete behaviours that are problematic. If things were getting better for them, how might those behaviours start to change? If the clients or people you thought of did start to make these behavioural changes, how would that impact on their beliefs about themselves, other people and about the world?

In the past, behaviourists have been accused of having a cold, mechanical view of therapy. More recently, however, they have developed more interpersonal sensitivity towards clients and opportunities for interpersonal change during therapy (Tsai et al., 2009). The behavioural tendency to regard only observable behaviour as a focus for therapy, though, probably put an artificial ceiling on what the approach could contribute. A breakthrough came with the recognition that, as well as observable external behaviours, there are also 'internal behaviours' such as thinking and remembering. This opened a wider perspective on factors that could be defined as behavioural triggers and responses. Claudette thought that 'People find me boring', for example, and this thought intensified her anxiety. With the concept of internal behaviours, behaviourists could develop a richer understanding of behavioural triggers and responses. They realised that people made evaluative appraisals of these triggers and responses. What one person regards as a reward, for example, another may not. These breakthroughs fostered a powerful alliance between the behaviourists and the emerging 'cognitive revolution' (Rachman, 1997). On the cognitive side of the alliance, Beck (1970a) and Ellis (Dryden, 2006) stressed the importance of working with behaviour. They realised, for example, that proactive behaviour was likely to have a positive impact on self-efficacy beliefs like 'I can take effective action on issues that matter to me' and 'I don't just have to accept things passively.' An additional interpersonal dimension has become evident in the fact that most behaviour relevant to clients' situations centres on how they relate to others. The therapeutic relationship can also be profitably seen as a key arena in which new and rewarding behaviours can be rehearsed and tested (Tsai et al., 2009).

Behaviourally oriented therapy began almost a century ago with the work of Watson (Watson & Rayner, 1920), Pavlov (1927) and Skinner (1965). It is now considered that the phenomena they explored are more complex than the original formulations (Ramnero & Torneke, 2008). Their work, however, remains important as signposts to the key areas of behaviour change. Pavlov and Watson both worked on the 'antecedents' (the 'what went before') of behaviour: they showed that one could change the way a person behaved by manipulating environmental conditions to trigger specific behavioural responses. Skinner, on the other hand, put more stress on the 'consequences' (the 'what came after') of behaviour that either may or may not reinforce it, so making it more or less likely to re-occur. A major thrust of more recent behavioural therapy has recognised the power of simple social reinforcement such as smiling, positive attention and praise – the fundamental building blocks of relationships (Spiegler & Guevremont, 2009). As CBT practitioners are concerned with human encounters, they can use an understanding of social reinforcement to point to rewarding interpersonal factors like attention, positive regard and intrinsic personal satisfaction as examples of reinforcement theory that greatly assist therapeutic change.

ANALYSING THE CLIENT'S SITUATION FROM A BEHAVIOURAL ANGLE

Behaviour therapists can now use the different concerns of Pavlov and Skinner as *both* playing key roles in most forms of learning. *Behavioural assessment* or *behavioural functional analysis* (ABC) aims to analyse clients' situations by identifying both the A triggers for key behaviours and the C reinforcing patterns that hold those B behaviours in place. The behavioural *ABC method* is a useful mnemonic for *functional analysis*: A stands for antecedents; B stands for behaviour; C stands for consequences. A blank version of the form used in Table 5.1 to apply ABC analysis to the situations of Matthew and Claudette can be found on the companion website for this book.

Table 5.1 ABC analysis

A: Antecedent	B: Behaviour	C: Consequences
What happened before what happened	What happened	What happened after what happened
Matthew worries that he may have another manic episode and decides that 'low-key' activities such as reading and walking may help to stave such an episode off.	Matthew 'buries his head' inside a book and/or goes out walking in several stretches covering 3 to 4 hours during the day and evening.	Matthew's reading and walking means that he has no time to undertake any of the tasks on his 'to do' list – so the list gets longer each day. The solitary nature of the tasks he does undertake means that he becomes more and more isolated from his family and friends.
Claudette worries all the way to the office party. She thinks, 'People will think I'm weird'.	Claudette goes to hide in the loo. Later, she walks through trying both to be unobtrusive and to look as though she were enjoying herself.	Claudette feels anxious throughout the evening and bad about herself afterwards. Some fellow workers notice her behaviour and think it odd.

Table 5.1 shows that different types of triggers, observable and unobservable, can act as 'antecedents': overt external events could include meeting people or facing the challenges of the day's tasks, whereas covert internal events could include thoughts like 'Nobody will want to be with me while I am so miserable' and physical feelings of tiredness. Furthermore, laying things out like this helps us to identify things that might be changed or modified, and targets for change can focus on any or all of the A, B and C columns. Matthew did not initially respond to help from his community psychiatric mental health team (CMHT) but liked the fact that the team social worker, who was asked to help him 'find some social activities', listened respectfully to him. The social worker was interested to try some formal CBT with him:

Matthew decided, in collaboration with this practitioner, that he would:

◆ deal with his negative thoughts in a different way (A);

◆ limit his reading to one-hour periods and do a socially enjoyable activity with his wife and/or children and/or friends once or twice a week (B);

◆ undertake daily one half-hour task from a list of jobs he was behind on and devise a behavioural experiment to test his thought that nobody wants to be with him (C).

Claudette, working with a health centre counsellor, decided that she would:

◆ be less worried if she believed she could be with people at least minimally (A);

◆ build up tolerance of her anxiety in social situations – first for 5 minutes and then for increasingly longer periods – and practise conversations in safe situations, such as therapy, and gradually extend this to other situations; if confidence grew during these tasks, she could practise taking the initiative in social situations (B);

◆ learn a powerful and genuine way to break the ice socially by admitting how nervous she was. Doing this as a *behavioural experiment* would allow her to test her belief that few other people were nervous like this and that saying she was would put people off (C).

We can also notice that some aims will be to do *less* of some activities – e.g. less reading for Matthew, and *more* of others, more social contact for Claudette. All these strategies proved able, eventually, to help Matthew and Claudette to make at least some improvement in their situations.

Suggestion *Behavioural exercise – figuring out an ABC pattern*

Form: Individual or in small groups

Aim: To become familiar with using the ABC pattern

A client recently told me that he was worried about his drinking and wanted to do something to bring it under control. We agreed to start by analysing what he thought was his most difficult situation regarding drinking. He said this: 'Now I am on my own I tend to get home to a lonely house. It is worse when I get home late and tired after a gruelling day at work, and my routine has been to grab some cans and fags and plonk myself in front of the telly. It helps me to relax but I get to bedtime having drunk more cans than I intended and I don't sleep very well either.' Using an ABC format like the one shown in Table 5.1, by yourself or in a group, see if you can target some areas for change as shown on p. 92.

Developing ABCs is really a simple type of 'behavioural formulation' and follows a similar process to that explored in Chapter 2. As we noted earlier, formulation is something that can be used even in the earliest CBT sessions. Deliberative behavioural assessment can help compensate for the fact that practitioners seem to overlook behavioural factors in CBT formulation quite often. Comprehensive approaches to clients' behaviours are needed because if problematic behaviours go unchecked they tend to spread across ever-wider areas of clients' lives. Fearful behaviours, for example, can seep into more situations as clients lose confidence. A wide understanding of client functioning gives practitioners more opportunities to encourage change in clients' current problems. Small changes in relatively easy areas can in turn make wider and harder changes more possible as confidence rises. We saw in Chapter 3 how it is essential for us as practitioners to develop awareness of our own behaviour; such awareness will also be helpful to clients. It can therefore be beneficial to encourage clients to develop behavioural awareness by learning and keeping a diary of ABC analyses of their own patterns as an on-going part of the therapy, especially during early phases. This analysis can help clients' awareness of potentially tricky situations and offers target behaviours for change. We have already mentioned the importance of goal formation as the culmination of the assessment phase of therapy. Goals are often the flipside of problems: this can be seen clearly in the strategies that evolved naturally from the ABC analysis of both Claudette and Matthew's presenting difficulties. Questions likely to be helpful in ABC analysis are shown in Table 5.2.

Table 5.2 Useful questions when formulating ABC analysis

A questions:	B questions:	C questions:
What happens just before you ...?	*How exactly do you react?*	*How do you end up feeling? Any relief?*
Were there any body sensations ...?	*Any avoidance behaviours?*	*How do other people react?*
Any thoughts?	*Any safety behaviours?*	*Are there any longer-term consequences to you behaving that way?*

Letting behavioural awareness do its work

Self-monitoring and diary keeping

It is best for therapists and clients to do initial ABC analyses together in session. As clients grasp the task, it can then become a useful homework assignment. As ABC analysis is carried out over a number of weeks, it takes the form of behavioural self-monitoring, along with other tasks aimed at developing cognitive and emotional awareness. The suggestion that the client should take up self-monitoring carries powerful meta-messages that clients can:

◆ be active partners in therapeutic activities

◆ do things that could make a difference

◆ develop a different relationship to the way they are living, becoming reflective observers of themselves as well as active doers

◆ change, but this is likely to involve 'work and practice' (Dryden, 2006).

It is worth spending time and effort to introduce this important task and to prepare clients for any problems that might arise. The following dialogue occurred between Claudette and her workplace counsellor with regard to developing more assertive behaviours:

Practitioner (P1): Could you keep a diary to help identify situations at work where this comes up? ... You can use ABC analysis to identify situations when it is hard for you to be assertive. Try to record at least one instance for each day. When you realise that you've been put down, figure out what happened just before you felt that and write it here (A column), then how you felt or what you did here (B column) and then what happened next in this column (C). This will help us find areas that we can work on. Before we go any further, how do you feel about me asking you to do this?

Client (C1): Okay I suppose. I mean I can see the point of it ... but I wonder if I will do it, when I feel low, I may not be motivated ... it may be easier to go along with things.

P2: It is good to be realistic – it could be difficult. Do understand though that it is not a pass-or-fail thing: anything you do is helpful. Even if you do nothing, we can try to figure out why it was difficult. Some clients only remember late on and then scribble down things for the whole week – always useful though.

C2:	So is it best to write it down as soon as it happens then?
P3:	Ideally, but that's not always possible, so whenever you can find time … it should get easier as time goes on.

Practitioners should go over the rationale for ABC analysis before starting. Everyone has favourite ways of giving and responding to rationales. They can be expressed in ways that make links with clients' interests (such as golf in the example below) or style of expression (such as metaphors). The following points can be made:

◆ It is often helpful to step back from an upset and think, 'What is this really all about? What is actually happening here?'

◆ It is good to stop bad reactions at an early stage: 'Problems can be like boulders rolling down a slope: the further they roll, the more momentum they develop and the harder they are to stop.'

◆ It is good to spot trigger events that give you problems: 'Forewarned is fore-armed'.

◆ It is good to develop several ways of dealing with difficult situations: 'You don't want to be a one-club golfer, trying to get round a big golf course with just a putter!'

Practitioners should consult with clients about how they might like to do self-monitoring and what they would find helpful to keep track of. I have found it useful to encourage clients to obtain a diary that they are likely to feel good about, perhaps with a nice cover and pages for drawing in. Diaries can work in highly flexible ways to record feelings, behaviours, thinking, physical reactions, substance use and social behaviour – but also 'musings about the universe'. They can be quite light-touch interventions that inspire clients to figure out for themselves the changes they could make. They can also be used in a more overtly directional way – to forward plan things for future days and weeks. We now examine the use of a more intentionally directional type of diary that is well known in CBT: the activity (or activation) schedule. Observations of behavioural self-monitoring and ABC analyses can now be used in the more directional interventions of behavioural activation.

Encouraging behavioural awareness to do its work: behaviour activation in depression

The body language and posture of depressed clients often signal the extent of behavioural deactivation: the shoulders become hunched, and the more depressed the person, the more the shoulders turn in on themselves, until he or she may seem to be shrinking before our eyes. The self seems to turn away from the world and the body slows down in unison. As the body dips below levels of optimal activity, performance drops below par as well: memory, concentration, appetite and sleep all suffer; movement and motivation seem to take more effort. Extreme inactivity may take on the form of a desire to stay in bed. Some clients believe that this will make them feel better – unfortunately this hope usually proves illusory. Beck et al. (1979) suggested that therapists might counter this tendency by encouraging clients literally to get up and get going. A realistic plan for gradually increasing behaviour levels is often the most effective way to go. Very depressed clients may respond best by following a simple behavioural programme. This is especially so for those with impaired concentration, who may find cognitive work just too difficult (Fennell, 1989; Emery, 1999). Well-known strategies for such an approach are *activity scheduling* from the cognitive therapy tradition of Beck (Beck et al., 1979) and *reward planning* from the behavioural tradition of Lewinsohn (Lewinsohn & Gotlib, 1995). Recent approaches to behavioural activation have also stressed the importance of reactivating formerly proactive behaviours that are now avoided – especially when they require interpersonal engagement and effort (Martell et al., 2001; McCullough, 2006).

Activity scheduling

We need to think about both the *quantitative* (how much) and the *qualitative* (what kind) dimensions of our clients' activities; both dimensions suffer when people become unhappy for prolonged periods. As clients become more depressed and de-motivated, they may well be withdrawing from everyday activities; often those things that have made life worthwhile in the past. Recent approaches to behavioural activation have stressed the benefit of generating activities that help clients enact their most cherished values (Martell et al., 2001). If clients are just 'going through the motions', life becomes a humdrum, low-temperature existence lived without passion. Our life passions may, however, be highly individual to us. One client was embarrassed about how absorbed he had once been in stamp collecting: he feared that it meant he was 'uncool' and 'an anorak', but as he described the stamps' different colours, styles and historical significances, he showed a real sense of passion. Therapists can help clients in these situations by affirming their right to be their own persons regardless of fashion or chic.

The activity schedule has a simple format but it is one capable of having a variety of different and even sophisticated uses. We can choose where to start on this spectrum but may do so with a combination of *quantitative* aspects of behaviours ('*doing more things*') and their *qualitative* aspects ('*doing things that count*').

Behavioural work: helping clients make qualitative improvements

When building up the activity levels of depressed clients, Beck et al. (1979) make the useful distinction between 'mastery' (M) and 'pleasure' (P) oriented activities. 'Pleasure' is often linked to the highly valued activities mentioned earlier. 'Loss of pleasure' is a criterion of depression in *DSM-IV-TR* (APA, 2000) and depression often seems to drain it out of clients' lives. Depressed clients often no longer enjoy activities that they had enjoyed previously and might be completing them 'with gritted teeth'. The addition of the 'mastery' rating appreciates perseverance in activities that depression has made more difficult. Perseverance is an important aspect of recovery. Thus ratings for mastery (M) and pleasure (P) can be added to the client's activity schedule. See Figure 5.1 for Matthew's schedule with M and P ratings.

	Friday	Saturday	Sunday
0600–0700	Sleep	Sleep	Sleep
0700–0800	Breakfast	Breakfast	Sleep
0800–0900	Washing up and tidying up: M1, P1	Washing up and tidying up: M1, P1	Sleep
0900–1000	Reading: M1, P2	Took the kids to the park: M1, P4	Breakfast
1000–1100	Reading	With kids in park: P5	Reading: M1, P2
1100–1200	Reading	Park/ got lunch for kids: M2, P4	Reading: M1, P3
1200–1300	Made lunch: M1, P1	Reading: P2	More work on shed: M5, P2
1300–1400	Out for a walk: M1, P2	Cleared part of shed: M3, P1	Made lunch: M2, P2

Figure 5.1 Activity schedule with basic self-monitoring (scaled down)

Matthew presented his schedule to his social worker five or six times before it showed any sign of a 'breaking good'. The social worker sometimes wryly wondered if Matthew feared reporting any pleasure at all, including pleasure from fulfilling his therapy tasks. Week after week he grimly reported the same monotonous list of activities that included only low ratings for both mastery and pleasure and excluded any mention of completing any tasks from his 'to do' list. The social worker was following a protocol (Emery, 1999) but felt reservations about this – even using the one that had been highly recommended to her. One of the strengths of this protocol, however, turned out to be the convincing rationale it offers for 'staying on track' even if results are not forthcoming. It advises patient inquiry into why clients are not able to do certain tasks, and these queries eventually uncovered the vital insight that these activities evoked bad memories for Matthew – they had been part of a big set of tasks designed to help him to 'catch-up' on his life around the time of his last manic episode. He thought that he had got very 'wound up' by the tasks and this had contributed to his breakdown at that time. After this was aired, however, Matthew seemed more able to try things, and the couple of hours he spent with his children in the park, as shown in the schedule in Figure 5.1, was in many ways a turning point. It confirmed that Matthew's role as a father had high significance to him and provided a reliable source of positive reinforcement for future activities. The social worker's ability to listen patiently to Matthew once again paid dividends at this point.

As with diaries, activity schedules can be used to review how any particular week has gone (*retrospectively*) or as a way of forward planning an upcoming week (*prospectively*). Simple mood monitoring can also be added by asking clients to record how they feel during each segment of each day.

In reviewing a week, therapist and client can look for periods of relatively high or low activity and/or periods of feeling depressed (low mastery and/or pleasure scores) or good (high such scores). They can work collaboratively to see if there are patterns that it may be helpful to clarify and work on: typically things like bad starts to the day or early evening dips in mood. Insights generated from this kind of review – e.g. 'I generally feel better if I can start the day with relatively undemanding tasks' – can be used to forward plan a new and better pattern in the upcoming week. Such a plan may be very much a case of trying things to see how they work, and can be thought of as *behavioural experiments:* for example, do I feel better if I load activity into the morning and take it easier in the afternoon or vice versa?

Suggestion *What do our behavioural patterns look like and how could they change?*

Form: Individual or counselling pairs (counsellor and client) or trio (practitioner, client and observer)

Aim: To experience skills of using the activity schedule

Using the form for the activity schedule, trace out the daily patterns for the last few days. Look out for patterns and rhythms within and between the days. Go for as much detail as the client seems comfortable with. Be prepared to offer some personal feedback on how the patterns compare to your own and how you might feel about days structured like that. Ask the client if there is anything about their patterns that they might like to change. Devise a brief two- or three-point plan for making such a change. Finally, take brief feedback from all the participants in the exercise.

Weekly behavioural reviews can be linked with other aspects of the CBT work; for example did working to counteract thinking of oneself as a failure produce any behavioural bonuses? Sometimes more general, 'across the week/s' or 'across situations' patterns show themselves. Reviewing schedules with clients over the years shows that how clients start a day is often a crucial influence over the way the rest of the day develops. Matthew reported that he often awoke with instant negative thoughts – such as 'How do I feel today? Am I going to feel lousy all day again?' He would then scan his body and mind and could usually find some minor negative feeling to latch onto and amplify. A good strategy to counter this tendency is to suggest that clients can postpone evaluation of how they are feeling. It is relatively normal for people to feel quite disoriented immediately after waking. The best response to this is often to get up, move around, do some things and see how you feel later. The majority of clients who have been able to do this report that they find that they are okay later, presumably because they have avoided negative rumination by making a shift in attention. Although this intervention is specific to dealing with waking up, it frequently turns out that the negative self-focus demonstrated by the client's reaction to waking is reflected in negative self-focus and over-evaluation in other salient areas of the client's life.

PLEASURE PREDICTING

Pessimism is another criterion for depression in *DSM-IV-TR*. It is good to tackle pessimism early in therapy because it has the potential to undermine the whole therapeutic enterprise with beliefs like 'Nothing will help me', 'It could work for others but not me' and 'There's no point in trying'. Sometimes the client's more specific pessimistic predictions – typically beliefs like 'I won't enjoy doing that now I am depressed' – will undermine the client's efforts to build up activity levels. The technique of *pleasure predicting* is an effective intervention to counter this. When confronted by pessimism, the practitioner can go back to the pragmatic CBT default position: 'Well, that's possible but shall we see?' Here we can see how negative thoughts and behaviours have mutually reinforcing effects on each other; conversely, we can hope that encouraging change in either one may influence change in the other.

It is realistic to think that depression makes it hard to enjoy things but depression can also make it hard to even imagine enjoying things that one might. We can explore the latter possibility with a behavioural experiment such as that for Matthew described below:

Matthew thought initially that he would never really enjoy any of the things that he had enjoyed in his life before, and he also feared that he risked going into a manic episode if he started to feel a sense of joy again. After finding out that he *had* enjoyed playing in the park with his children, he contemplated whether he could go along with their request to go to a fairground. This seemed particularly risky to him as fairgrounds 'seem quite manic'. He and his social worker worked on developing a 'plan B' that could be put into practice if he started feeling distressed. This plan centred round helping the children to understand that they would need to go 'if Dad started to feel funny'. In the event Matthew did feel the need to go after about an hour, and the children did not much like leaving. Nevertheless Matthew felt pleased that they had all enjoyed the trip while it lasted – wryly noting that going early had saved them all money! He later used the same principles to go to a football match with a friend.

FACING UP TO FEARED SITUATIONS

CBT methods vary according to the specific presenting problem and/or transdiagnostic issue being targeted. We began looking at behavioural activation, which is used predominantly with depressed clients with their characteristic problems of under-activity. The next skill area we will look at is exposure, often used to overcome over activated safety behaviours of anxious clients.

Early behavioural therapy worked on the notion that noxious anxiety responses might be extinguished by being paired with incompatibly pleasant experiences such as relaxation. This concept was called 'reciprocal inhibition' and was operationalised in a therapeutic strategy called *systematic desensitisation*. For this strategy clients are exposed to feared situations, either for real or in imagination ('*in vivo*' or 'imaginal'), while practising the relaxation response at the same time (Wolpe, 1958). This proved to be a successful treatment. Another tradition of behaviour therapy that was imported into CBT was that of the scientific, empirical evaluation of therapy (Rachman, 1997). Evaluation of systematic desensitisation showed that the relaxation element did not add to the overall effectiveness of the exposure element and, since those findings, CBT has naturally focused more on the exposure element of the treatment (Hazlett-Stevens & Craske, 2008). Exposure therapy contributed to helping Claudette in two ways, first by working with a series of problematic situations that triggered her acute social anxiety (Claudette I) and later when she asked if she might use the same principles to work on a separate fear – of bridges (Claudette II).

Claudette (I) was inspired by reading Gillian Butler's (2009) self-help book for people with social anxiety. The book gives many helpful cognitive and behavioural strategies that one can use in social situations. Claudette's problem, though, was that she simply could not get herself into a social situation and stay there long enough to be able to put these strategies into action. She and her counsellor therefore decided to work on this aspect first and to build a hierarchy of increasingly distressing situations – using the subjective units of distress (SUDs) method described below – and then to get Claudette to remain in them for increased periods of time so she could practise some of the skills in Butler's book. Claudette felt that she wanted 'good back-up' when doing this so her practitioner also worked with her on having 'plan Bs', again discussed below.

Claudette's hierarchy of feared situations (extract)

Activity	Time	SUDs rating
1. Going into the common room	5 mins	10
5. Going into the common room	40 mins	50
6. Going for a drink with colleagues	15 mins	60
10. Going for a drink with colleagues	60 mins	95

The term 'SUDs' is fit for purpose here because what we need is a way for clients to report on their *comparative* feelings in different situations at different points in time. We help clients to establish SUDs ratings to go with their hierarchies, first, by asking them to brainstorm a list of situations that trigger their fears, and then by asking which is scariest. We then ask, 'If 100 represented the *most* scary feeling you could feel, how would you rate the feeling that would come up in this situation?' We can follow this by asking a similarly slanted question about the *least* scary feeling and use these initial ratings as anchors from which the client can estimate SUDs for the other items on the list: *So having to spend an hour in the bar with colleagues is the scariest feeling and you rate that at 95; how would you rate this one – being in the bar with them for 15 minutes?* You can observe the SUDs rating process in action on the DVD by Wright et al. (2006) listed at the end of this chapter.

Exposure can be carried out in imagination or in real life (*in vivo*). Generally real-life situations seem to produce more effective results, though if a client is not yet ready then imaginary exposure can be helpful as a build-up to that. Reproducing aspects of real-life situations in session (*simulation*) can also be useful; an example of dealing with client *Karen's* emetophobia (fear of vomiting) with simulation was presented in the first edition of this book (Wills, 2008a, pp. 102–3) and is available, along with a similar example with client *Jana,* on the companion website of this one: https://study.sagepub.com/wills.

Claudette was keen to proceed with these exposure exercises so the next step was to set a time scale for attempting them. This could have been as long as several months but she set herself the comparatively short-term time frame of 2–3 weeks. She also showed strong determination by saying that she intended to press on with the tasks, even moving up through them without necessarily completing all of them in strict order. Her practitioner decided to support her intention on this but also suggested a 'plan B': that she could revert to a slower timetable should that become necessary. They did use session time to simulate some practice of interpersonal skills that Claudette thought might be helpful for potential difficulties during these social encounters – e.g. refusing to be plied with drinks, dealing with over-personal remarks and coping with lulls in conversations. Though not appropriate in this situation, practitioners do sometimes accompany clients into exposure situations, and this can involve expeditions to supermarkets, civic amenity sites, driving on roads or catching trains. Of note here is the importance of checking with your professional indemnity insurance cover! Some colleagues have accompanied clients to zoos, and on to ferries and aeroplanes. Devising appropriate plans can involve therapist and client creativity.

In Claudette's situation, the plan was that she would tackle her exposure situations by herself and then use therapy sessions to make a progress report, fine-tune the plan and practise interpersonal skills as described.

How clients progress through hierarchies will obviously vary between them. Progress is usually not completely smooth. Problems in getting started are common and there are also often 'plateaus' in progress even when a start has been made. Claudette started well but became stuck when she needed to go beyond just having a 'quick drink' with colleagues. In the event, however, and by good fortune rather than by plan, this triggered a significant advance. Richard, a sympathetic male colleague remarked to her that he had noticed that she would 'never stay very long'. To this he added the interesting comment that the fact that she left quickly drew more attention than if she had stayed longer and 'it would be nice if she could stay longer sometimes'. These comments had a great impact on Claudette, who had previously given herself the name of the *Viz* comic character, 'Billy No Mates'. Claudette told Richard a bit about her problems coping with social situations. This discussion helped her feel more of a sense of belonging in the group and that made the *amount* of time she spent there seem less relevant.

C1: It just feels different now. I am not sure it matters how long I stay there.

P1: That does not matter because …?

C2: It's more important to be there — truly there — for 5 minutes or 5 hours.

P2: It sounds like you were proactive, and managed to tell Richard how you felt — well done.

C3: Yes — and he did not run a mile! And you know what else I have realised? These are some of the skills discussed in the self-help book: so I have got there anyway!

P3: What's happened to poor old Billy No Mates?

At this stage, Claudette's focus shifted in an interesting way. She felt that she had got 'pretty much where she wanted to on the problem of social situations' but felt that she wanted to finish off her therapy by using the idea of exposure to face up to another fear she had never discussed before — of heights and crossing bridges. As the practice centre was quite near a famous suspension bridge and she felt the fear acutely there, she asked if they could do a one-off 'exposure walk' across the bridge.

Claudette's (II) walking pace accelerated markedly as she and her counsellor approached the bridge. The footpath across the bridge is single file and as the counsellor fell in behind Claudette, she noticed that Claudette's walking style had become stiff and awkward and that she stumbled constantly. Claudette's legs seemed frozen with fear. The counsellor talked softly over her client's shoulder, suggesting ways for Claudette to loosen her legs and calm her thoughts and feelings. Eventually she stepped round Claudette and adopted a loose-limbed, 'monkey walk' and said, 'Like this'. Claudette managed to loosen her stance and they now progressed quickly, and after a short debrief were able to cross back over the bridge. Claudette was exhilarated and amused by the whole event but felt she had taken a big step forward.

Several important points about exposure can be noted by comparing these examples of its practice — with Claudette's fears of social situations and bridges respectively. They both ran within a time period that was shorter than is usually associated with exposure — varying here only from several weeks to one day, as opposed to much other exposure work that can last for months. The single-session version on the bridge resembles 'flooding' (short, sharp, all-in-one-go exposure) whereas the version for social situations was more like standard 'graduated exposure'. In both the practitioner adopts a warm and supportive relationship that encourages task completion but also tolerates problems in doing so.

There seem to be no universal rules governing practitioner behaviour during exposure exercises. Clients do not like unnecessary distractions during exposure and so report that they prefer therapists to keep a low-profile presence with fairly sparse, low-key

Table 5.3 Therapist skills for *in vivo* exposure therapy

Skills	Comment/variation
Giving a rationale for exposure	Not too elaborate; there is often a need to 'get on with it' – too much explanation can build up anticipatory anxiety.
Setting up a hierarchy with the client	Brainstorm and reiterate – keep revisiting before and after sessions to review in light of latest experience.
Asking SUDs questions	Follow a loose TOP-BOTTOM-MIDDLE order but be ready to just follow the client's thoughts.
Negotiating a time scale	Veer towards conservatism and realism but be prepared to give clients their heads.
Discussing skills that might be needed by client	Think of difficulties that could arise and whether rehearsal or a new skill might forestall problems.
Setting up a 'back-up' plan B	Suggest, 'We will probably never need this but ...'
Keeping a low profile	Don't give clients another problem by demanding too much of their attention when their attention might be transfixed on the task.
Maintaining a reassuring presence	Keep making positive noises and comments.
Asking about thoughts, feelings and urges during exposure	Do have some presence; low-key questions that you would ask in sessions anyway are fairly 'normalising' and give you quite useful information on how things are going.
Dealing with hiccups during exposure	Generally encourage clients to 'feel the fear and do it anyway' but be ready to 'pull the plug' quickly if necessary. Also be prepared when possible to restart after a break.

interaction. I find that asking about thoughts and feelings, as well as asking for on-going SUDs ratings, seems a natural and useful thing for the therapist to do, although one should be wary not to enter any new elements into the situation that have not been pre-agreed. Unexpected things can throw the client off track. It is important to stay with the exposure situation until SUDs ratings have come down – ideally to minimal levels. There are, however, some situations when this does not prove possible. It is sometimes suggested that practitioners plan extra-long (one-and-a-half- or even two-hour) sessions to take account of complications arising from the client becoming over-aroused. This may be increasingly hard to do as demand for CBT increases: therapists now usually have tight schedules themselves. In practice, I have found that the client can nearly always suggest a fall-back plan for continued uncomfortable feel-ings if asked beforehand. One client I worked with decided that if she still felt upset and had to go on to work, for example, she would call her office and tell them she was unwell and then have some quiet time at home. Clients' fall-back plans usually work well: the aim, after all, is to move the client towards self-practice at the time that seems best to them. Table 5.3 lists therapist skills for conducting exposure.

Suggestion *Facing up to a fear*

Form: Therapy duo or trio (including an observer)

Aim: Practice giving rationales for facing up to fears on a graduated basis and in constructing a graduated hierarchy to shape a new response

Instructions: Give the client a rationale to explain why a step-by-step approach can help in facing up to fears then help the client identify an area in which they have some kind of phobia or fear. End by asking clients if they can nominate a date by when they will have completed the first step. Take brief feedback from all participants in the exercise.

Helping clients to develop interpersonal behaviours

More recent approaches to behavioural activation have stressed that it is important to ensure that quality of behavioural engagement is addressed. In particular, it seems important that the avoidance of interpersonal interaction is tackled, as this sometimes plays a subtle role in contextual maintenance of depression:

Matthew followed up the success of taking his children to the fairground by tak-ing them to a T20 (short game) cricket match. He had been a keen sportsman when younger but unfortunately reported afterwards that he had not greatly

---

enjoyed this particular experience. There was a large crowd at the match and he'd got irritated with his kids for 'wandering off all the time', raising anxieties that they would 'get lost'. In going over this experience, practitioner and client were able to discern that Matthew had an *off* day and that actually he had been quite cut off from the kids. He had focused on inessentials such as scorecards and lunchboxes and not really on sharing the experience with them. Though this was a negative experience, it proved useful because one will have off days, and it was useful to think how to deal with them.

The progress of Matthew shows that there are frequently ups and downs in the recovery processes. Regaining previous functioning can seem a big step, and just as we would phase a person back into work who had been off sick, so the client can plan to return to more usual functioning at a slow but steady rate. Beck et al. (1979) illustrate how one small change can lead to another. They describe a hospital patient who said she could not read – previously a favourite pastime. Beck found her the shortest book in the ward library and asked her to read some of it to him. She eventually agreed to read just one line but actually managed a whole paragraph and some hours later she had finished the book. We can break things down into manageable units and allow success to feed on success, and we can 'shape' behaviour towards desired ends by moving in successive degrees closer to the final goal. Clients can be encouraged to know that, as long as they keep moving towards the goal: even by small steps, they will keep improving. These gradual steps can also work with rebuilding relationships after absence or illness. The importance of the interpersonal aspects of behaviour is often fundamental: maintaining friendships, meeting new people and taking the initiative when appropriate are at the core of proactive social behaviour but often very distant from clients immobilised by depression, stress or fear. Such a natural step-by-step framework for reconnecting with people was discussed with Matthew to help him shape his resumption of a more interpersonally connected life:

◆ re-contacting already established friends

◆ taking small initiatives with established friends

◆ taking larger initiatives with established friends

◆ finding out about places where new friends might be contacted

◆ taking small initiatives with new friends

◆ taking larger initiatives with new friends.

Practitioners can negotiate this kind of framework with clients as a series of low-risk steps. Realistic expectations should always be applied to such steps because success will depend at least partly on the reaction of others – something we can never completely rely on. It is therefore helpful to get clients to think about having a plan B: how for example could they cope with getting unfriendly responses in any of the above steps.

Focusing on rewarding behaviours

We have already discussed in Chapter 3 how both depressed and anxious clients can easily become 'unrewarding' to those closest to them. In this they may often only be mirroring their own reluctance to reward themselves sufficiently. Managing the rewards of one's behaviour both to oneself and to others are self-control strategies that help recovery from depression (Martell et al., 2001; McCullough, 2006). The most effective 'rewards' are not necessarily material. People often seem most rewarded by social reinforcers, such as smiles, recognition and attention from others. Clients sometimes need to refind and practise skills that may have become rusty, in order to participate in social situations. Therapists can help them for example by setting up role-plays and 'slow motion' interactions in which they can practise listening and taking turns in speaking with people. Therapy can act as a safe arena where ways to deal with these issues can be practised and monitored after efforts to implement them outside therapy. Most clients like having the feeling of support 'in their corner' and appreciate the chance to lick their wounds if something they had planned to try out did not quite work to plan.

> *Matthew's* plan to obtain the help of friends to put up a shed on his allotment ran into the sand when no one seemed able to help at the required time. It turned out that Matthew had quickly become frustrated when they did not seem to show the response that he had expected. He had stormed off and then felt bad about how he had spoken to them but was too embarrassed to try again. In replaying the interaction in the next session Matthew had been surprised to realise how hurt he had felt but also began to understand the hurt as part of his depression. His social worker helped him to feel okay about feeling this, even though it was a bit 'irrational', but also helped him to reflect more on the nature of his hurt. He then re-contacted some of his friends and explained 'where he had been coming from', and this cleared the way for a rearrangement to erect his shed.

It is more helpful for practitioners to stress that clients can strengthen aspects of their existing coping strategies than to talk of remedying behavioural deficits. It is rare for clients to have no aspects of most coping strategies – though we know these may be distorted by current problems and symptoms. The development of assertiveness skills is a crucial base on which a well-rounded set of interpersonal skills is founded.

Building assertive behaviours

It is striking how often a lack of assertiveness plays a role in maintaining anxiety and depression. This may be because assertiveness skills rely on emotional and cognitive awareness of needs, an ability to articulate these needs and, finally, the ability to negotiate and compromise with others on how they are best achieved. These skills and qualities are often the 'first casualties' when anxiety and/or depression occur. A good way to help clients to develop assertiveness often mimics the prospectus of a good assertiveness-training group course:

◆ consideration of assertiveness rights

◆ learning various templates for assertive communication

◆ practising individualised versions of such templates to fit specific problematic areas.

Almost all assertiveness texts devote some coverage to assertiveness rights and often use them to distinguish between aggression, assertiveness and passivity (Lindenfield, 2014). The main thrust of these 'rights' – which are obviously not legal but moral rights – is that you have the right to ask for what you want or need. We do also have to consider that other people sometimes also have an interest in what we want. While it is therefore valid to want almost anything, we also have to take responsibility for the consequences of wanting what we want; and if we also believe in some kind of good society then we must also recognise that we very often need to negotiate with others about how we can best get what we want without trampling on the rights and needs of others. So we can see that in these considerations we are starting to build a set of interpersonal skills that have a wide utility – recognising our feelings and our values and recognising those of others too, being able to communicate clearly and being able to give good clear attention and respect to others. In light of these, even when we want the whole cake, we may feel satisfied to settle for half of the cake or none at all at times. The premise is that when we are clear about what we want and about the rights of others to have wants and needs, then the greater the chances are that the

---

1. The two key skills of assertiveness are:
SAY WHAT YOU WANT + NEGOTIATE WITH THE OTHER PERSON

2. It is best not to back the other person into a corner as this
may make them go into 'retaliatory mode'.
USE EMPATHIC ASSERTION to 'prepare the ground'.

3. SAYING WHAT YOU WANT
Be direct – keep it clear and simple, don't apologise or offer
anything up before the negotiation has started.

4. NEGOTIATING WITH THE OTHER PERSON
Be open to the fact that the other person may also want something and let them say what it
is. If both parties have said what they really want then negotiation will have at least
started on a 'cleaner' basis – unspoken wants usually muddy the water.

FOR EXAMPLE:
I hope I don't sound like I am taking this too seriously but I felt angry
when you just decided that we would all …
I'd like to start the whole process again, giving everyone a say this time …
The other person might object: THAT WOULD TAKE AGES …
RESPONSE: Okay, I don't want to take ages either but let's just
have a quick round – I'd like …

Figure 5.2 Assertive communication template

negotiations will be 'cleaner' – i.e. uncontaminated by hidden needs and wants. A typical template for assertive communication is shown in Figure 5.2 and used, not altogether successfully, in the case example below.

Claudette (III) articulated a lack of confidence in her ability to assert her views and needs in social situations as she and her counsellor reviewed interpersonal skills that might be needed for interacting with colleagues on social visits to pubs and cafes. She did not particularly like drinking alcohol and naturally preferred fruit juices, but had noticed that some people in the group tended to press drinks on people and implied one was a bit weedy if they were refused. Claudette and her counsellor were discussing the template for 'empathic assertion' shown in Figure 5.2 when an interesting situation arose. They were working in a quiet room at the back of the counselling centre when some scaffolders began to make a great racket as they erected scaffolding next door – to the point where client and counsellor could hardly hear each other. The counsellor felt somewhat obliged to demonstrate her skills and stepped into the back courtyard and shouted up to the scaffolders, 'I know this might be a pain but I am working down here and it is terribly noisy now. I'd really appreciate it if you could keep the noise down.' The scaffolders laughed at her rather cruelly and said there was no way they could make less noise. Judging that there was nothing further to be gained, the counsellor came back in and said to Claudette, 'You win some, you lose some.'

Claudette was intensely interested now to process the event with the counsellor just as the counsellor had processed Claudette's attempts to be assertive in the situations shown in Table 5.4. Having moved to a quieter part of the centre Claudette was especially interested to understand how the practitioner did not appear to feel 'put down' by this situation. The counsellor reminded Claudette of their discussion about what the nature of assertiveness really was and the counsellor's own working definition that 'Assertiveness is about *saying* what you want, not *getting* what you want: *getting* what you want is something else – and usually it involves negotiation.' In this situation the other side did not appear open to much negotiation so the counsellor had been left with choosing whether she wished to escalate her demands – calling in the centre management and so on. She made a rational decision that it was not worth it on this occasion. Others might have chosen differently. The point that was really helpful to Claudette though was made when the counsellor said, 'The thing is that I did say what I wanted. The worst thing for me is to not even say what I wanted. You know, like when you have been served a rubbish meal and the waiter comes round to ask if it was okay and everyone says "fine" or "lovely".' Claudette could remember many times when she had walked away from a situation of being put down and felt bitterness inside that she had never said a word about it. She felt a resolve to try her best never to let that happen again, and if she did manage to say what she wanted then that surely increased the chances that, on some occasions, she might have things go her way!

Readers will find many textbooks in which the basic skills above will be listed in technical bullet point fashion but I hope that what will also be of value in this particular example is the very human and interpersonal context of the way things are played out. I do not suggest that practitioners should deliberately switch roles during therapy but when it occurs naturally, interesting possibilities for learning arise on all sides. In fact situations like this have cropped up in my work not infrequently. When we are able to use CBT skills alongside natural interpersonal skills then we are getting close to the mode of interpersonally informed CBT that this book aspires to describe.

Table 5.4 Assertive situations hierarchy

Assertiveness task	Difficulty rating
1. Telling the boss I can't do something	100
2. Telling peer I can't do something	80
3. Asking the boss for extra resources	75
4. Telling peers I want extra resources	65
5. Not clearing the coffee cups	60

Suggestion *Assertiveness*

Form: Therapy trio or duo

Aim: Practise giving rationales for building new behaviours and constructing hierarchies of testing situations

Instructions: After giving a rationale for developing a new behaviour to the client, devise a hierarchy of four or five situations in which you would like to act more assertively. Help the client review his or her *old plan* pattern for dealing with these situations and then devise a *new plan* pattern for how they could be dealt with more effectively. Take brief feedback from all participants in the exercise.

CONCLUSION

As noted earlier in the chapter, behaviourally oriented therapy has been developing over a long time period and this, together with its technically precise nature, means that there are very many skills, methods and technical procedures that work from a behavioural perspective. A single chapter like this one can only aspire to convey the essential skill-related factors of a limited number of interventions that CB therapists are likely to find they need to work on. As clients for therapy present with a very wide range of problematic behaviours, readers are likely to find much further help in behavioural texts; I have listed some that I have found most accessible and helpful in the further reading and resources section at the end of the chapter. I began the chapter by suggesting that we short-change clients if we do not have effective ways of addressing the need for behavioural change, but I end it with the hope that I have shown this can be done in ways that are creative and interpersonally sensitive.

PRACTICE TIPS AND TROUBLESHOOTING

Sometimes as we read about these interventions, we may ask, 'Where is the skill here? Isn't this just a question of giving a rationale to clients and just following step 1, 2, etc.?' This is a good question. My answer might surprise some. It is because these skills are potentially so mechanical that the importance of a therapeutic delivery of the exercise is so important. We referred earlier to the myth that a CB style is cold and impersonal. There has been a wealth of evidence from Sloane, Staples, Cristol and Yorkston (1975) to Keijsers et al. (2000) that CB therapists can be just as warm and interpersonally skilled as other therapists. It may be that CB therapists even find this stance easier than other types of therapists because the concepts they work with are more user-friendly and collaborative than can be the case in other approaches. Using pre-set formats potentially *frees up* therapists both to let therapy run itself and to concentrate on the interpersonal relationship that runs alongside the use of technique. Interpersonally sensitive behavioural work first requires that clients understand what they are asked to do and why they are asked to do it. Explanations should be matched to clients' learning styles and levels of understanding. For example, with scientists we can talk about the scientific dimensions of CBT, while with clients who had a bad time at school, we can make the experience as unlike school as possible. The need for collaboration shows itself as practitioners fit the style of CB therapy to the needs of clients – rather than forcing clients to fit the therapy model. Procedures like exposure can be demanding for clients, and practitioners may need to stand firm if questioned about their usefulness. The therapist may also need to guard against being 'talked out': allowing time to drift so that the task cannot be embarked upon. The art is to strike a balance between support, understanding and challenge (Egan, 2013). A task may be a bit beyond the client's comfort zone. Therapists can underestimate the degree of challenge that clients can take. Listening empathically to clients paradoxically enhances the ability to challenge them when necessary – by understanding what they can take and what motivates them. There may be fears about doing the exercise 'right'; one should convey that it is not about getting it right but about learning, and that therapists are also fallible.

Finding the right degree of reassurance

Clients with anxiety problems frequently seek reassurance from those around them. CB therapists have tended to see this as a type of 'safety behaviour' to be gently challenged (Sanders & Wills, 2003). It can seem harsh to refuse reassurance so perhaps the tone to be striven for is one of 'regretful and limited reassurance'. It is also useful for therapists to know that exposure therapy does not always work. A small minority of clients do not react well to it and some of them go through a period of setback, sometimes showing marked deterioration in mood. It is helpful to alert clients to this possibility and devise a strategy for dealing with setbacks and other approaches to the problem. My experience is that clients may at times benefit from a short holiday from exposure. Often a gentler hierarchy of steps can be devised so that clients can try again, and, having learnt from the previous experience, succeed.

FURTHER READING AND RESOURCES
Books

Addis, M., & Martell, C. (2004) *Overcoming your depression*. Oakland, CA: New Harbinger.

Emery, G. (1999) *Overcoming depression: client's manual*. Oakland, CA: New Harbinger. (Also available as *Overcoming depression: therapist protocol*. Oakland, CA: New Harbinger, 1999.)

Lindenfield, G. (2014) *Assert yourself*. London: Thorsons.

O'Donohue, W., & Fisher, J. (2008) *CBT: empirically supported techniques to your practice*. New York: Wiley.

Ramnero, J., & Torneke, N. (2008) *The ABCs of human behavior*. Oakland, CA: New Harbinger.

Spiegel, M.D., & Guevremont, D.C. (2009) *Contemporary behaviour therapy*. Belmont, CA: Cengage/Wadsworth.

Watson, D.L., & Tharp, R.G. (2007) *Self-directed behavior* (9th ed.). Belmont, CA: Thomson Wadsworth.

DVDs

Persons, J.B. et al. (2006) *CBT: activity scheduling* (DVD). Washington, DC: APA.

Wills, F. (2009) *CBT for depression: behavioural activation and cognitive change* (DVD). Newport: UWN. (Available from www.counsellingdvds.co.uk)

Wright, F. et al. (2006) *Learning CBT*. Washington, DC: APA. (Book and DVD; includes exposure)

6

SKILLS FOR WORKING WITH EMOTIONS

Anyone can become angry – that is easy, but to be angry with the right person and to the right degree, and at the right time and for the right reason, and in the right way – that is not within everybody's power and is not easy. (Aristotle, *Nicomachean Ethics*, Book II, Chapter 9)

INTRODUCTION

Cognitive behavioural practitioners need good skills for working with both clients' and their own emotions because therapeutic work that does not evoke feelings is likely to be ineffective. This chapter will describe the nature and functions of emotions – taking account of findings from current research in neuroscience and from research on the role of emotions in therapy. Although emotions are in the main adaptive, when emotional regulation fails, problems can arise on the one hand from overwhelming negative emotions and, on the other, from emotional avoidance. CB therapists therefore need skills for helping clients to practise emotional regulation based on emotional intelligence. Processes involved in helping clients to develop emotional regulation skills will be illustrated in two on-going case studies – one of an avoidant client who needs to get more in touch with feelings and another of a client who needs to regulate overwhelming negative emotions. Therapeutic skills for working with such clients include facilitating emotional awareness and expression, and working to transform problematic aspects of emotional functioning for more adaptive living. The two case studies will illustrate these skills in action.

THE NATURE AND FUNCTIONS OF EMOTION

Emotions are complex and involve physical and affective feelings, behavioural responses and thoughts. Emotions are generated by complicated brain networks yet are closely connected to basic body functions. This means that emotions are thoroughly 'embod-ied' and most usually first experienced in the body. They are often experienced only briefly so that a different term – mood – is used when they become enduring. Persistent negative mood is described as being 'chronic'. Feelings often occur below consciousness, so another term – affect – is used for the more conscious aspects of emotion. Emotions are best understood as sending information to tell us that some-thing significant is happening inside us or in our environment and that this may need our serious attention. Fear, for example, often draws attention to possible threats in the environment and therefore has survival value. In this sense even negative emotions can be functional, so it is often important for practitioners to help clients to foster accept-ance of emotions as a first step. Attempts to suppress emotions often have the ironic result of making them yet stronger (Wegner, 1994).

Emotional reactions occur much faster than the more deliberate and conscious processes of cognition, though it is hard to explain emotional reactions entirely without at least some fleeting and perhaps non-conscious element of *appraisal* – the key explanatory concept of the role of cognition in emotion. Emotions are also *motivating* and have built-in behavioural or 'action dispositions'. We move towards things when we experience them as good and move away from them when we see them as bad – reactions usually termed as 'approach and avoidance'. These responses happen so quickly that we usually identify the sequence only in retrospect. From a physiological viewpoint, emotions move in and around the body and may change form and meaning as they do so. What we say about our emotions never quite fully expresses the visceral reality of them. All in all it seems most reasonable to assume that some kind of complex reciprocal interaction operates between emotions and thoughts.

Emotions guide and protect though they can also run out of control at times. They play a key role in helping humans to identify their needs. Physiological processes are deeply involved: anger, for example, triggers many different bodily reactions as well as psychological ones. Anger may mobilise us to try things to put situa-tions right. Similarly, anxiety activates awareness of danger and drives us to seek safety. Such action may need to be taken urgently – hence the compelling drive that comes with anxiety. Our bodies do not want us to feel comfortable at these times. Discomfort feeds the imperative to act, though it does not necessarily result in helpful behaviours.

Many theories of emotion now use an age-old metaphor to describe the two brain tracks involved in the generation of emotional reactions – one a track of the '*heart*' (direct emotion) the other of the '*head*' (cognitively mediated). Sometimes 'heart' and 'head' act in harmony but at other times they conflict, and this conflict can be a major factor leading to emotional problems. Some earlier CBT formulations have seemed to suggest that there are linear relationships between cognition and emotion. Clients, however, are more likely to be aware of emotions first and be much less aware of any thought accompanying them. Thus a thought reported by a client may be an artefact of an emotion. Thus CB therapists must accept that clients often correctly report experiencing feelings apparently without any thoughts going with them.

Decreases in negative mood do not necessarily lead to increases in positive mood and vice versa, so that separate strategies may be needed for working on these two aims. There is only a limited number of basic emotions – fear, anger, sadness, happiness and disgust (Power, 2010). Complex emotions can be seen as involving mixes of these basic emotions; obsession-linked anxiety for example seems to involve a mix of fear and disgust. Emotions are linked to evolutionary processes and goals – especially when important goals change. For example, clients may have much invested in maintaining a relationship, so that if the relationship is threatened, they will feel highly anxious and fearful. If at some point the relationship ends, however, they may easily *switch* into sadness and depression. The implied shifts in cognitive appraisals fit with Beck's (1976) concept of 'cognitive specificity'.

HOW EMOTIONS CAN BECOME PROBLEMATIC

Some 'head v. heart' conflicts are caused by the fact that emotions are typically triggered more quickly and strongly than cognitions, so that often we are more aware than we 'know' (Damasio, 2000). Strong emotions are especially attention fixating – this is, after all, what these 'emergency signals' are designed to do – but they can also overwhelm and disrupt the cognitive system, inhibiting its balancing role. The speed of emotional reactions can mean that subtlety and accuracy in the perception of personal needs are sacrificed. These mutually interfering processes may mean that the cognitive mind functions less effectively – making the characteristic 'errors' of those gripped by strong negative emotions. Fear of anxiety thus produces more anxiety. Anxious clients typically become over-vigilant for danger and so over-interpret possible environmental signals of threat as indicating a clear and present danger that is actually not there.

One key function of emotional regulation is to achieve balance in emotional-cognitive processing. The emotional side of the balance allows us to feel the healing elements of negative emotions fully and this can start a self-correcting process. The cognitive side can offer additional help by guiding us to make realistic appraisals of risks detected by the emotions. We can for example decide if, when we feel anxiety or fear, the situation really *is* dangerous enough to justify action. If there *is* clear and present danger, however, there may not be time for lengthy consideration. Additionally, if the cognitive system is not given sufficiently strong emotional reactions to activate it, then the cognitive system has less chance to process negative experiences.

Two further problems often prevent fully functional processing – avoidance and negative interpretation of emotions. Not only can the emotional and reasoning systems go out of balance, they can sometimes act independently of one another; for example, a person can 'act calmly' while ignoring danger signs rather than face them. If however emotions are avoided then it is difficult to see how they can be processed. Sometimes we ignore emotions because we may believe them to be 'wrong' – *I should not be angry*. Furthermore, memories may be encoded in bodily sensations and emotions out of conscious awareness so that, in Bessel van der Kolk's (1994) memorable phrase, 'the body keeps the score' in trauma. In PTSD for example, the body may be 'tricked' into reacting as if the trauma were happening now even though the mind 'knows' that this cannot be. Thus emotions are embodied and body awareness is inextricably linked to emotional awareness, emotional intelligence and healing. People who believe that they should always be strong may be particularly vulnerable to PTSD because they cannot accept the feeling of powerlessness, and therefore cannot process negative emotions that go with PTSD. Another key area in PTSD is the way that interpretation and meaning of traumas can maintain trauma-based emotions – seeming to confirm the relevance of cognitive appraisal in the generation of emotions. After trauma a person's world can be 'shattered' so that people who previously saw themselves as 'strong' cannot accept the weakness they experienced during traumas. This again reminds us that, despite the new emphasis on emotions, thoughts and beliefs continue to have relevance for therapeutic work.

Ray was a professional sportsman who approached his club doctor feeling low, flat and out of sorts. He also revealed that he was having problems in the relationship with his partner. The club doctor wondered if he was 'depressed' and suggested anti-depressants but Ray was not keen. The club doctor then suggested seeing a GP colleague who had a counsellor attached to his practice. This counsellor had recently trained in CBT so when Ray saw her they began by helping him work on his negative thoughts, which were many and included 'No one really cares about me and what I have to say.' Early work focused on trigger situations, mainly connected to arguments with his partner and some people in his club. Ray eventually said, 'I don't know if I am depressed, I just don't seem to feel anything.'

Chrissie was a nurse specialist who approached her occupational health unit (OHU) for help with some 'emotional issues'. She explained that she worried about confidentiality but less so at this time because she was moving to a new job and second marriage in a new area. The OHU counsellor noticed that Chrissie seemed irritated by having to wait a few extra minutes in the waiting room and then that she continued to show strong emotions throughout the session. Chrissie described having a 'rough' first marriage but then meeting a 'marvellous new man' about two years ago. It 'all seemed like a dream' but now the closer they got to marriage the more they argued. Chrissie worried that she would 'make another big mistake with a man'. Her counsellor also noticed that she looked very sad when she left after her initial appointment.

LETTING AND HELPING EMOTIONAL AWARENESS TO DO ITS WORK

Exploring and assessing emotions

In a similar way to how we approached cognitions in Chapter 4 and behaviours in Chapter 5, we will here also explore work with emotions by way of a continuum of skills and methods moving from 'letting emotional awareness do its work' to 'helping emotional awareness to do its work'. Beginning at the 'lighter-touch' end of the continuum, we will first examine assessment and exploration of emotions. Here clients become aware of feelings, so a meta-emotional effect can kick in: *Oh, so this is what I have been feeling!* The client has now stepped outside the emotion and is not only aware of it but is also simultaneously aware of being aware of it. This is really a form of mindful awareness and therefore makes the skills of mindfulness relevant to this area. Shifts in emotion – sometimes therapeutically helpful ones – can happen spontaneously during initial encounters, even during assessment. It is helpful for practitioners to be alert to such shifts and to have the skills to understand and capitalise on them. Emotionally sensitive practitioners learn aspects of clients' emotional development from their history – in effect learning about their emotional schemas. Leahy (2011) offers a comprehensive system for assessing and working with 14 emotional schemas, shown and defined in Table 6.1.

Table 6.1 Leahy's emotional schemas

Emotional schemas	Typical questions
VALIDATION	*Do the important people in your life understand and accept your feelings?*
COMPREHENSION	*Do your emotions make sense to you?*
GUILT	*How okay is it for you to have the feelings you have?*
SIMPLISTIC VIEW	*Can you hack it with feelings that are vague at times?*
HIGHER VALUES	*How do your feelings relate to what is most important in life to you?*
CONTROL	*Do your feelings often feel out of control?*
NUMBNESS	*Do you often feel numb about things?*
NEED TO BE RATIONAL	*Do you think you should be rational and logical in most things?*
DURATION	*Do you often worry about how long a bad feeling could last?*
CONSENSUS	*Do you think that when you have bad feelings, so do most others?*
ACCEPTANCE	*How easy or difficult is it for you to accept uncomfortable feelings?*
RUMINATION	*When you are down do you find the same thoughts and feelings going round and round your mind?*
EXPRESSION	*Do you think that you can express most of your feelings openly?*
BLAME	*Do you think most of your bad feelings are caused by other people?*

Ray explained that his inability to feel came from his 'unemotional family'. Both his parents were 'people of few words' and usually those few words were about the practical side of life. Furthermore they looked down on people who displayed emotions as silly and weak. Showing true northern disdain, his father had once responded to one of Ray's teenage feelings by asking him, 'What does tha' know about selling horse muck through parlour window?' – roughly translated as 'Your opinion counts for little'. Emotional blankness also extended to family crises. Ray was the one boy from his village who had to travel to secondary school by train. As an outsider the other boys mercilessly bullied him. He remembered stepping off the train scratched, bruised and dishevelled after his first day at the school. His mother met him at the station but made no comment whatsoever on his condition. It is unsurprising that Ray concluded, 'Nobody cares about what I think and feel. I just have to *crack on* with my life.' Luckily he could protect himself from bullying but it was the start of an emotionally and interpersonally quite lonely phase of life.

This history mainly influenced Ray's ability to express his emotions – in Leahy's (2011) terms he was limited by an emotional expression schema, believing that *It is not safe for me to express my feelings openly.*

For clients to do emotional work there has to be an empathic and safe therapeutic relationship. Before Chrissie's therapist could begin to assess and work with her emotional schemas, however, a therapeutic incident – such as those discussed in Chapter 3 – arose that put a safe relationship under immediate threat.

Chrissie's counsellor scrutinised his notes in preparation for their second session. He noted that Chrissie had displayed three emotions in the first session – anxiety, anger and sadness. These emotions ran high and shifted constantly during the session. The counsellor reasoned that as Chrissie had stated that her main concern was worry about the upcoming marriage it would be appropriate to offer that as a starting point in the second session. Chrissie readily agreed. She then revealed catastrophic thoughts such as *Jim* [her first husband] *destroyed my trust in my judgement forever*, and, *I'm heading for relationship hell again.* The therapist drew up a nice clear 'vicious cycle' diagram of this and expected positive feedback from the client. Instead Chrissie delivered a stream of invective along the lines of 'That's just rubbish … CBT shit with arrows … why don't you listen to me and stop telling me how I should feel?!' It was all the therapist could do not to respond in kind. The session ended in confusion but at least with agreement on the therapist's suggestion to 'Give each other a few days to think about what happened and what we should do about it.'

The next day Chrissie sent an apologetic email acknowledging that she had 'really lost it and gone off on one'. She confirmed wanting to stay in therapy and indeed asked if it were possible to meet again as soon as possible as she'd like to apologise in person and explain some context about how she had been feeling that day. This meeting went ahead a day or two later. Chrissie explained that

(Continued)

(Continued)

in fact that she had always had a problematic temper and the more stressed she got, the worse her temper became. She had inherited this temper from her mother, a 'difficult woman' who had in fact phoned to 'badger' her shortly before she came to the previous session. Chrissie commented, 'In one sense, my whole life has been a journey round my mother.' She had known that Jim, her first husband, was 'bad news' but his one virtue was that he could always 'top' Chrissie's temper with his. This had, however, turned 'destructive in the end'. Her new man was gentle – but even they were arguing now, 'So it seems like I carry some really bad karma'. Oh – and her wonderful new man, by the way, had trained as a person-centred counsellor and was highly sceptical that CBT could help her!

We can see that our intrepid CBT practitioners are involved in working with negative emotions but if they thought it was going to be a straightforward matter of identifying an emotional focus with a distinct cognitive profile on which to base their interventions – it is starting to look a bit more complicated. Ray reports a lack of feeling rather than depression as his main problem, and has not shown any real tendency to report negative thoughts or beliefs. Admittedly flat affect is often closely related to depression so perhaps sad mood is a prime focus. Chrissie originally reported anxiety as her problem but it seems now as if anger is also in the frame.

CBT theory has actually always acknowledged that a variety of emotions can be prevalent in emotional disorders (Emery, 1999) but it has been slow to give a general therapeutic role to the processing of emotions (Wills with Sanders, 2013). We can however draw further help here from an idea that has been better articulated in emotion-focused models – that of primary and secondary emotions (Greenberg, 2011). Primary emotions are relatively unadulterated and so, even when unhealthy, they may be processed in ways that lead to therapeutic gain. Secondary emotions are more problematic because the secondary element, e.g. fear of anxiety, and subsequent avoidance may prevent the processing of underlying primary emotions. It can be hard to pick one's way through the complex twists and turns of problematic emotions and this probably necessitates a lot of trial and error. Finding an appropriate focus for work with emotions, however, can be facilitated by the skills of identifying the bodily felt elements of emotions and by finding the right descriptive word, phrase, metaphor or 'handle' for them.

Focusing on the bodily felt sense of emotions

A floodtide of findings from research in neuroscience and on emotions in recent years has greatly enhanced our understanding of how our brains are emotionally wired and the intimate connection between the brain and body processes. The autonomic nervous system plays a particularly prominent role in regulating arousal, and this arousal is felt first and most strongly in the body, especially in the 'core' of the body – the guts, stomach, heart, chest, throat and shoulders. There is particularly striking evidence suggesting that heartbeats become unhealthily disorganised by emotional distress and healthily recalibrated by emotional healing (Servan-Schreiber, 2005; see also the HeartMath website, www.heartmath.com). The brain–emotion–body connection is reflected in the everyday language of emotion – *heartfelt*, *shaken to the core*, *weight on our shoulders*, *nervous throat* and so on. These feelings, however, may be relatively non-conscious and vague, and our more conscious brain may be aware of them only as murky stirrings. The urgings of negative emotions can be intensely strong and there are good arguments for rolling with them rather than resisting them – mainly because the more they are resisted the stronger they seem to become.

CB therapists have not always been encouraged to explore the inner world of embodied emotions but a newer stance is emerging in the practices around accepting and developing mindful awareness of feelings and thoughts in third wave approaches to CBT. Additionally, learning emotional methods from other models enhances CBT practice (Wills with Sanders, 2013) and shows a technically eclectic approach in the tradition of Aaron Beck, who commented, 'If it is effective, it is cognitive therapy' (Leahy, 2006).

Bodily awareness of emotions can be helpful in and of itself but it can also be extended into other areas such as expressing emotions by naming them, using metaphors and images in conjunction with bodily awareness to promote emotional change, and developing more deliberate techniques for processing emotions. All these therapeutic activities have matching therapist and client skills. These are shown in Table 6.2, and descriptions of using these skills in client case studies follow.

Table 6.2 Matching therapist and client skills in emotion-focused work

Therapist skills	Client skills
Facilitates expression of feelings	Expresses feelings
Helps client understand the flow of feelings	Accepts the flow of feelings
Teaches mindful attitude to feelings	Accepts and tolerates feelings
Helps client to use thinking to regulate feelings when appropriate	Uses cognitive skills to regulate when appropriate
Clarifies link between feelings and actions	Uses emotions to drive adaptive behaviours
Clarifies links between feelings and values	Uses feelings to live by highest values

Mindfully accepting emotions

Approaches based on acceptance of negative emotions have been associated with mindfulness practice – one of the most exciting developments in CBT. This is generally not seen as a spiritual practice within CBT, though it may offer useful links for those who – like myself – do have an interest in spiritual practice. Here, however, I will examine a limited but highly practical application: helping clients to manage anxiety. This involves using the AWARE strategy described by Clark and Beck (2012, p. 142). This strategy is a five-step process that involves the client learning to:

1. **a**ccept the anxiety

2. **w**atch the anxiety

3. **a**ct with the anxiety

4. **r**epeat steps 1–3

5. **e**xpect the best.

The reader is recommended to read the full version of the strategy. Looking carefully at the steps, we can see, however, that the AWARE exercise invites clients into a new relationship with anxiety. Anxiety is often regarded as something to be avoided at all costs; ironically this can empower it. Acceptance opens clients up to what emotions have to teach them. Once accepted, anxiety is 'watched' and acted with rather than suppressed. Clients can thereby 'ride the waves' of anxiety, shifting from 'worried suppressers' to 'detached observers'. The last step adds a cognitive finale, suggesting that it is wise to expect the best because what one fears the most rarely happens.

The AWARE strategy can be used in various ways – for example, as a behavioural experiment to test the effects of staying with emotions rather than trying to make them go away. Clients often think that emotions will get out of control if they do not suppress them. In the experiment they can find out the effects of suppression and avoidance – seeing for example whether they do make anxiety rebound more strongly. Another way of using AWARE is as a regular exercise for practice at home. It is usually helpful to introduce it in a session by asking clients to close their eyes and get into a relaxed state by using *progressive muscle relaxation*[1] and then to read out the AWARE strategy script in a gentle voice. This exercise often has a helpful impact on clients, and going through it with them raises the chances they will be able to practise at home without undue problems. It is also helpful to reinforce the method by continually coming back to it in sessions, especially if the client is feeling anxious or an anxiety attack spontaneously arises during the session. It can also be used in conjunction with exposure tasks. Some clients report that AWARE has been a mainstay tactic for dealing with anxiety symptoms more mindfully.

Chrissie's apologetic email to us had really stuck in her counsellor's mind – especially the phrase 'going off on one'. In subsequent sessions he noticed how well the phrase described Chrissie's style of communication when she was discussing her anxieties as well as when she was angry. It represented a forceful way of describing her experiences. The counsellor also noticed how this style of communication affected him – making him feel on edge – as if Chrissie were somehow passing the anxiety on to him. The counsellor put it to Chrissie that 'going off on one' could be a way of avoiding the anxiety, and

---

[1]Many written and free YouTube downloads on how to do this can be found by using this phrase as a search term on the worldwide web.

there might be an ironic 'white bear' suppression effect (i.e. trying NOT to think of a white bear makes it difficult not to think of one) that made the anxiety worse. Chrissie surprised her counsellor by taking this potentially difficult feedback on board and responded well when they tried the AWARE exercise together in the session. Chrissie began to use this exercise regularly and also explored mindfulness exercises in sessions and at home using self-help texts and CDs. She began to report feeling much less anxiety and coping better at work and in her relationship. Job done – well, not quite!

Focusing practice

When we talk about 'visceral' emotions we acknowledge not only that these feelings are fundamental and deep but that where we feel them is likely to be located in the part of the body we know as the 'viscera' – which the dictionary tells us is 'the soft contents of the principal cavities of the body; esp., the internal organs of the trunk'. There is a sense of softness and opening here and, by association, a liquid responsiveness. When we experience important life events our viscera may well make sounds, even 'sing' or 'scream'. We can often get an internal sense – *a felt sense* – but we can sometimes hear and see such body reactions, both in ourselves and in others. I have come to believe, like Gendlin (1996), that we can enhance our therapy practice with relatively simple interventions such as asking clients, 'When you are talking about this, what seems to be going on in the middle of your body?' We can expect roughly half of clients to respond by searching for emotional experiences within themselves but the other half may simply be puzzled. Even the latter eventuality is useful information – this client cannot experience a 'felt sense' *yet*. This may be because the person does not feel safe enough to feel and or reveal that yet. After all, what they only half experience may still leave them feeling vulnerable.

The therapist's main role here is to encourage clients to maintain an inward focus and to avoid distracting them by being 'too busy'. Gendlin (1996) advocates a light touch for doing this and, if clients cannot 'go there', to just gently return to what they and clients were 'talking about' and then wait patiently for the next opportunity to explore and experience the feeling. Emotion-focused therapists like Greenberg (2002) seem happy to offer a little more guidance and direction, as suggested in previous references to the 'zone of proximal development' (see Table 6.2).

Focusing technique also encourages clients to 'give feelings words', in the words of Shakespeare's *Macbeth*. These words, phrases and images can act as 'handles', and naming them can offer opportunities for further development in the experience of emotion. Creative devices such as metaphors and narrative development may also be used to extend this work. This extension of feeling and meaning progresses by a kind of oscillation between words and feeling: the sequence often takes the form of 'Is that the word for the feeling? Not quite. How about this word? Still not quite but closer.' The range of therapist and client skills used in these exchanges are shown in Table 6.2, though it is important to note that there is no strict matching across the columns – any skill in one column may match up to any one in the other. The whole process of matching therapist and client contributions is shown in the dialogue that flows and counter-flows in the next client case study.

Ray made good progress in therapy. He and his partner decided to separate but managed this in an amicable way. Ray's depression gradually lifted and thera-peutic meetings were reduced to occasional sessions to 'check in'. About a year later and some months into a new and seemingly promising relationship, Ray had a sudden sharp downturn and asked for an urgent appointment. His new partner had revealed some 'baggage' from an old relationship that Ray found very hurtful and difficult – not so much the baggage itself but that he had found out by chance what he felt his new partner should have told him. He retreated into paralysing sadness and could hardly explain what he felt – another source of distress because he reckoned he was now better at expressing feelings. The following dialogue took place.

Practitioner (P1):	So remember that we have talked about being able to use your emotions sometimes: what are you feeling inside down there now?
Client (C1):	Every bit of me just wants to walk out.
P2:	That's what you feel driven to *do* – what are you feeling?
C2:	I cannot believe that she did not tell me this when we had our 'clear out' right at the start of the relationship … (*Now the counsellor simply pointed down to his body*) I don't know what you mean … (*The counsellor makes another body signal and asks Ray to 'speak from there'*) … I guess I feel pretty twisted up inside … (*asked what was twisted*) … like a hot thing that could explode … anger, I'm angry!
	… (*A little later in the dialogue*) …
P3:	Remember that old image we had of you when you feel emotionally overwhelmed and you want to walk away, hide away actually … *the bear in the cave* … and now it seems like the bear is fighting off a rage.
C3:	Yes – I'm scared if I go into a rage, it'll finish off the relationship for good … and I am unsure if I have the right to tell her how to live her life – is that being over-assertive?

By getting Ray to 'stay with' (P2/C2) and enhance via imagery (P3) his *'felt sense'*, the practitioner accelerates therapeutic movement and new space is gained – the 'stuck' feeling is freed up and is now flowing – but there are dangers. The anger released could indeed be destructive. Ray may be over-whelmed by it in the session or later with his partner so we need now to find

---

the healthy form of adaptive anger. Ray's statement at C3 probably conceals a self-critic – 'You should not be angry' – and this probably inhibits his capacity to allow anger and to find a healthy version of it. The counsellor attempts to 'soften the critic' by responding to Ray's fear that he has no right to be assertive in relation to his new partner's emotional life, by suggesting that what is at stake is not just the partner's life but also 'their life' together, and asks Ray if he feels the right to have a view on that. Ray thought he did and so can now be more accepting of his anger. He now surprised the counsellor by remembering from a previous discussion the quotation from Aristotle at the start of this chapter. This facilitates a calmer and more reflective discussion about the rights and wrongs of this situation and how Ray might go about being assertive to set the things right.

It is instructive for us to pause for a moment and reflect briefly on how else the exchanges in these last case studies could have developed in CBT work less oriented to emotional awareness and emotional intelligence. Chrissie's anxieties concerned predictions about how her marriage might go wrong. We could easily see these predictions as catastrophisations based on evidence from the past rather than present-day realities. It is, however, all too easy to imagine her responding to cognitive restructuring by saying she could see that she was catastrophising but still felt worried; after all, a marriage is a very significant life event and probably worth at least some worry. By helping her to use the mindful AWARE exercise we have taken her fear seriously and had some discussion about how to act on the realistic part of her worry – developing a long-term plan not to 'end up in relationship hell'. We have also introduced her to some skills that are likely to have benefits across many areas of her life. Technically, we may also have enhanced the effects of any cognitive interventions that might follow. With Ray, instead of assuming that he feels just depressed, the counsellor invites him to express what else might be there and we are somehow not too surprised when anger emerges. Aaron Beck's development of cognitive therapy began by challenging the old psychoanalytic idea that depression was retroflected anger (Beck, 1967). It is true that, despite drawing attention to the benefits of expressing anger (Beck et al., 1979, p. 171), Beck's more general suggestions for dealing with it in therapy run more in favour of cooling anger down and helping the client to feel empathy for the person with whom they feel angry (1979, p. 180). Yet, on re-reading the debate about retroflected anger, it now seems to me that Beck's argument was really contesting both this view of anger in the context of it being anger against the self, and the further assumption that depressed clients have a 'need to suffer' (Weishaar, 1993) – a psychodynamic concept no longer current even in that model. In Ray's case, he does feel hurt, i.e. both sad *and* angry. Helping him to use anger to clarify what he wants and to energise himself to seek what he wants (after due reflection) seems a more positive approach than either focusing on his evident negative thoughts about himself or attempting to help him to put aside his anger and approach his partner in an entirely reasonable way. Some passion surely seems in order when in pursuit of saving a passionately felt relationship – and so it proved.

Suggestion *Focusing*

1. Find some space, physical and mental. Listen to the breath in your nostrils. Whenever your mind wanders, and that's what minds do, come back to the sound of your breath.

2. Sit comfortably, breath steadily from your diaphragm and relax.

3. Scan your body all over. Get the general feel of your body and then begin to notice different parts of it. Are there knots of feeling? What are they telling you?

4. Gradually come to focus on what is your major concern as you sit there right now.

5. See if you can put words to what you are feeling – give it a clear descriptive word. If it is hard to find words, go back to the body sensations and ask them what they are saying. Keep going back between the sensation and the words that are forming. Sometimes this will come to a crescendo feeling of 'Yes that is it.'

6. Keep checking if the words are right. Let the words and the meaning flow and change if that is what they seem to want to do.

7. Keep receiving the sensation and feeling words and phrases. Let them flow and keep telling you what you are feeling and what you need.

8. Let the experience come to a close: Is it okay to close now? Afterwards check (especially with clients): Was it really okay to close? What will you do if these feelings crop again before we meet again (safety procedure)?

CHANGING EMOTIONS THROUGH EMOTIONAL EXPRESSION

Clients can often benefit from bringing their verbal expressions of emotion in line with their embodied emotions. Though verbalisation and 'intellectualisation' of emotions can play a role in avoiding the full experience of them, language can also play a crucial role in 'sealing the deal' for successful emotional work. There is an ancient spiritual principle that certain things can only be fully understood when they are finally and correctly named (Whitehead & Whitehead, 2010). It is not that there is only one true word that properly describes emotions in any universal sense; it is more that for *this person in this situation and at this time* there may be a word that captures the essence of their being more closely than any other. There is also something inherently healing in the effort to find the words or phrase or metaphor or narrative that can do this. Emotions are in this sense constructed by the person experiencing and seeking to articulate them. Finding the 'true name' in spiritual narratives is often associated with the idea of 'quest' – a kind of heroic struggle or journey that tests the person on the quest. Thus this co-creative process between client and therapist has a satisfying element of empowerment, and challenges the notion that clients are passive victims of their emotions.

Chrissie needed to work on naming a troublesome emotion just a few weeks before her wedding as she sought help with an overwhelming panic. She described looking across a room at her fiancé and thinking, 'I don't really love him. I am about to make the biggest mistake of my life …' It was when she found the word *terror* to describe her feeling that she finally could put words to the depth of her anxiety. This however seemed to help her to 'lance the boil' and to find the courage to take the risk that she felt was really right for her.

Ray similarly became preoccupied with finding 'handles' and metaphors that linked with his situation. We left Ray struggling to find out how to feel the anger that was 'right' in the sense of the words of Aristotle that opened this chapter. During this process he became so frustrated with the situation that he did something unprecedented – he got angry with his counsellor – furiously saying to her, 'You said that I should feel my feelings but if this is feeling my feelings, well – f--- that for a game of soldiers!' The counsellor later confided to him that when he said that, she had thought to herself, 'And if this is what teaching you to feel your feelings is like, then f--- that for a game of soldiers too.' This mutual recognition of an 'only too human' set of thoughts and feelings led to amusement between them and to a liberating discussion about the fact that perhaps life actually is a bit of 'a game of soldiers'.

DEALING WITH SECONDARY EMOTIONS

Insufficient attention may perhaps have been given to the fact that the original premise of cognitive therapy was *not* focused on the idea that clients had *solely* negative thinking but that they often had *two* streams of thinking running in parallel with each other – either of which might underlie either the dominant emotion or any other emotion they might be feeling (Weishaar, 1993). Quite often we see people in therapy who may be feeling an unexpressed primary negative emotion that if expressed might be successfully processed: for example, a person who feels highly understandable sadness at the end of a relationship. This person may be unable to express that sadness fully because they fear being overwhelmed by the tidal wave of emptiness that could follow in its wake. They therefore end up expressing a less threatening emotion such as anxiety about the future – in this case because it is an externalising feeling – or even anger at the person who has 'abandoned' them. The clue to this situation is often in how the anger and/or anxiety feels to the therapist; secondary emotions often feel like the person expressing them is going 'over and over … old ground' and thus is 'not going anywhere' that is actually helpful to the client. In effect what we have here is a competing set of thoughts and feelings that might be experienced by the client as 'two voices in my head'. This is a difficult experience and can even feel slightly schizoid to the client. In this situation it is often therapeutically helpful to 'give both of these voices air time': ideal methods for doing so are found in 'empty chair' and/or 'two-chair' work, pioneered by Fritz Perls, which is now very much part of emotion-focused therapy (EFT; Greenberg, 2011). Work that gives emotions a voice and uses symbolic chairs is also used in compassion-focused therapy (CFT; Gilbert, 2009a).

Ray recognised that his struggle to find a 'right' anger about the fact that his new partner, Tonya, had not told him about the baggage issue partly reflected his own struggle to deal with anger about himself. When he became stressed or down about himself he became very self-critical. His counsellor had raised the idea of being self-compassionate but they also identified a belief that blocked him from doing this – 'I'd like to go easier on myself but if I did then I'd be guilty of just making excuses.' Statements like this are good indicators of a conflictual split and suggest that two-chair work might be useful. When the counsellor put him into a chair scenario, Ray called his critic 'Roundhead' and in the other chair – the one who makes 'excuses' – 'Cavalier'. Battle was quickly joined between the two and the English Civil War was being symbolically fought out across the therapy room floor.

C1: (*as Roundhead*): You're just so cheap – in your fancy clothes and big words. You just make excuses because you can't be bothered to be disciplined and work hard. It's people like us that have to do the hard work – you swig your wine and live the life of Riley. Don't come looking to me for sympathy.

P1: Okay, come over to this other chair and tell him, *really* tell Roundhead, what it's like to be talked to like that.

C2: (*Cavalier to Roundhead*) That's harsh – give me a break! All I am doing is trying to help us enjoy our life a bit more – I mean, don't be so relent-less – can't you see you're driving us down – you will make yourself ill and I don't want that – you are my brother! ... (*Roundhead*) That's all very well, yeah we can talk about that but can we also talk about why I have had to pull you out of a hole so many times ... (*Cavalier*) You know I wasn't well – I was never so strong as you or as handy with my fists. You know I really am grateful for how you have helped me over the years.

We can see that there are two sides of an argument here and that neither side seems completely right, yet it is always interesting to ask the client about which side appeals to him. Ray thought that Roundhead expressed the 'suck it up' attitude to emotions he'd learnt in his gritty northern family and was impressed by its strength, but Cavalier had all his sympathy. In this dialogue some kind of constructive engagement has, how-ever, got under way and raised the hope of some agreement, and with that the prospect of a more rounded and integrated internal feeling within Ray. In P1 the counsellor maintains the emotional level and tension by switching relatively quickly from chair to chair. We can note the tone of voice in both practitioner – '*really* tell' conveys urgency and the need to communicate emotion as well as words – and client – 'that's harsh' conveys the emotional effect of the other's words.

It is also of interest how the idea of a brother was drawn into this dialogue. Ray explained that this related to family history. The 'Roundhead' attitude reflected the rather austere and stoical style of parenting Ray had experienced. We have already noted how in some ways this served quite well – certainly in how it helped him nurture self-discipline in the sporting context. The fly in the ointment for Ray, however, was more that his parents did not seem to extend the same attitude towards his younger brother.

There were times when this 'two-chair' work more resembled 'empty chair' work. 'Empty chair' work is more associated with attempts to transform the effects of abuse and neglect and will be described in the next section alongside another helpful idea from EFT – transforming emotions with emotion.

TRANSFORMING EMOTIONAL EXPERIENCE

Therapies oriented towards emotional processing, often in conjunction with at least some element of cognitive processing, as in the eye movement desensitisation and reprocessing (EMDR) model (Shapiro, 2001), have exerted major influence in the therapy field in recent decades. We noted earlier in this chapter that decreasing negative feelings does not necessarily lead to increases in positive emotions, and interest has grown in developing methods to achieve a more radical sense of 'transforming' negative emotions. EMDR has been used especially in PTSD with striking transformative results at times (Servan-Schreiber, 2005). A more generic approach to transforming trauma is presented in the case study of '*Bes*' in the first edition of this book (Wills, 2008a, pp. 116–21) and also on the book's companion website for this edition. Another form of transformative processing, using an 'empty chair' framework, is presented here in the work with Chrissie. This work focused on the idea of changing emotion with emotion and being able to 'shift' out of emotions.

Chrissie settled and was getting towards the point when her move to a new area would mean that she had to finish her therapy. She said that as a final piece of work she wanted to look at how her anger problems related to her past and present relationship with her mother. She seemed to have 'airbrushed' any mention of a father out of her accounts of her early life. It was only when the counsellor questioned this that Chrissie revealed some significant but previously unrevealed aspects of her childhood. Chrissie's birth father had died when she was 5 and she seemed to have almost no memories of him – one of them was, tellingly, of ripping up a photograph of him. Her mother had remarried but Chrissie described her stepfather as 'more evident in his absence than in his

(Continued)

(Continued)

presence' and 'a worm'. She pulled out an old photograph from her handbag. In it she could be seen aged 15 or so accompanied by another teenager, Jo, her stepfather's daughter by his first marriage. Jo was smartly dressed and strikingly coiffured whereas Chrissie was in a dowdy raincoat and with an almost 'pudding basin' haircut. 'That says it all, doesn't it?' Chrissie remarked, 'He did not want me and he wouldn't give Mum any money to buy me nice things.' The visual confirmation of this interpretation was shockingly brutal – and the counsellor felt his breath catch as he looked at it. Chrissie added, 'That's why I feel so mad with Mum – she never seemed to fight for me and just accepted his meanness.'

Chrissie's accusation against her mother is a classic indicator of 'unfinished business' with a key significant other in one's interpersonal life. The themes of neglect and trauma suggested, however, that opening this out could be deep and disturbing work. Chrissie seemed to insist on wanting to 'go there' but the counsellor felt that she should first consider the case for *not* doing so. The debate focused on 'going there now' or 'going there later' – an important issue given the fact that Chrissie also faced imminent transitional life changes: marriage, new job, new town and, just as importantly, the end of therapy. The factor that influenced their joint decision to 'go there now' was in the end Chrissie's insistence that she was 'as ready as I will ever be' and her question 'If not now, when?' Chrissie put her mother in the empty chair but initially things seemed to fall rather flat. She told the other chair of her hurts and resentments but in a noticeably flat voice and with a seeming lack of passion. At the end of the session, she reflected, 'No, I am trying but I cannot seem to get my anger really up and I keep thinking that it wasn't her fault: it was *him* – my stepfather – as ever hiding behind her.' She also remembered that her mother had on occasion fought her daughter's corner, even winning the odd concession. She saw also that her mother had been in a very vulnerable position after Chrissie's natural father had died. They decided then to have another try – this time with her stepfather in the chair. Again, however, Chrissie seemed to baulk. She turned away from the other chair and addressed the counsellor:

C1: … I can't do this, it's too mean: he is sick and old now – dying actually – and anyway he will not change.

P1: It is not really about how he is *now*. You are really talking to the man as you remember him *then* and how he lodged in your mind – that is what *can* change …

After a little more discussion, Chrissie tries again but finds that she is so choked up with feeling that she cannot speak.

P2: Take a breath, take your time … speak from what is finding it hard to speak …

C2: Oh my God, I just feel so … so … ragged … so orphaned … so shamed …

P3: Tell him – this is how I ended up feeling because of what you did …

At P1 the practitioner helps the client to engage with the task by providing material for her to resist her interrupting thought that it would be 'mean' to express anger towards, even symbolically, a sick old man. The counsellor essentially reminds Chrissie that the target at this time is healing her internal process – her stepfather and his motivations are separate issues and may or may not be addressed at another time. She is coached in how to undertake the emotional task in P2 and then given direction by the counsellor's prompt at P3. A little later she is able to direct a full stream of anger at the empty chair, culminating in the words, 'You systematically stripped me down … and people expect that I should feel sorry for you now – they really have got to be joking.' After this Chrissie felt exhausted and at her next session, which turned out to be her last, she said she felt 'cleansed' – for now at least – of *some* the pervasive shame that she had felt for so long. She was aware that there could be more to do but thanked the counsellor for letting her go so far. It is not known at this time what has happened to her since or whether she chose to go on working with these issues.

CONCLUSION

Before moving to our final concluding thoughts on working with emotions in CBT we need to note that we have read of two clients, a man and a woman, who in these instances began by taking the opposite routes in dealing with emotions than are usually described by 'genderised' accounts of emotional functioning (Power, 2010), partly because cases that defied gender stereotypes were deliberately chosen. It is probably still more socially acceptable for women to internalise anger as sadness and for men to externalise sadness as anger with others – ironically not borne out on our case studies – showing that stereotypical responses can be changed. Emotionally intelligent strategies seem to offer both genders better ways forward and hopefully this could become a unified emotional project for men and women to take together and, when appropriate, to help each other with.

Servan-Schreiber (2005) makes an overwhelming case for how emotional intelligence can contribute to massive gains in both physical and mental health. There appears to be momentum building up behind emotionally focused psychological therapy at present, but it is noticeable that emotional intelligence and emotionally focused therapy by no means ignore the crucial contributions made by cognitive and behavioural change. To some extent, however, the impact of new emotional approaches is such that CB therapists cannot just ignore them. We should be open to what we can learn from these approaches and this could be as simple as merely learning to ask clients, as suggested on page 121, if they are feeling their problems in their bodies. Changes in those body feelings can then be regarded as giving us good information about how well our work with them is going. As before, we have used a continuum to suggest a range of skills stretching between those associated with relatively non-directional methods linked to mindfulness and acceptance, and more directional methods such as 'empty chair' and 'two-chair' interventions from emotionally focused therapies. I am hopeful that the coming years will see increased cooperation between CBT practitioners and those who practise models that at first sight may not seem to be easily compatible with CBT. I believe that therapists from all models should be open to learn from each other, and I think that there may be rich prizes available for such efforts. I hope I may have inspired readers at least to try emotionally focused methods to enhance their practice of CBT.

PRACTICE TIP AND SUGGESTION

Format: individual exercise or group discussion

In Chapter 1 we considered a set of principles associated with the practice of CBT and you were asked to think about the extent to which you felt able to 'sign up' to them as principles to guide your practice of helping people with psychological problems – in whatever context of helping people you work or would like to work. Below I have taken a set of principles associated with the practice of emotionally focused helping and rewritten them as a series of brief 'practice tips'. As in Chapter 1 you are invited to consider each principle or tip and, first, consider how enthusiastically you would be able to 'sign up' for them. Second, can you also identify any reservations that you might have about using them personally, as a helper, with your particular clients or in a particular helping agency in which you do actually work or would like or aspire to work? Compare and contrast some of your responses with those of other people in the group.

Principles for working with emotions in CBT

1. Therapists are well advised to observe and appraise the way their clients express and use emotions.

2. Therapists are well advised to observe and appraise the way they themselves express and use their emotions.

Observing and appraising emotions facilitates

1. increased awareness of emotions

2. increased acceptance of emotions

3. more flexible and helpful expression of emotions

4. more flexible and helpful use of emotions

5. more flexible and helpful ways of regulating emotions

6. more potential for the transformation of emotions and healing

7. more potential for strengthening the self

8. more potential for using emotions to generate new meaning

9. more potential for generating corrective emotional experiences in the therapeutic relationship.

FURTHER READING AND RESOURCES
Books

Elliott, R. et al. (2004) *Learning emotionally focused therapy*. Washington, DC: American Psychiatric Association.

Greenberg, L.S. (2002) *Emotionally focused therapy: coaching clients to work through their feelings.* Washington, DC: American Psychiatric Association.

Greenberg, L.S. (2010) *Emotion-focused therapy*. Washington, DC: American Psychiatric Association.

Power, M. (2010) *Emotionally focused cognitive therapy*. Chichester: Wiley.

Servan-Schreiber, C. (2005) *Healing without Freud or Prozac*. London: Rodale.

DVDs

Greenberg, L.S. (2004) *Emotion-focused therapy for depression*. Washington, DC: American Psychiatric Association.

Greenberg, L.S. (2007) *Emotion-focused therapy over time*. Washington, DC: American Psychiatric Association.

7

SKILLS FOR WORKING WITH ENDURING LIFE PATTERNS

Everything depends on upbringing. (Leo Tolstoy, *War and Peace*)

INTRODUCTION: THE PAST, THE PRESENTING PAST AND THE CONSTRUCTED PAST

Films of yesteryear that feature psychoanalytic psychiatrists often showed them making some complex Freudian statement about the patient's past only to be greeted by the patient's unbelieving incredulity. On the one hand there is the psychiatrist's Godlike certainty in his own 'interpretation of the case'. This interpretation is held to be *the* truth and if the patient cannot accept it then he is 'resisting analysis'. The patient thinks that it is all 'poppycock' but does also wonder if the doctor might just be right after all. These may be old-fashioned views expressed in rather archaic language but versions of them are still sometimes heard today. In some senses I do have a little sympathy for both the psychiatrist and the patient here. We have just read at the end of the last chapter how the client Chrissie's past impacted on her present-day problems – there was 'unfinished business' with all three of her parents. It is often difficult, however, to formulate exactly how such past experiences influence the present, and sometimes the subjects themselves may be too much 'in the wood to see the trees'. On the other hand, the patient has after all lived the past under discussion and only he can fully know the many complications it contains. Even the most insightful interpretation may get it somewhat wrong, and the more run-of-the-mill interpretations often sound lamentably unconvincing.

The aim of this chapter is to review the skills needed by CB therapists to work with issues and problems that are significantly rooted in the client's past history. It will begin by focusing on the significance of the schema concept for this work, and will show how the characteristics of schemas influence the way in which they are best addressed. We focus first on the way assumptions contribute to problematic schema-based functioning and suggest ways in which clients' awareness of assumptions can contribute to the change process. Practitioners can aid this process by using the downward arrow technique and then by helping clients to formulate assumptions flashcards. Flashcards lead naturally to goal setting in relation to areas where valued behaviours can be encouraged to address and overcome problematic patterns related to dysfunctional assumptions. A similar set of procedures to target problematic core beliefs and other aspects of schema functioning is then described. Two key case studies will follow the path of two clients, *Bruce* and *Antoinette*, through CBT methods based on changing enduring life patterns. As we do this I suggest that the reader retains both some of the scepticism of the patient described in our opening quotation and some of the enthusiasm of the psychiatrist to understand and formulate the problems. At the same time, we should realise that our memories of the past are always somewhat incomplete and somewhat constructed – and no less valid for that. By retaining both these qualities and by understanding the relationship between them, I believe that therapists can establish a way of working with clients' past experiences that is both informed but also somewhat conservative in its reach. We can develop deep and nurturing therapeutic relationships with clients in ways that should ensure that our understanding does not become oppressive to them. Human experiences, especially those of trauma and abuse, are always just beyond our understanding and to pretend otherwise is to short-change our clients.

How the past affects us

Counsellors and psychotherapists are sometimes guilty of 'psychologising' when we try to account for the way our clients have come to be how they are (Gordo & De Vos, 2010). The term 'psychologising' in the field of critical psychology implies that psychologists over-extend their framework to explain aspects of human functioning in solely psychological terms and thereby ignore the crucial influences of the social and political environment. At its worst, psychologising may collude with powerful forces in the status quo that do not want the effects of such factors to be understood, debated or changed. Critical psychologists tend to direct this argument against many aspects of psychology and psychological therapy in general, and it is to me ironic that there has been a tendency among other schools of psychotherapy to point the finger at CB therapists as supposed agents of the status quo without seeming to consider their own role in this respect (Hall & Iqbal, 2010).[1] An intelligent approach to our

---

[1]Further discussion on this point can be found at https://study.sagepub.com/wills and at www.frankwillscbt.co.uk

work does require us to appreciate how macro social forces do often have oppressive influences on the lives of our clients. We can however still help clients to make what sense they can of their situations. We must also consider our own role in these essentially socio-political matters. We should never forget that people are dealt very different cards at the start of their lives – some of which make the possibility of psychological problems much more likely – for example, from discrimination related to disability, poverty, gender and ethnicity. The majority of such people do not of course have psychological problems but, statistically, they are both more likely to have psychological problems and more likely to have more serious ones too – personality disorders (PDs) for example (Coid, Yang, Tyrer, Roberts & Ullrich, 2006). In this chapter we will explore how some of these disadvantages get encapsulated into schema-focused problems – areas where clients may exhibit symptoms related to personality difficulties. The chapter cannot offer comprehensive analysis of all kinds of disadvantage or give satisfactory coverage of schema therapy for working with PDs, which must be sought elsewhere – see 'Further reading and resources' at the end of the chapter for suggestions. I do believe, however, that there are large grey areas between different categories of psychological problems, and this means that schema-related and personality problems related to early experience are relatively common (Coid et al., 2006) and are found in many of our clients who could not be seen as remotely near exhibiting PDs. This pragmatic view of psychiatric classification is described more fully elsewhere (Wills with Sanders, 2013). The aim here, then, is to describe everyday client presentations, focusing on particular schematic aspects of them relating to early experience and to show how CBT skills are adapted for use in these situations.

Key case studies

Bruce, now in his thirties, had been born premature and was regarded as unlikely to survive his period in intensive care. It seemed a miracle when he did and then developed into a normal healthy little boy. He was brought up in a tough working-class area but nonetheless did well in primary school and was soon reading better than most of his classmates. Areas of development that were not so good were in his mouth and teeth. His teeth were under-developed and caused severe problems in his mouth. Unfortunately all his teeth had to be removed so that, from the age of 9, he had only false teeth. This did not bother him too much at first as his classmates regarded his false teeth as a novelty. It troubled him at secondary school, however, where he was much teased about it. He found girlfriends difficult and suffered constant anxieties about how and when to tell them about his teeth. He obtained a degree and a good job but the problem with relationships persisted and he began to fear he would be 'left on the shelf'. After a rather traumatic end to a relationship of which he had great hopes he developed acute anxiety, insomnia and depression and was referred for psychological help from a community psychiatric nurse (CPN).

Antoinette was also in her thirties and was of mixed heritage and a care worker. Her father had migrated from Jamaica to the UK in the early 1960s and later

---

married an English woman. Antoinette was born some years later. Antoinette's father was unfortunately killed in a tragic industrial accident when she was 7. Her mother took his loss badly: she sank into grief and depression and was eventually subject to compulsory treatment of electroconvulsive therapy (ECT). Antoinette went to live with her mother's sister. Removed from the stress of an unhappy home, Antoinette flourished at her aunt's and began to do well at school for the first time. After a lengthy stay in hospital her mother continued to be frail and it was decided that Antoinette would stay with her aunt. Her mother later remarried and grew quite distant from Antoinette. Antoinette qualified as a care worker but found it difficult to have relationships. By this time she seemed to have a difficult relationship with her aunt too and lived a rather lonely life. She came for more specialist counselling after receiving help from a voluntary agency that identified her as needing longer-term work.

CB therapeutic work for people with enduring life patterns is very much centred on the concept of early maladaptive schemas (EMSs) – henceforward simply termed 'schemas'. The theory and nature of schemas has already been described in some of the previous chapters, and for our purposes here we will use a metaphor to regard them as a *neighbourhood* in which aspects of the way a client functions are likely to 'gather'. Furthermore they are neighbourhoods with a prevailing atmosphere where we might breathe the very air of, for example, unworthiness or failure or entitlement. We will in this chapter particularly focus on the beliefs we find tucked away in the corners of these neighbourhoods – previously described by the terms 'assumptions' and 'core beliefs' – again described earlier. The case study of *Bruce* will explore the way assumptions operate in enduring life patterns and that of *Antoinette* will explore similar territory for core beliefs. I will show how CBT skills are used to raise awareness of assumptions and core beliefs and then describe deliberate strategies for modifying them when possible.

The nature of early maladaptive schemas in CBT

The word *schema* was probably first used in a psychological context by Bartlett (1932) in his work on memory. He used his famous example of a story called 'The war of the ghosts' to show that memory worked on the basis of straight recall *and* story reconstruction based on previous memory structures, 'schemas'. Beck et al. (1979) used the early maladaptive schema concept to theorise how certain clients would have a vulnerability to think with a 'depressogenic' bias, especially in relation to the 'cognitive triad' of negative thoughts about the self, the world and the future. The bias did not show itself all the time but could be triggered, especially when clients were already in a negative mood. Although schematic bias is a highly plausible concept, it is only fair to say that it has been hard to demonstrate it experimentally and there is a 'chicken and egg question' quality about the idea that the 'cause' of depression is only evident once depression has begun. As in other aspects of CBT, work on cognitive and schematic processes is helping us to build a more sophisticated version of what is already a useful clinical concept (Wells, 2000). It is probably wisest to regard the early maladaptive schema concept as a useful clinical metaphor. I also agree with Ian James's (2001) cautions about schema-focused work in that it seems to induce in some neophyte therapists an alarming tendency to engage in 'amateur psychoanalysis'. There is much in schema work to be excited about but there is also much to be modest and cautious about.

In the original formulations of cognitive therapy, the term 'schema' covered both what we now think of as 'assumptions' and 'core beliefs'. Now, although this terminology is not completely universal, most CB therapists describe early maladaptive schemas as being an overall 'structure' that contains unconditional beliefs (e.g. 'I am bad') and conditional beliefs (e.g. 'If I can please people, then people may think I'm okay'). Both these beliefs may, for example, occur within a 'worthlessness' schema (Young et al., 2003). There is an increasing understanding that schemas are relatively indistinct entities and are often associated with vague, gut and visceral feelings about the self. This is probably because they were laid down in early experience, sometimes before the client had much vocabulary to describe them. They have therefore been recorded in consciousness only as physical feelings.

In time, negative experiences may be retained as core beliefs: that is, with a characteristically dichotomous nature, and may be related to the dichotomous thinking associated with early childhood cognition. Early maladaptive schemas can therefore be particularly difficult to change. There seem to be various schema maintenance processes that strengthen this resistance to change. Negative schemas may operate in a homeostatic way: for example, by distorting more positive data with more negative bias so that they do not have to change. Positive data seems to bounce off schemas and is not therefore noticed or stored by the client. Data that does enter the schema tends to be distorted along lines similar to the operation of the cognitive distortions described in Chapter 4.

We need to think of *weakening* problematic schemas as a first step, while at the same time building up more functional, alternative ones. Once these new structures start to attain some critical mass, even if in only a small way to start with, there is then a neighbourhood in the brain which positive data can inhabit. It is important to build alternative schemas into relatively robust structures that can keep on developing. Because they have been encoded at deep levels, however, we need to prepare clients for the likelihood that they will never be completely eradicated. It is more useful to think in terms of clients developing a different, more insightful and accepting relationship with them.

Therapists may experience more resistance from clients undertaking schema work (Leahy, 2003). Clients may hook themselves and their practitioners into playing along with their schemas and may need to have a strategy for consciously weaning off schematic behaviour. A negative schema may be compared to a relationship with an old acquaintance that always seems to have a negative hold over us. At some point we realise that we don't get anything out of this relationship. We may now avoid them but we can't always stop them from popping up in our lives every now and again. They will keep trying to exert the old negative hold over us but we can at least inhibit them from doing that by, first, not engaging with them any more than we have to, and, second, by giving less weight to the old negative jibes in their voices – e.g. 'You are so useless, you don't deserve to enjoy yourself.' Sometimes we can even take the initiative and give them a bit of their own back: 'Says you – well I am not going to allow you to have that power over me, thank you very much!'

WORKING WITH NEGATIVE ASSUMPTIONS (CONDITIONAL BELIEFS)

One way of thinking about negative assumptions or 'rules of living', as they are also called in CBT, is to see them as compensatory devices that help people cope with their negative core beliefs. Thinking things like 'I am bad' and 'Other people will not help' and 'The world is a hostile place' are themselves bleak beliefs to have to live with. If people really believe them, then only a minimally satisfying life may be possible. Even within these bleak landscapes, however, the human spirit will often reach for hope so that it would be natural for people to start to think, 'Okay, I may be a bad person, but perhaps there is some way that I can get other people to see me as at least okay and, if I can, perhaps I may even be okay in some kind of way.'

Bruce was troubled by a pervasive sense of carrying a flaw around him, and of course in some senses he was. He took consolation in reading and enjoyed the feeling of getting lost in the world of literature. He read one book about an 18th-century radical called John Wilkes, who was well known for being ugly but also for being able to make positive impressions on people. When asked how he managed this, Wilkes replied that in order to win people round he needed 'a half hour to talk away this face' (Cash, 2007). Bruce had nothing like this confidence in the power of his 'silver tongue' but he did take Wilkes' statement as some encouragement that he could at least make favourable impressions on people by using his personality; 'If I can be interesting then perhaps they will overlook my flaws.' He did have some successes with this assumption-driven strategy as he tried to find a satisfying relationship. When we consider this assumption we can perhaps see that it is not entirely problematic; it seems useful to think about being interesting to people. We can also perhaps see that assumptions often conceal an accident waiting to happen. Here we can see that this one still retains the schema-based idea of being flawed. The if/then formula also has the possibility of failing – if I *don't* seem to interest people then they *will* see my flaws. Sometimes assumptions can be victims of their own success: if we are being driven by fears then we tend to overuse strategies that seem to work sometimes. Thinking this over, Bruce reflected that he realised that he had become a little 'bumptious' sometimes – an impression that was in fact far from how he felt. The accident finally happened one day when he overheard two young women in his office talking about him. One asked, 'Has Bruce done his *hilarious comedy* routine with you yet?' and the other replied, 'Yeah – I just hope his teeth don't fall out'. Life and people can indeed be cruel at times, and at this moment Bruce felt the strategy that was based on his assumption had bitten the dust and so he was driven back to his core belief and schema of defectiveness.

From a therapeutic perspective this moment of defeat however also contains a potential opportunity. If Bruce can allow himself to be vulnerable in a relationship, he is then 'daring to be himself' – warts and all (Dryden & Yankura, 1992). This in all likelihood is a prerequisite for the deepest types of relationships.

Identification of assumptions via the downward arrow technique

When working with a client's negative automatic thoughts, a therapist may often wonder exactly *why* they make the client feel quite so bad. The answer to this question may well be that something even more disturbing lurks beneath the negative thought and that thing may well be an unhelpful assumption. The method for identifying unhelpful assumptions is through the 'downward arrow technique' (Burns, 1999).

When things in his life were going okay Bruce could forget about his 'flaw' to some extent. In times of stress, however, he constantly felt very conscious of it and was always fearful that people would find out. He tried to cover this up and initially did not even tell the therapist about it: despite the fact that it was a major driver for his social anxiety. He came for help after a relationship that he had been hopeful for had broken up out of the blue. In a 'Dear John' letter his girlfriend told him that she was sorry but she no longer felt the same about him.

Practitioner (P1):	So when you were feeling so fed up and thinking about your girlfriend, what was going through your mind?
Client (C1):	I was thinking that she has really seen me, you know, *seen* me for what I am and she couldn't possibly want me.
P2:	She has seen you for what you are and does not want you? What was so bad about that?
C2:	You're joking! I wanted her and she didn't want me!
P3:	Yes, I can see that is bad but what is so very bad about it that makes you depressed?
C3:	It's one more example of someone not wanting me. It looks like no one will ever want me.
P4:	And if no one will ever want you, what then?
C4:	I'll be on my own always and for evermore. And that will prove I *am* flawed.

The unhelpful assumption is that 'If I'm flawed then I will always be left alone.' As well as revealing this as a 'rule of living', the sessions moved forward because Bruce clarified his feeling of being 'flawed', an unusual word and one pointing to a 'defectiveness schema' (Young et al., 2003). The CPN reflected the word back to Bruce and this finally led him to tell her about his teeth: a big step forward for him.

Using flashcards

The activation of unhelpful assumptions often plays a key role in psychological problems. Looking at most longitudinal formulations,[2] one can see that the part of the map where significant events trigger unhelpful assumptions is like a long thin passage between the historical 'old stuff' of schematic memories and the current 'here-and-now' symptoms and reactions. Being long and thin, this is a good place to block the reaction. Therapy flash-cards can help clients by taking insights generated in the 'downward arrow' process and keeping a prepared card to hand, using it as a device to look at in order to mentally step back from negative assumptions and thereby defuse the automaticised reactions associated with them. Bruce and his CPN built the following flashcard from the identification of the assumption about 'being physically flawed' that was rooted in early experiences of shame.

FLASHCARD

I sometimes make the assumption that: If I am not very interesting, people will reject me.

It is understandable that I make this assumption because: I have had an invisible physical problem since I was a boy. I had to learn to hide this problem because people were sometimes cruel about it. I found that I could sometimes win them round by the use of my wit and intelligence.

The assumption works against me because: I get nervous in company because I worry about whether I will really be able to win people over. This undermines my confidence and this means my problem is spreading across more areas in my life.

The assumption is wrong because: Most people who know me well do not seem that bothered when they find out about it. They like it when I am funny but I can also be serious and just neutral with them too.

The way forward for me now is: To see that people who would reject me because of my disability are best kept out of my life anyway. I can learn to be more proactive in telling people about it and work on helping people to accept me for what I am, without trying to please everyone all the time.

Figure 7.1 Bruce's assumptions flashcard

The flashcard aims to help the client to use cognitive prompts to help him step aside from the immediate experience of distress – 'It is understandable that I feel this way but it is not wholly right' – and enable him to react more reflexively – 'I am entitled to feel some sadness about this but it doesn't say everything about me and my life, and it doesn't help me to go and seek my goals after I have allowed myself to feel moments of distress.'

Suggestion *Practising the downward arrow technique and developing a flashcard*

Most of us can identify an assumption that is not so very functional in our lives. (If you have trouble finding one for yourself, try 'I must not fail as a practitioner'.)

(Continued)

---

[2]See Chapter 2, pp. 29–30 for such a formulation.

(Continued)

Try using the downward arrow technique on this assumption, either by yourself or with a partner, to get to the 'bottom of the ladder': what would be so bad about failing as a practitioner for example? You may also wish to try developing a flashcard for the same assumption. If working with a partner, it might be helpful to review how sensitive use of the downward arrow felt. It can sometimes feel a bit relentless. Think about what makes it okay and not okay to keep going on 'down the ladder' with downward-arrow-technique questions.

Working to change assumptions: developing new adaptive standards and assumptions

Rules that have been followed habitually for years are hard to give up until a newer, more adaptive rule is in place. Therapists can facilitate this process by initiating a debate that opens out the client's previous strategy:

Practitioner (P1):	Bruce, I'm wondering if can we open up to scrutiny this issue about having to hide away from being yourself? You know, at present, you have this pretty omnipresent anxiety that if people see you and who you really are – that you have false teeth – they are not going to want to be friends with you. This problem is at its sharpest with female friends, whom you fear may be put off you, but it is also a problem with male friends: you said that you sometimes go along with what they want in case they start to make fun of you.
Client (C1):	That's right. I don't know why I cannot stand up for myself at times like that; I just seem to get self-conscious and it is easier to let other people make the running.
P2:	So that's one thing, isn't it? It would make sense to have a rule about how you show yourself to others depending on exactly who they are and what you want to do with them: in other words, a more varied rule.
C2:	To some extent I do that. Some of my friends know about my problem: they have found out somehow or other. Like when I was out drinking with Tony and I was sick and my bloody teeth came out *(laughing)*. He was okay actually, he just picked them up and said, 'Here, your teeth came out, mate' and handed them back smart style. As far as I know, he never said anything to anyone else: Tony is good as gold though.
P3:	So some people can know and it's okay but others, you're not so sure?

C3:   Yeah, I mean it's one thing a mate knowing but I would find that so difficult if it was a girlfriend. I never told Jean anything about any of that.

P4:   What do you think might have happened if you'd told her?

C4:   Well, the worst would have been that she finished with me and that happened anyway …

In this dialogue, new elements and new rules are emerging:

◆ It might be possible to take the initiative with some people.

◆ There might be good and bad ways of revealing himself.

◆ Acting first might help to bring things to a head sometimes.

◆ Taking the initiative might help Bruce feel more in control.

◆ He might not be able to control the fact of having false teeth but he can control how he does and doesn't tell people about it.

As this dialogue unfolded, an interesting issue arose in the CPN's mind. She was rather older than Bruce and their relationship was always boundaried and respectful but she did wonder what she would say if he had asked her about how she would feel if she discovered a potential male partner had false teeth. She discussed this in supervision and concluded that she hoped that such a thing would not spoil a relationship that felt right – but she was bound to concede that she could not be completely sure without actually being in such a situation. Therapeutic discussions over matters like the above tend to go on over several months and can sometimes be helpfully combined with a behavioural experiment like the 'survey method' – asking a sample of people what they think would happen if one told a potential partner about something like having false teeth.

WORKING WITH EARLY MALADAPTIVE SCHEMAS: SCHEMA–DRIVEN INTERPERSONAL PROBLEMS

There are two main ways that practitioners might engage with therapeutic work primarily targeted at schema-driven patterns. One is to use the formal CBT-oriented models specifically designed to target personality disorders (Arntz & van Genderen, 2009; Beck, Freeman, Davis & associates, 2004; Layden, Newman & Morse, 1993; Linehan, 1993) and/or early maladaptive schemas (Young et al., 2003). The second way is to adapt CBT to schema-based issues as the natural flow of therapy focuses attention on the necessity to address them. It is best to approach learning the more formal models by reading source literature and seeking appropriate training. Here we address the second way and describe the adaptation of methods to work appropriately with a client introduced earlier as Antoinette.

How would we know when the natural flow of therapy is taking us into schema-driven territory? We have formal classification systems that give guidance on identifying PDs and schemas. We have already noted that many believe that such systems are still far from robust in this respect – so that many experienced practitioners rely more on clinical rules of thumb, often described as follows:

◆ Clients may reveal considerable previous attempts to seek help.

◆ A certain strain in therapeutic work often becomes apparent – as if the therapeutic container can barely hold the issues.

◆ Clients reveal many core beliefs and schemas – often in multiple forms.

◆ Schemas and core beliefs are acted out across many areas of the client's life.

◆ Schemas and core beliefs are acted out during therapeutic sessions.

◆ Clients' strong reactions to life triggers often seem disproportionate.

Antoinette's counsellor eventually discovered that his two periods of therapy with her, both lasting around 12–20 sessions, were the third and fourth periods of therapy within five years. She had also had counselling while a student and probably later, and her counsellor suspected that she would come for more in the future. There is evidence that although many clients do well with relatively brief therapy, a small percentage need more and an even smaller percentage, estimated at around 5%, will have multiple periods of therapy over many years (Cummings & Sayama, 1995). Not all of this even smaller group have PDs or schema-driven issues but it is likely that many of them do. Practitioners should put some effort into exploring previous episodes of therapy because they may contain important information on how the client perceives help and also highlight what has already been identified as significant – thus saving time and unnecessary duplication.

Initial contacts with Antoinette were tense with continually shifting emotional atmospheres. Antoinette came in smiling and looking exaggeratedly grateful. Then she seemed to move into some kind of 'business mode': *I have got this problem – you are the expert, fix it!* The presenting problem was that she felt very anxious on dates with men and she felt this was preventing her from finding 'the one'. Antoinette looked disappointed when the counsellor said he would like to explore this more, and went into a disengaged sulk – *Please tell me when this boring bit is over and you are ready to come up with something useful*, and *I thought CBT was supposed to be good at fixing things; why aren't you getting on with it?* In an effort to meet her at least half way, the counsellor described some CBT concepts and methods for working with anxiety. The only reaction from Antoinette was that she began to look at her manicured fingernails. The session ended with the counsellor feeling that he had failed to engage her and expecting that she would 'sign off' therapy or at least simply not turn up next time. He was amazed when Antoinette said that she had greatly enjoyed their meeting and asked if they could meet again the next day, as she would 'like to get on with things'. She did however eventually accept the more conventional formula of weekly meetings. Later, when a colleague observed that the counsellor seemed to look tired and headachy, he said, 'I feel completely wrung out.'

Antoinette's second session went much better, especially after she had redefined her problem as 'I long for intimacy', and this led her to give a deeper account of her history. After moving to her aunt and uncle's house, Antoinette said she had really regarded her uncle as her father. He had particularly supported her engagement with education and helped her all he could. It also became apparent that things between him and her aunt were far from good, and he seemed to turn more to Antoinette for some sense of intimacy. Her aunt became jealous and wrongly accused them of improper relations. It turned out, however, that he was having an affair with a neighbour and eventually he left his wife for this neighbour. Antoinette felt betrayed by his behaviour but ironically was accused by her aunt of leading her husband 'astray'. Her uncle's new partner was also suspicious of her so that gradually her uncle too became estranged from her. Antoinette's situation became so difficult that she had to live with relatives in Jamaica for a year before finally coming back to the UK to live independently and to finish her social care training.

Antoinette's return to the UK at the age of 19 marked the start of a remarkably stable and dichotomous pattern of, on the one hand, professional success, and on the other, loneliness and long-term mild depression (dysthymia) in her personal life. As she recounted these past and present troubles, over 20 core beliefs and 5–6 schemas were articulated. These and the phases of therapy when they emerged are shown in Table 7.1.

Table 7.1 Antoinette's core beliefs and schemas

Face data	42 years old; social care manager; Christian; **Presenting problems**: Anxiety, dysthymia/ cyclothymic (I am only living half a life); low Beck scores; people pleasing; impulsive spending; shame; solitude; 'emptiness'. **Desperately wants to FIX self**
History	Father died when Antoinette was 7 – mother broke down and cut herself off. Antoinette went to live with her aunt and uncle; Antoinette 'idolised' her uncle but when he left her aunt, he shut himself off from her. *I have watched the impact of endings on others*
Schemas and core beliefs	**MISTRUST/ ABANDONMENT** **DEPENDENCE** SHAME/ VICTIM MODE *I'm not attractive* *I cannot trust others* *I cannot trust men* *Men are bullies, selfish and lack emotional intelligence* *I cannot trust in male roles* *I cannot sort this out myself*

(Continued)

(Continued)

	I have to find 'the one' *I can't be myself in relationships* *If I change my mind, men will get aggressive* *I am only living half a life* *It's hard to say what I want* *I cannot be seen as a 'negative' person* *I have to be the/a 'go-to person'* *I'm crap* *I have to do it all myself* *Others are hostile* *People will dismiss me*
Triggers	Getting close to a man Ending with a man 'Frolics' with a man Chanel bags Setting boundaries with a man Promotions/interviews 'Wily Geordie' 40th birthday Weddings Criticism from others – esp. professional men

This is obviously a lot of material for both therapist and client to handle so it is helpful to try to articulate a central driving mechanism that may underlie them all. The counsellor reviewed this with his supervisor and they decided that a schematic sense of shame seemed to do this. Shame is strongly associated with a 'defectiveness schema' (note the presence of *I'm crap* and *I'm not attractive* in Table 7.1) but also with other schemas and modes (Young et al., 2003) and enduring life problems (Gilbert, 2009a). This focus coincided with the following dialogue in therapy:

Client (C1):	(*Describing going to a wedding*) It was in a place that's difficult to get to and I was dreading going. It was like almost the last one of my college mates that wasn't married – making me feel 'left on the shelf' … I came late and the only space left was on the front row … I felt so exposed …
Practitioner (P1):	So what was going through your mind?
C2:	I was thinking that they will see me on my own and they will all think I look tarted up and they will see that I am desperate …
P2:	And how did you feel?
C3:	Oh so awful … like shrivelling up inside … I just felt like a piece of left unwanted baggage … deep, deep shame …

Antoinette described her characteristic responses to experiencing acute shame. On the way home she passed through London and went on a spending spree in expensive shops. Her haul included a Chanel bag and, in all, cost her several thousand pounds – an amount she could not afford. On getting home she also contacted a man she would only refer to as 'the wily Geordie' or 'WG' – a man with whom she had what she termed as 'occasional sexual frolics'. These were usually unsatisfying but also oddly comforting for her. On this occasion WG could only manage to visit on Sunday evening and she did not feel she could meet him after going to church earlier in the day. Her sad reactions to these events, however, did help practitioner and client formulate goals for therapy:

◆ to learn how to comfort herself in less destructive ways when she was sad;

◆ to learn how to resist giving herself away too cheaply by people-pleasing.

Both Antoinette and her therapist retained good boundaries in these sessions but she continued to blow very hot and cold during them. On the one hand she enjoyed experiencing the practitioner's acceptance and empathy but on the other she got irritated with him for not 'fixing' her. These two tendencies finally blended in a more harmonious way when she arrived for a session only to announce that she planned to end therapy and move to a new job in New York. The context of this revelation is now described and is followed by the ensuing therapeutic dialogue:

> *Antoinette's* impulsive spending had actually gone on for many years and she now explained that she had serious debts. She was paying very high interest rates to service her debts and was thus, despite her good salary, in a cycle she could not free herself from. She had seemingly secured a high-salary job in New York via the influence of a friend, and she imagined that by moving to New York she would soon start to clear her debts. Another factor that clinched the plan in her mind was that there would be more Christians in New York and that she would therefore find it easier to find the 'right' man for her. The counsellor became alarmed when she euphorically told him of the plan and then added the detail that she had actually resigned from her job. Antoinette was very forceful in this mode and it took the counsellor a lot of effort to cut across her and point out some of the downsides to her plan – principally the great expense of moving to and living in New York and the loss of friends and colleagues here. Antoinette did not thank him for making these points but did at least agree to consider the idea of withdrawing her resignation to allow a little more time to think through her plan more carefully. At their next session, the following dialogue took place:
>
> *Client (C1):*   … I did withdraw my resignation (*P:* That sounds sensible) and I do want to thank you for talking me down last time … you really helped me to think it through more carefully … (*P:* I
>
> *(Continued)*

(Continued)

> talked you down?) Yes, well, I was pretty well away with the fairies there wasn't I? ... But I really appreciated it that you cared enough to argue with me. I know that it is difficult when I get like that ... and that's what I haven't had much of ... you know, someone looking out for me ... someone who thinks I should give proper priority to my own true needs ... it feels real cheesy to say it ... but someone like a father ... I hope it does not worry you for me to say that.

Practitioner (P1):	No – in fact I wrote in my personal notes *It's like I am being her father ...*
C2:	I mean my uncle was like that ... for some years at least and especially about school and all that. He had massive belief in education and went to parents' evenings and bought me books ... we talked about missing my real dad ... but it was lovely having a bit of that then ...
P2:	You had some priority then – what you'd like from partners now...
C3:	Yeah – and still from him now and that's why I felt so hurt when he turned away from me ... but this is weird, isn't it ... saying you are like a father sometimes – a bit Freudian!
P3:	I guess ... but I think it is okay for some of that to come into this work ... we do need to remember the '*like* a father' though – I'm not actually your father ...

Young et al. (2003) discuss the role of 'limited re-parenting' in schema therapy, and we also discussed an understanding of transference and 'corrective emotional experience' that is compatible with CBT in Chapter 3 of this book. Whatever we may think of this it did seem in this instance to coincide with Antoinette being more 'settled in' to therapy, and she did begin now to work in more measured ways on her goals. She worked on being more accepting of her feelings and picked up some ways of self-soothing (Linehan, 1993). She also got some very effective debt counselling via the local Citizens Advice Bureau (CAB) and this led to rescheduling her debts in a way that began to make her everyday life easier. She began to learn too that in her words, 'If you give yourself away too cheaply you lose your market value.'

This phase of therapy was mainly based on raising awareness of how schemas and core beliefs operated in her life – often using interpersonal awareness of how they influenced the way she worked in sessions. After a while, however, Antoinette felt that she needed some time to 'run on her own for a while'. This did not necessarily mean that she would return to therapy but neither party was surprised when she did, about 18 months later. Her personal life now seemed more stable and she said that she wanted to work on issues related to her employment. During this phase of therapy the practitioner turned to more formal use of technique and this is illustrated below with a description of their work using the continuum method (James & Barton, 2004; Padesky, 1994).

WORKING WITH SCHEMA CONTENT: CONTINUA

Antoinette had now reached the lower rungs of middle management in her organisation and was gearing herself up to apply for promotion to the next level. Her main strategy to achieve this was by making herself into a 'go-to person'. Most of her fellow managers were women but as she rose higher, male colleagues became more evident and one in particular, Steve, now seemed to stand at the gateway of her promotion. Her sheer hard work and earthy humour that worked so well for her female colleagues seemed to cut less ice with Steve. Sometimes he encouraged her to 'think big' about what she might aspire to. At other times he seemed distant and critical – confirming her belief about men that she had articulated previously, namely that *men are bullies, selfish and lack emotional intelligence.*

Antoinette told her practitioner that she was well aware that Steve 'pushed her buttons' and activated schematic responses in her that related to the feeling of being taken up and dropped by people. Even so she remained convinced that eventually Steve would drop her because she believed that *People in the end will dismiss me.* This made her feel on edge and sulky in his presence and often precipitated tetchy arguments between them. Her practitioner told her how such beliefs could be explored using the continuum method and the prejudice model. She agreed to give these ideas a go.

The continuum method uses a written format to work on 'softening' the hard and inflexible categories that lie within core beliefs and schemas. It does this by clarifying the often rather narrow nature of their field of operations. Clients are asked to map out problematic beliefs by comparing them to their functional opposites and by breaking them down into specific criteria. This helps to 'stretch out' and soften them in a way that naturally leads to the formulation of more functional and adaptive alternative ways of thinking, feeling and doing. The process is illustrated below by reviewing continua work with Antoinette's belief that *People dismiss me.* The actual continua drawn are shown in Figure 7.2.

0% Accepting	50%	100% Accepting
Uncle's second wife: Aunt: Uncle (now): Mother?: Some colleagues:	*WG: Steve:*	*Most colleagues: Church friends: Uncle (past)*

Figure 7.2 Continuum method (worked example)

Practitioner (P1):	Okay so we are going to explore 'People dismiss me' first by establishing – what is the opposite …?
Client (C1):	I guess that would be 'People accept me', perhaps 'People respect me' …
P2:	Okay – let's go with 'accept' first … so let's draw a line across the page stretching from 'People accept me' here (*points*) to 'people dismiss me' here (*points again*) … now let's think about people we have talked about … and any others who seem relevant, and place them on this line according to how accepting or dismissing they are of you …
C2:	Let's put Steve right there because sometimes he accepts me and sometimes he dismisses me … (*writes in Steve over 50% mark*) … (*They then add in other people as shown in Figure 7.2*) …
P3:	Okay so now you have done that, have a look at it – a good look at it. What do you see?
C3:	(*Smiling*) It is interesting, isn't it – very interesting. I am most struck by the fact that the most dismissive people on it are women – that bitch who married my uncle for example! I am pretty sure she poisoned my uncle against me.
P4:	Okay, but I was also being a bit sneaky … I left out one of your words – 'eventually' … (*C: Why?*) … because 'eventually' is hard to disprove. It might not have happened all year but it could happen on 31 December.
C4:	Oh you sneaky thing! But I do get that – it's kind of how I feel a lot of the time: 'Just cos something bad has not happened yet it does not mean it won't any moment now' … And it can work the other way round too – I remember you saying that one minute before you met your wife you did not know you would ever meet her …
P5:	It is interesting to think that things are okay now but they could still go wrong, because in a sense it is true but it may just not be a helpful thing to think … for the moment let's just note that that is sometimes how our minds work. I'd like to try something else now …

At this point practitioner and client turn to using another aspect of the continuum method – breaking down the definition of a problematic term in an unhelpful belief and examining each criterion in turn (see Figure 7.3).

Practitioner (P1):	(*Looking first at the factor connecting 'People who dismiss me'*) What does it mean actually to 'dismiss' or 'accept' people? What would it look like if we were watching someone dismissing or accepting another?

NON-ACCEPTING	50%	ACCEPTING
Does not listen to me		Does listen to me
	STEVE	
Non-affirming		Affirming
STEVE (BLUNT REJECTIONS)		STEVE (AGREES WITH PRAISE)
Destructively critical		Constructively critical
BLUNT STEVE (Occasional)		NICE STEVE (More often)
Does not like my company		Does like my company
SPARKY STEVE		NICE STEVE

Figure 7.3 Criteria continuum method (expanded worked example)

Client (C1):	People who accept me listen to what I have to say … they affirm me in what I am doing … they might criticise me but it would be constructive criticism, not destructive criticism … and they like me, you know, enjoy my company … they would not look down and be judgemental with me … and I guess they'd respect me … if that isn't saying the same thing.
(Having set continuum as shown in Fig 7.3) P2:	Okay, now we are going to put Steve on all these continua lines – just Steve this time. We can see if we can learn any more about how he accepts you and how he dismisses you. Are you up for this? (*C*:Yes) Okay, where would you put him on the listen/not listen line?
C2:	Quite high – he does listen to me most of the time but also sometimes he does not really do that … in fact if he's busy he might even ask me to go away … (*The practitioner goes on down the continua lines for each one of Antoinette's answers.*)
(Affirmation) C3:	He has backed me on some ideas: he agreed with my point about how the house cleaners have been operating … but he told me my ideas on training were both 'expensive' and 'a bit naff' – I didn't like that.
P3:	He can be a bit blunt at times. What do you think of that?

C4:	I'm not too bad on that – I can be a bit like that myself but he does it perhaps a bit too much so I would put him towards the non-affirming side: there maybe (*pointing*) …
(*Constructive criticism*) C5:	Well again – okay actually – he did make some suggestions on how I could get my training ideas to what he called 'realistic' and within the budget … I haven't had a chance to work it all out yet but I think I will …
(*Enjoy my company*) C6:	He can be quite nice with me sometimes but I almost feel like he has to come down on hard to compensate for that too …
P6:	I get the feeling it is a bit sparky between you and him … a bit difficult … but never dull perhaps?
C7:	(*Dry laugh*) Yes – I heard someone say once, 'an enemy worth having', and I think we both feel that about one another …

Practitioner and client worked down the continua shown until it looked like the final Figure 7.3. It seemed that her relationship with Steve was difficult but actually quite dynamic and in some ways creative for her. They would never be the closest of colleagues but in some ways Antoinette got more challenge from him than from her other colleagues and she did accept that he did not 'dismiss' her in any outright way. She never did get the promotion she hoped for but did make a good sideways move and was hopeful that in this other section of the organisation she would get the middle management post she craved. After this move she again felt that she wanted to 'run on her own' and has not, as far as is known, come back for more help – *yet*.

USING ENACTMENT METHODS IN SCHEMA–BASED THERAPEUTIC WORK

The two phases of therapeutic work described both worked on aspects of the client's history and present situation. Given Antoinette's history, in which she was 'abandoned' to a lesser or greater extent by four different parent figures (five if we include her uncle's second wife), it would be surprising if she did not have an on-going vulnerability to rejection and abandonment. She had developed a compensating sense of autonomy – *I have to sort things out myself* – but also had periods naturally of thinking, *I can't do all this alone*. This latter belief can be seen as helping her to ask for assistance, be it therapy or some other form of support, and this feels as healthy as someone with an on-going medical vulnerability seeking out top-up help from a doctor. To some extent the same ground is trodden in each episode of therapy – acknowledging the presenting past and dealing with the present – though hopefully with some new ground being gained. Although the second episode described here was more focused on present-time issues there were still moments when the pain of the past would erupt and transfix the client's energy, and on these occasions it was helpful to facilitate contact with the emotional power of the past to offer further chances of emotional processing via enactment methods. These include methods such as imagery rescripting (Hackmann, Bennett-Levy & Holmes, 2011; Stopa, 2009) and the empty chair method, as described in the last chapter. These methods seem to work because they help the client access the emotional feeling of certain key episodes of their life, and this emotion can then become a motive power for change.

In a famous account of his life of hell in an English prep school, George Orwell (1953) recalls how he came to the belief that he was 'in a world where it was not possible for me to be good' because he was beaten for something – wetting the bed – over which he had no voluntary control. He says that he does not want to claim 'that this idea flashed into my mind as a complete novelty at this very moment … [of a double beating … but that it constituted] … a turning point, for it brought home to me for the first time the harshness of the environment into which I had been flung' (p. 6). Orwell goes on:

> To grasp the effect of this kind of thing on a child of 10 or 12, one has to remember that the child has little sense of proportion or probability. A child … has no accumulated experience to give it confidence in its own judgments. On the whole it will accept what it is told, and it will believe in the most fantastic way in the knowledge and powers of the adults surrounding it. (p. 17)

Schemas and core beliefs seem to develop in this same way – they are not completely consciously formed at a specific time but there seem to be key moments that symbolise the point at which a growing realisation of them starts to intrude into consciousness. Chapter 2 described the idea that it was good to get clients to tell 'stories' that seem to encapsulate their childhood experiences, and we go to that same idea here for facilitating schema-oriented work, not just for their narrative but for their power to aid transformative change too. A key memory for Antoinette had always been of the occasion when she had visited her uncle soon after recommencing her social care training on her return from Jamaica to the UK. By this time her uncle was now living with his new partner and Antoinette realised that he would be in some ways different, but nothing had prepared her for him being as indifferent as he proved to be. She was in fact hoping that he would sponsor her for a particular event connected to her training placement. All this involved was him signing a form for her. He met her at his front door and did not even invite her inside. She became flustered but still determinedly asked about the form. He said, 'I can't do those things for you any more, girl – no, please go away and don't you come back again.' She said she walked the streets for hours with tears in her eyes after this and then eventually trudged her lonely way home. 'That was when the great loneliness began' was how she summed up this moment and its meaning.

Antoinette's counsellor explained the various ways they might review this experience and she chose to put her uncle in an empty chair. One again the tears rolled down her face as they had on that night years ago. The counsellor encouraged her to tell 'her uncle' how she had felt during this encounter and the effect of the loneliness of her life that followed. She also told him that she thought he was afraid of his new wife and that she had heard this from other people who knew the couple.

(Continued)

(Continued)

Most of all she condemned him for the 'meanness' of his silence: 'Not one word, not even one little word of recognition or support over all these years.' She also named his offence – 'betrayal.' One more to add to others she had experienced in her life. Antoinette seemed utterly drained at the end of the session. The therapist stressed that Antoinette could use her self-soothing skills and also get in touch to update him on how she was feeling over the next few days. Some days later she called to say that she had spent most of the following day crying and had considered going on long-term sick from work. Then she began to feel lighter and better and, if anything, was now even keener than ever to get back to working on developing skills to work on her thoughts and feelings – especially on learning to tell people what she really wanted, and learning to negotiate effectively with them on that.

CONCLUSION

We noted in the opening chapter that the CBT model had an inclination *initially* to work with present-time issues but that its capacity to address more enduring problematic patterns with their roots in the past has expanded with new models such as schema therapy (Young et al., 2003) and with adaptation of past-oriented methods such as imagery rescripting (Hackmann et al., 2011). This became necessary as CBT has expanded in wider problem areas but also because a denial of past influences has seemed to fly in the face of working sensitively with clients who will themselves frequently want to talk over and work with such issues. We noted certain signals become evident when therapy is approaching schematic issues – although these signals can also be more simply translated as being guided by clients themselves, who are often quite able to tell practitioners what they need to work on and what their capacities for doing such work are. The skills described in the chapter are based on the ability to help clients make emotionally intelligent contact with their past experiences and to understand how they may be impacting on their present lives. The client is thus empowered to build a 'new plan' to – put at its simplest – *believe and think* something different, *feel* something different and *do* something different.

FURTHER READING

Hackmann, A., Bennett-Levy, J., & Holmes, E.A. (2011) *Using imagery in cognitive therapy*. Oxford: Oxford University Press.

Linehan, M.M. (1993) *Dialectical behavior therapy for borderline personality disorder*. New York: Guilford.

Wills, F. with Sanders, D. (2013) *Cognitive behaviour therapy: a practitioner's guide*. London: Sage. (Chapter 7)

Young, J.S. et al. (2003) *Schema therapy: a practitioner's guide*. New York: Guilford.

8

MAINTAINING AND DEVELOPING CBT SKILLS

All the world's a stage,

And all the men and women merely players,

They have their exits and their entrances … one man in his time plays many parts … At first the infant, mewling and puking in the nurse's arms … then the whining schoolboy creeping unwillingly to school like a snail … then the lover sighing like a furnace … then a soldier, full of strange oaths and … seeking the bubble reputation …

(Shakespeare, *As You Like It*, II. vii. 139–52)

These words from Shakespeare's play *As You Like It* are often referred to as 'the Seven Ages of Man'[1] speech. The speech finishes by reminding us that we end our lives 'sans teeth, sans eyes, sans taste, sans everything'.[2] Here we will explore seven stages common to developing CBT skills. The characteristic challenges of each stage will also be charted, along with some suggestions on how to meet them. I have always been fascinated by lifelong learning and will draw on discussions with colleagues and trainees over the years and on my research and my own experience of developing skills. Although I am now in the later stages of my development, I would suggest that the overall experience has not left me quite so bereft as that described by Shakespeare. This quotation is apt in another way too: it reminds us that although psychological therapy often seems an intensely private business it does always proceed on the 'stage' of the public domain. This public profile does affect the practice of psychological therapy in many ways – for instance we operate in politico-legal and organisational contexts.

There are, however, many aspects of CBT skill development and in order to avoid trying to say too little about too much I will focus on three specific developmental issues:

---

[1]Being from the Elizabethan age, the speech inevitably shows masculine bias.
[2]'Sans' means 'without'; i.e. we end up as old people with no teeth, no eyesight, no taste – with nothing!

◆ ways of handling the anxiety that affects trainees in the earlier stages of their training and career

◆ developing 'mastery' of skills in the middle and later career stages

◆ making a contribution to the wider field of psychological therapy.

In this final point I will suggest some benefits that could rise from developing our model by being open to learn from other approaches to therapy.

DEVELOPMENTAL ARCS OF CBT SKILL DEVELOPMENT

There are two ascending and overlapping arcs of development in learning CBT skills. The first is the *rise to competence* – developing basic competence – and the second is the *climb to expertise* – going beyond the basics to proficiency, expertise and mastery. The gradient of the first ascent of development is steep but can be climbed quite quickly. The second is usually more gradual and lengthy, having some resemblance for those familiar with hill walking to the experience of reaching what seemed to be the hill top only to find another slope tucked in behind.

There has been much research that suggests there are a number of clear stages in competence and skill development that are common to many professional areas. These begin with a novice stage and go through to the stages of expertise and mastery. The stage concept has been applied to learning CBT by authors such as Derek Milne (2009) and James Bennett-Levy (2006). For our purposes I have extended the usual range of stages slightly to produce my own 'seven ages' of CBT development:

◆ *Pre-novice stage*: Practitioners here may be contemplating training in CBT.

◆ *Novice stage*: Practitioners are actually undertaking the early stages of CBT training.

◆ *Advanced beginner*: Practitioners have now successfully completed training.

◆ *Competence stage*: Practitioners now get recognition as being competent and can get posts that may allow them to extend that competence.

◆ *Proficiency stage*: Practitioners develop expertise and may now be asked to help develop the practice of others.

◆ *Expert stage*: Practitioners' skills are at a level deemed capable of contributing to the development of the model itself.

◆ *Mastery stage*: Practitioners may now make contributions to the whole field of psychological therapy.

THE RISE TO COMPETENCE

Pre-novice stage

> At first the infant, mewling and puking in the nurse's arms … (*As You Like It*, II. vii. 142–3)

Prospective trainees do not usually throw up at the prospect of training in CBT, although as we will see in our next section, anxiety seems to rear its head quite often during training. An issue that may often concern prospective CBT trainees, however, is the degree to which what they will be learning would fit with their pre-existing skills. In most CBT training situations, many of the trainees will have experienced some previous professional practice and/or training. In fact it is still a requirement of professional CBT accreditation in the UK to have a recognised qualification and training in a recognised 'core profession' – for example, as a clinical psychologist, psychiatric nurse, counsellor or social worker – in addition to training in CBT. Atherton (1999) has shown that people make distinctions between training that they regard as *additive – i.e. skills that can be added to those one already has* – and training that could be regarded as *supplantive – skills that should replace those one is now using*. Attitudes towards additive training are usually quite relaxed but people can get nervous if they think that any training will require them to stop doing some of the things they do now and replace them with things they don't yet know how to do. They can thus feel a sense of uneasy transition and such a state is naturally anxiety making. Additional negative ideas may emerge when people are faced with learning CBT in particular. The following quotations all come from my research into how trainees experience CBT training:

> One fear that I had about CBT training was that I would be turned into a CBT automaton.[3]

> I feared that CBT might be cold and regimented … and … that I would lose all my individuality as a therapist.

Some trainees will of course be motivated by other, less-than-positive, factors:

> To be honest I was not that into CBT to begin with … I thought, I'll just keep my head down – and get a CBT qualification – it could come in handy these days![4]

---

[3]Quotations in this chapter are from my doctoral study on CBT training (Wills, 2008b) unless otherwise indicated. Further information on this study is referenced at the end of the chapter.

[4]It did indeed – I recently heard that this interviewee went on to get a doctorate in CBT!

Table 8.1 Stages in the development of CBT skills

Developmental stage	Characteristic challenges	Potential problems	Possible solutions
Pre-novice stage	Being aware enough of gaps in one's current practice that could be improved by learning CBT skills.	Buying in to negative stereotypes about CBT, CBT skills or CBT training.	Seek informed but friendly advice from a range of sources about the reality of CBT training and how such training might be integrated into your practice.
Novice stage	Engaging in CBT training in an open and productive way.	Being thrown into anxiety by the disabling experience of 'conscious incompetence' and/or the 'awkward' feeling of 'conscious competence'. Being disabled by the thought 'I am just not doing it *right*'.	Seeing some 'deskilling' as a necessary part of learning and that new skills take time to 'bed in'. Thinking that it may be helpful to 'play with' the model for a while rather than getting stuck in a 'fight for competency'.
Advanced beginner stage	Completing all the necessary tasks for successful CBT training and to 'get the piece of paper'.	Applying CBT skills to the situations in which you are required to implement them. Wondering at what stage you will have 'joined the club' you seek to be in.	If possible begin practising CBT in limited situations with just a few clients then slowly expand that scope. Explore your therapist beliefs and schemas about doing CBT with your clients. Confidently assert your new identity in a way that is comfortable to you.
Competency stage	Applying and experimenting with CBT with a widening variety of contexts and clients.	Feeling limited by 'protocol-driven' CBT. Missing the support of the training situation and the concomitant danger of 'reverting to the mean' of previous practice.	Keeping audio recordings of CBT sessions for supervision and for yourself. Maintain some contact with CBT-specific organisations and/or groups.

Developmental stage	Characteristic challenges	Potential problems	Possible solutions
Proficiency stage	Extending CBT skills for supervising and teaching others.	Feeling the pressure of thinking, 'Now more than ever I must *get it right*.' An awareness of 'clunkiness' that may be related to 'the limits of technical rationality.' Seeing how to use complicated research findings in practice.	Encouraging supervision that has creative use of the model as a principal aim. Using research as a *starting point* that will lead onto the work with the *individual client* before you (Persons, 2008). Doing your own research – using single case studies and reflective journals.
Expertise stage	Developing and applying a specific set of CBT skills to a particular problem or client context with the potential for making an original contribution to the development of the CBT model.	Idiosyncratic client reactions – usually driven by complex interpersonal factors – to CBT interventions.	Developing a more relaxed, and at the same time more interpersonally informed, style of practice. Take the same interpersonal and relaxed style into the wider debate about therapy with colleagues in other modalities.
Mastery stage	Developing a CBT skills model that will enhance the standing of CBT in the wider field of therapy while being open to 'other voices'.	'Wild eclecticism.' The complacency of 'Done it all and got the tee-shirt'.	Developing the skills of improvisation. Allowing 'positive doubts'. Searching for new skills more widely. Finding 'fellow spirits'.

I have learnt however that these seemingly negative approaches to training do not rule out positive outcomes for the trainees concerned – indeed all three trainees quoted above *did* move on to complete training successfully. These attitudes do though have the *potential* to lead to poor training outcomes. If these attitudes are evident before training then they are worth taking seriously, and if possible such trainees should be encouraged to talk these attitudes through with an appropriate person. When training courses in CBT at the University of Wales Newport first developed in 1995 we felt that we could not insist that all our trainees had CBT-qualified supervisors – mainly because such people were thin on the ground then. Often trainees had an existing non-CBT supervisor and sometimes asked if they could continue with that person. Our advice was: 'You should look for a CBT-qualified supervisor but in the meanwhile you may continue with a non-CBT supervisor – provided they are not *hostile* to CBT.' By and large this worked well, often in the spirit shown by the trainee cited below:

> When I discussed my doubts about the model with my (non-CBT) supervisor, she said that I should be like her – put my doubts aside and then we could both see what we could make of it. She said she looked forward to the experience, as she wanted to learn more about CBT for herself.

I have sometimes found supervisors like this one are better for trainees than some types of 'true believing' CBT-qualified supervisors who may supervise didactically and overwhelm supervisees with too much jargon. In contrast the supervisory attitude quoted above does allow supervisees to be active in articulating the model for themselves, and this can help them clarify what it really means for them, increasing a sense of ownership of the model – and of being able to do CBT in a way that really fits with them.

Suggestion Imagine that you are sitting in a café with a friend who is thinking about doing some training in CBT but who also articulates some of the negative fears about it that are illustrated in the quotations above. What points would you want to make to them?

If you are working in a group, do this in pairs first and then draw the whole group together to compare the responses people gave.

The novice stage: the joys and struggles of coming to terms with the CBT model during training

> ... the whining schoolboy creeping unwillingly to school like a snail (*As You Like It*, II. vii. 146–7)

Most of us know that when we learn a new set of skills we are likely to move from something like 'unconscious incompetence' to 'unconscious competence' (usually via the states of conscious incompetence and conscious competence). Such progress is likely to involve struggles of some sort. Furthermore, we may need to let some old skills go, to make room for new ones. We can appreciate this point intellectually but to know it experientially however is another matter. Perhaps we are in this respect like clients who say, 'I know I am not a failure but I still feel like one.' I am sure that all types of training have their difficulties but learning CBT perhaps may carry other factors that add to the stress of this kind of experience – for example, tutors who see strict adherence to protocols as the main way to practise. Adapting the words of Philip Larkin's immortal poem,[5] perhaps some trainers can 'give you all their faults and add some extra – just for you!' As I have argued throughout this book, CBT is essentially a set of ideas and methods that can be practised in varied ways. A mythology has however developed among some that there is only 'one true way' of practising CBT, and in this mythology such a way of practice is based on protocols – an unattractive and seemingly uncreative prospect for many. Yet it may be necessary to adapt this approach or something like it during some phases of training.

Suggestion/exercise: *Syllogism time is here again!* Syllogisms are used in a type of reasoning developed in philosophy. The practice is to take two statements that may at first seem to be contradictory. The aim then is to explore the two statements and the potential relationship between them in order to reduce the apparent contradictions and even to aim to bring them together into a single extended statement. I suggest my own particular solution to this one in the next paragraph so try not to read further until you have tried the exercise for yourself or with a group of others. The two statements here are:

You have to learn to do CBT by the book
and
You can't do CBT by the book

Like all myths, the one about the supposedly robotic nature of CBT has at least a grain of truth. This grain of truth can in my view be stated like this – *You have to learn CBT by the book* at first – but later *You may often do it better by deviating from that book*. The point here, however, is that the one time that CBT probably does come close to its negative stereotype may be during training. This is because students do need to get the *working model* of CBT skills firmly in their minds so that they can practise these skills in a more relaxed fashion later. Unfortunately some authorities on CBT do not necessarily share my view of this and insist that CBT practice should mostly *follow the protocol*. While there are some practice scenarios in which this may be a valid approach, there can also be unfortunate and probably unintended consequences during training, partly because it can trigger trainees' anxieties about 'doing it right'.

---

[5]'This be the verse' (in Larkin, 2003), with its famous first line 'They f—k you up, your mum and dad'.

> I was really struggling about half way through the course because I thought I had to do CBT like 1, 2, 3, 4, 5 … I could not *play* with it … (*Later*) … I thought *I'll just have to try to do it my way … if the tutors don't like it, tough …*

Many other trainees have echoed this kind of experience, and understanding this dilemma better has helped the author to improve his training and teaching practices. Just as CB therapists should be wary of trying to 'talk clients out' of their ideas, even if those ideas are 'negative', so should trainers be similarly wary of being over-persuasive when trainees reveal apparently 'negative' attitudes to their experiences of learning. Collaboration is a much better stance for therapists' work with clients *and* for trainers' work with trainees (Padesky, 1996). It is usually more effective because, as we have noted in previous chapters, trying too hard to change people and their ideas often leads to resistance. In my early days in CBT training I suspect that I was guilty of 'bulldozing' trainees at times and only later realised that a key tutor attribute is the ability to help trainees to be free enough from anxiety to 'play with CBT' – i.e. to experiment with it and 'try its skills on for size'. When students are freed up in this way, in my experience, the chances of successful learning increase.

Geoffrey Masson (1990, p. 245) once accused practitioners and trainers in psychological therapy of being 'the bland teaching the un-bland to be bland'. While this is a bit harsh we can agree with it to the extent that helping trainees to achieve initial basic competence can involve some 'blanding' of them. Tutors may, for example, want trainees to drop their more quixotic ideas and practices but what this achieves can at first look and feel like a rather conformist brand of practice, like 'doing it by the book'. Furthermore, although this is probably an essential stage of development, it can often seem to trainees that they have only received what some educational researchers have called 'inert knowledge' (Bransford, Brown & Cocking, 2004; Bransford, Franks, Vye & Sherwood, 1989) – that is, knowledge that is not easily transferred to real-life situations. We can understand this by returning to some of our discussion on the relationship between cognition and emotion – some knowledge is 'declarative' (essentially factual) and some 'procedural' (more intuitive). Declarative knowledge of CBT skills suggests they can be learnt in steps and stages, whereas procedural knowledge for skill usage is subtler and concerns matching skills to the needs of individual clients. Declarative rules and basic skills can be learnt quite quickly whereas learning the subtleties of applying them is a much slower process. As one trainee put it:

> I found it difficult to move from very consciously applying skills to a more natural form of CBT practice.

Most trainees find themselves in this more uncertain place at some stage during or after their courses and this can lead to anxiety:

> [in the … later stages] … I went through my 'crisis' with CBT. I had passed the first assessments without too much problem but I had trouble finding the right clients to work with and began to wonder if I would ever get a good enough audio recording to submit …

In the amusing spoof paper on CBT training by I.M. Worthless, U.R. Competent and O. Lemonde-Terrible (2002) the 'authors' point to the anxiety-making effects of assessment of CBT trainees using the Cognitive Therapy Scale (CTS: Young & Beck, 1980, 1988) or its more recent version from the University of Newcastle, the Cognitive Therapy Scale – Revised (CTS-R: James et al., 2000). These scales are multi-item measures of competence in CBT. They both have a General Therapy Sub-scale and a Cognitive-Behavioural Sub-scale. Further information on these scales and manuals for rating trainees using them can be found at the end of the chapter. Unsurprisingly, the CTS has generated much debate and has strong supporters who argue for its efficacy, and equally strong critics who argue against. In my experience the CTS and its manuals are invaluable *aids to* the assessment of trainees for CBT competence but are best used alongside other criteria and within course-specific guidelines. CBT tutors should constantly develop and share their assessment skills among each other in light of developing expertise in this area. References related to the use of the CTS and CTS-R are offered at the end of the chapter.

Suggestion/exercise *How would you start to generate criteria to assess the skills of agenda setting?*

You will have read in Chapter 2 that CB therapists are encouraged to set an agenda for each session. On first consideration this seems simple enough – yet a surprising number of trainees struggle to do it. Draw up two columns; in one write down ways in which you think agenda setting might be done badly, and in the other, ways in which it can be done appropriately and well. Finally decide for yourself or discuss with others in your group whether it might be possible to use these two lists to construct assessment criteria of this item of skill assessment. (You may compare your answers with those of the manuals of guidance for CBT skills assessment shown at the end of the chapter.)

Among trainees I have interviewed anxiety is a common feature of student experiences during CBT training – especially when it comes to any kind of assessment of competence and even more so at the prospect of skill assessment using the CTS. Worthless et al. (2002, p. 369) for example suggest the possible use of a 'safety behaviour' in the form of 'recording your grandmother's Bing Crosby album over the tape to be submitted for assessment'.

Anxiety can also have some more seriously disabling effects on skill performance. A number of trainees have for instance described negative metacognitive thoughts like 'I must keep reminding myself to perform this skill otherwise I will forget to do it', rather like the trainee below:

I had a real block on setting an agenda. It was difficult for me because I'd had previous training in Rogerian therapy and setting an agenda sounded a bit like bossing people around to me. So I kept telling myself 'I must do it, I must set an agenda' over and over again. I'd get so anxious – and that would often result in me forgetting to do it …

Anxiety may obviously increase when assessment is involved because then it is even more important to remember to do it – at a time when nerves will be on edge anyway. Interestingly, trainees with a Rogerian background did tend to have significantly more problems with agenda setting than trainees from other backgrounds (Wills, 2008b). In an interesting contrast, however, they had fewer problems setting homework at the end of a session. It could be argued that homework setting is also a directional method, but I would guess that trainees have fewer problems with it because it tends to come at the end of sessions whereas agenda setting is of necessity at the start of sessions. Perhaps novice therapists feel more nervous at the start of sessions but by the end had used their natural skills to create a situation where therapist and client were more settled and at home with each other. This was certainly the case for many students as they approached the end of the course:

CBT is more directive but then I thought, 'Well you don't have to go in with hobnail boots on' … it got easier after that.

We might think that it is puzzling that we CBT practitioners don't seem able to help ourselves with this type of anxiety. The discussion also raises the possibility that there may be specific beliefs about learning CBT that make it more difficult. Persons, Gross, Etkin and Madan (1996) have written about helping trainees with previous psycho-dynamic training overcome their reservations about CBT. They also feel it is helpful to encourage trainees to surface their feelings and to encourage them to 'try CBT for themselves' rather than by demanding that they do it in 'one true way'. Interestingly, trainers in other models have also reported these factors at work (Mackay, West, Moorey, Guthrie & Margison, 2001) and again stress the desirability of encouraging trainees to find their own way to 'play with' new methods. We might think too that a more open style of training would offer a good model of CBT practice to trainees since it would be based on collaboration and on 'guiding discovery' rather than 'changing minds' (Padesky, 1993).

Suggestion/exercise *How can we help CBT training courses to encourage students to 'play with' the model?*

How do you react to the idea that trainees should be encouraged to 'play with' CBT as a way of finding 'their own way of doing it'? If you agree, can you suggest any ways that courses could allow such a spirit to develop in training? As with a previous suggestion it might be worth jotting down ideas under two headings – 'Allowing students to find their own way' and 'Having students learn it in a uniform way' – and see if any ideas emerge from such a comparison. Questions that might structure some responses around might be:
What could facilitate such an atmosphere in training courses? What about staff–student relationships? What activities would help? What about assessment?

The advanced beginner ('the lover sighing like a furnace …') and the competence ('the soldier, full of strange oaths and … seeking the bubble reputation') stages

One reason why I think it is highly desirable to encourage an atmosphere in which trainees can 'play with' learning CBT is that it makes for the most favourable situation in which trainees obtain feedback on their skills and practice. Good quality feedback is essential for learning CBT skills. Learners need to practise skills, be able to reflect on what happened, and get some feedback from others, including our clients, on 'how it went'. We noted earlier the role of feedback in the session structure for CBT. I think that Beck's emphasis on getting feedback from clients could prove one of CBT's most significant contributions to the helping professions. I once found myself using the next washbasin to Beck in the mens' room after a lecture he'd given. I should not perhaps have been surprised when he asked me for feedback on his lecture, though there could perhaps have been a better moment for such a request! More seriously, would it not be good if more professions were introduced to the idea of systematically seeking client feedback? For example if GPs routinely asked patients, 'What do you *really* think of the way I ran this consultation?' This simple question could produce a significant move towards a more democratic relationship between many professionals and their clients.

Trainees should be keen to seek user-friendly feedback on their skills that might be available in a well-organised course; such feedback may be so much harder to find after the training has finished. Equally, we all need to work on honing our abilities to give effective feedback, to find the balance between affirming each other – *You did that well* – but also challenging each other to do better – That *could be better and this is how you might try it*. Using video and audio recordings is a particularly effective context for learning skills. In my own training at the Oxford Cognitive Therapy Centre we were encouraged to record every session, and I remember feeling the same excitement as that described by Carl Rogers as I listened to my own work – the good sessions and the bad ones. Rogers (1980) pioneered the use of recording therapy sessions and tells how he and his colleagues gathered around their recording equipment to listen out for what learning could be gleaned from each passage of therapeutic dialogue. I learnt another good principle for skills training when some trainees informally told me how nervous they felt at having to use recording equipment for skills training. They asked if they could go to the studio for a '*play* around' with the equipment – without tutors present – so they would be less nervous next time. This worked like a charm and became standard practice for video learning sessions, and we see once more the positive role of *play* in learning: a role thoroughly endorsed by developmental psychologists (Dobson, 2004).

As they finish training, trainees often report a dilemma about how to now regard themselves. At its most basic this may be about how one answers the question, 'What do you do?' Can I for example now call myself a 'CBT therapist' or is there some further stage – for example, accreditation, or being given a post with CBT in the title – that must be undertaken before such a claim is valid? I was surprised by the sense of uncertainty that newly trained people often felt about this:

> I made sure that I got the title 'CBT therapist' on my business card but I felt shy about getting my department to put it on my staff profile – people might think, 'Who does she think she is?'

Another trainee correctly observed that there can be a lot of politics in these processes: does anyone have 'ownership rights' for CBT or does anyone think they do?

> I'm employed as a 'counsellor' but I see myself as a 'CBT therapist' … it is a tricky one … with titles – you get into a status thing …

Employers may resolve these issues by awarding titles or making rules. Many of these quotations come from the period just before the Increasing Access to Psychological Therapies (IAPT) projects commenced and after which CBT qualifications became more desirable. Many trainees then reported that their employers were largely indifferent to their training and/or unwilling to get too involved in awarding titles that could reward some but upset others. Meanwhile many trainees decided to come up with their own title and see how far they could push it:

> In the counselling world I say I am a counsellor but in the CBT world I say I am a counsellor who does CBT.

> I see myself as an integrated therapist but if I talk to a doctor I tend to say I am a CBT one.

> I call myself a counsellor who does CBT.

As trainees go into the post-training environment the title they give themselves may signal commitment to keeping up practice of the model, but more will be needed, especially if the idea of continued commitment to the development of practice is aspired to. There is much evidence that it is easy to 'revert to the mean' – i.e. gradually slip back into old ways of practice followed before training (Ashworth, Williams & Blackburn, 1999). Ideally, training organisations should take an on-going interest in the development of trainees after training and, speaking personally, it is always a great delight to me to meet with former trainees and find out what they are 'up to'. Trainers have an imperative to put more attention on new trainees, and it is often hard for them to persuade their employers of the desirability of giving 'follow-up' time to former trainees. This however may mean that trainers are not always well aware of the challenges that ex-trainees face in the post-training environment.

Many former trainees will seek accreditation – mainly through professional associations such as the British Association for Behavioural and Cognitive Psychotherapies (BABCP) and the British Association for Counselling and Psychotherapy (BACP). These bodies require therapists accredited under their banners to undertake a form of supervision and a certain amount of continuing professional development (CPD) each year. Sometimes CPD can seem more designed to benefit training organisations than the real needs of practitioners. The collection of CPD certificates can become a ritual – with some people definitely pursuing a strategy of 'exit-essentialism' after getting the piece of paper at the earliest opportunity! On the more positive side, BABCP for example, has many lively regional groups that offer on-going contact[6].

These are important methods that help people to avoid merely returning to their old form of practice or 'reverting to the mean' and/or 'drifting off message' into other directions after training. My research revealed, however, that a significant number of trainees do no more than the minimum required by whatever jobs, statuses or titles they have. This is not always because of lack of commitment and may be because of time, money or simple preference. One low-cost and relatively congenial way of keeping up contact with the therapeutic field can be to run informal groups with former trainees with whom one felt some fellowship during training. One such group did actually form to help me develop parts of this book, for example. I will discuss some fertile ways of development that such groups can follow later in this chapter but will for now ask readers to reflect on their own post-training experiences as a final suggestion here.

Suggestion *Forming a peer development group, individually, in pairs or in a group*

If you are currently on a training course or in a training group, have you yet given any thought to how you will keep up your skills development after training? One way is to discuss setting up a small group of people on your course with whom you think you might enjoy continuing contact. Think about how you would do this: Where could you meet? How often – monthly, every two or three months? What activities could you undertake that might act as a stimulus to maintain your skills or practice development? Last but not least, would it be good to have some kind of social element to this – a meal or some time in a café or pub?

THE LONG, SLOW CLIMB TO PROFICIENCY, EXPERTISE AND MASTERY

From proficiency to expertise

… then the justice … full of wise saws and modern instances … (*As You Like It*, II. vii. 154)

Trainees leaving their CBT training programmes should have achieved a level of basic competence – often set as achieving a satisfactory rating on a competence measure such as the CTS-R. Self-confidence is higher but many still seem uncertain on their ability to make a success of real-life practice. They are often still dominated by the idea of 'getting it right' and may feel the tutor's metaphorical voice in their ear. In some of my interviews the trainees did a little mock role-play using a nagging tutor's voice:

---

[6]Such groups can be found via the BABCP website: www.babcp.com

I could not deviate from the protocol – after training I was still saying to myself, *Now, you must remember to do your mood check and bridge …*

You want to do it like you have been told how to do it, and if you don't there is still a fear that you will be *told off!*

This 'conscious competence' is still dependent on declarative knowledge that 'follows the rules' and imposes 'official order' and 'sticks to plans'. This kind of competence, however, comes at a price, and before too long many of the trainees begin to think that the practice it allows is 'okay' but not really skilled, and in fact seems 'a bit clunky' and 'rather rigid and mechanical', feeling as if it is done 'by rote' or 'by the book'. As noted earlier, there can be a considerable drift back to previous practice after training (Ashworth et al., 1999), which may begin at this point perhaps because practitioners are encountering what Schon (1994) calls 'the limits of technical rationality'. According to Schon, technical rationality emerged as an aspect of positivism, and it advanced the development of professionalism in many work contexts from the mid-19th century before reaching its high watermark in the 1960s. Technical rationality is, however, particularly appealing to organisations and governments, who often (rightly) think about populations rather than individual clients and for whom it offers help in developing rational policies and practices. CBT became especially involved in such a project with the 'evidence-based practice' movement of the 1990s and then with the similar thinking that drove Lord Layard's report on depression (the Centre for Economic Performance, 2006). These trends were based on the idea that there were best practices supported by research evidence and that practitioners should read the research literature and make practice choices accordingly. The limitations of this approach became clear to me, however, when I attended a poorly organised evidence-based mental health conference in the late 1990s. In a key conference exercise we were given a case scenario followed by a 30-page collection of research abstracts to read and were then asked to make decisions about the case in light of the 'evidence'. The articles were dense and hard to understand and we were given a hopelessly inadequate half hour to digest and use them. Needless to say the subsequent discussion was not enlightening. This exercise seemed to be aimed at modelling good practice but to me only highlighted the massive problems for practitioners planning to use research findings. The only other thing I remember about that conference was that, in the cause of so-called empowerment, a client was invited to speak but went straight off message by saying that clients were more concerned with being treated respectfully than with the 'effectiveness' of their treatments.

Practitioners are often criticised for not reading research, but we may also ask whether researchers have made enough effort to make their work accessible to and useable by practitioners. The CBT research base could be characterised as 'outcome rich and process poor', and CBT researchers often seem wary of process research, as if it is contaminated by association with other models of therapy. The most that CBT practitioners can take from much CBT outcome research, however, is the ability to find a good *general* direction – perhaps via a protocol – on what effective work might look like. There is nothing like enough information on how to use protocols. Beutler (personal communication) has suggested that it takes at least two years of consistent use to learn how to use a single protocol in order to practise it well over a range of client situations; and he adds, tongue-in-cheek, that by the time you have worked your way through all the protocols that would be necessary for everyday general therapy practice it would be time to retire! More process research could possibly plug this gap but there has been a dearth of this in CBT. I have now become convinced that the only way such research is likely to develop is for practitioners to commit to doing it themselves at peer group level – ideally with some support from the more democratically oriented academic institutions (Wills, 2010). The key to such work would involve discovering more about how clients respond to different methods and whether there are identifiable 'response tracks' that would be useful for practitioners to know about – rather as an earlier generation of research in counselling revealed (Truax & Carkhuff, 1967). In addition it would be helpful if we could identify what 'tracks' practitioners find when travelling through this dense wood of uncertainty that characterises real-life implementation of methods and skills.

One interviewee offered the following colourful metaphor for this kind of work:

> It is like a client using a thought record and it just does not work – like blowing on a trumpet but no note comes out, never mind a tune … and the new practitioner can feel that too: *I learnt to play this instrument; how come we can't get a tune out if it?*

Clients can start to help us out with these dilemmas, however. Their problems may refuse to be neatly dealt with in the way the protocols describe. Clients may show resistance and apparently refuse to 'play the game', and this can push us to see that we are knocking on closed doors and that we need to try more creative solutions:

> One client I had just bristled at the sight of paperwork – a thought record was a no-no … but she would talk things through using the same principles, finding evidence and all that …

As trainees gain more experience and confidence they are more likely to report being able to trust their own preferred ways of doing things:

> I'd taken a lot from Rogers in my first training so I thought a lot about how the client's thinking was influenced by my 'way of being' – if I could be calm and clear in my thinking and see if that could have more influence than techniques …

This however could feel risky – NICE guidelines have little to say about 'ways of being' – so perhaps some will see such work as ineffective and too far 'off-piste'. This can leave practitioners in a 'lonely place', so that trainees often need significant support and encouragement if they are to deal with the necessary uncertainties of 'trial and error' that are bound to come with learning to 'play with' the model. Internal sources of support can come from supervisors, managers and clients. Understanding the stages and transitions involved in skills learning facilitates good, sensitive supervision. Supervisors can vary the balance of support and challenge to grant supervisees a gradually increasing sense of autonomy that is best suited to that supervisee's development. At first supervisees may follow the 'by the book' approach that may have informed their training, and may mistakenly think that they have to find a technical solution for every problem (because they may believe that there *must* be one). It has been my experience, however, that technical problems fade in importance as experience develops, because problems are more often to do with implementing skills and methods with particular individual clients – a continuing theme of most of the supervision that I do. Problems of implementation are most often interpersonal at base. CBT has been a little hampered in this area as many versions of it have downplayed the interpersonal side, with some notable exceptions (Gilbert & Leahy, 2007; Safran & Segal, 1990; Wills with Sanders, 2013). CBT has also done very little process research – a factor we will return to later. The sense of deviating from the protocol may also trigger some anxious therapist schemas (Leahy, 2007): *If I give this client homework she won't like me but if I don't it won't be proper CBT.* Light eventually appears at the end of the tunnel and a sense of more creativity and flexibility then enhances confidence; in the words of one former trainee:

> In any case experimentation is fundamental to CBT … and so trial and error must be so as well … you can say to a client 'I don't know for sure if this will work but we could try it – what do you think?'

It can feel weak to admit that we are not omniscient but such a stance in fact shows strength, supporting both therapist genuineness – owning what we know and what we do not know – and retaining a fundamental trust in clients' abilities to know what is likely to work for them. This growing confidence, to be fallible at times, allows a more holistic view of what should be priorities in practice.

This sense of 'fallible confidence' brings us to the gates of proficiency as competence becomes less conscious and is more relaxed, because it requires less deliberate and effortful 'work' and because it comes more naturally. Crucially it allows us to think what is required by the unique situation before us. Our theoretical approach can help us with that but should not determine what it should be. When practitioners have reached the stage where they can do this for themselves, they can often begin to step up to supervisory roles so they can help others reach this same place. Supervisory roles can help them take a wider view of the model in all its aspects – a necessary precursor of expertise.

From proficiency to expertise and mastery

> the lean and slippered pantaloon with spectacle on nose … last scene of all that ends this strange eventful history is second childishness and mere oblivion, sans teeth, sans eyes, sans taste, sans everything. (*As You Like It*, II. vii. 158–66)

A sense of 'positive doubt' – that neither one's practice model nor oneself has 'all the answers' and that this can be okay – is now perhaps twinned with a growing confidence that one has the skills to 'improvise'. Improvisation has been defined as the defining characteristic of mature expertise and mastery (Binder, 2004). The tacit knowledge that allows this confidence can be hard to articulate, however, and it may be this sense of difficulty in 'saying what one knows' that influences people to seek knowledge from outside their current knowledge base to help them do just that. One obvious place to start is to look at ideas from other models of psychotherapy that may have something else to add here. There has however been a built-in tribalism (Inskipp & Proctor, 1999) in the field of psychological therapy that can make such exploration hard to do for several different reasons. Besides the feeling of slight disloyalty to one's own tribe – it can involve time and effort to seriously explore other areas. The literature of psychological therapy is now quite vast and difficult to navigate one's way round when all of us seem to be pushed for time.

During the eight years that have taken up the writing of the first and second editions of this book, I have deliberately sought to train myself in some skills from models outside CBT, mainly to deal with aspects of the CBT model that I thought were not working as well as they could for me in my work. This self-training was aimed mainly at two main targets. First, I wanted to examine how more understanding of the time-limited dynamic therapy (TLDT; Binder, 2004; Levenson, 1995; Strupp & Binder, 1984) might help me understand and use some of the subtle influences that I had become more aware of in the therapeutic relationship. Second, I wanted to learn more about how emotion-focused therapy (Elliott et al., 2004; Greenberg, 2002, 2011) could help me deal with some of the more subtle aspects of clients' emotions that I felt I sometimes missed. In order to do this I attended some workshops, read all the main texts that I could manage and watched all the recorded examples of this type of work that I could lay my hands on. I also followed two practices that I think could be helpful at any stage of one's career – doing informal but systematic single case research and keeping a reflective journal round a particular theme of practice development (Wright & Bolton, 2012). Systematic single case studies are simple science projects that can help one follow the ups and downs of using a new method with a particular client (McLeod, 2010). Practice-based reflective journals on the other hand can take a more discursive approach to tease out what developmental issues are latent in one's current practice. Some examples from my efforts that relate to this book may be found on the book's companion website (https://study.sagepub.com/wills).

I have never been content to 'rest on my laurels' in either my practice or my writing and some people have been kind enough to tell me that I have retained the sense of adventure and enthusiasm that I have felt ever since beginning to work in psychological therapy over 40 years ago. I have found this phase, of writing reflective pieces on my practice while also writing these books, an exciting and stimulating period and do not for a single minute think it is over yet. The results of this 'self-training' are presented in the earlier chapters of this book so that readers will be able to judge for themselves what value may have been added.

As I have followed this developmental trajectory I have also become aware of other CBT practitioners of my generation travelling on similar tracks and so I have wondered if the distinguishing features of this journey – the courage to admit the limitations in one's current practice and the openness to learning from the 'other side' – are essential features of the mature practice of therapy (Goldfried, 2005). To return for a moment to our passage from Shakespeare, mature practitioners do in a sense 'lose some teeth' and may no longer look so 'dashing'. Perhaps, however, in our 'second childishness' we also rediscover the ability to play again and to feel some of the wonder of discovery, like children encountering the vibrant world at their feet.

Other CBT practitioners have for example reflected on the potential pitfalls of an overly cognitivised approach to emotions (Power, 2010). Paul Gilbert (2010, p. 6) refers to the fact that there are clients who say, "'I understand the logic of CBT … but I can't feel any different" … This is a well-known issue in CBT.' As we discussed earlier Paul has used insights from his knowledge of neuroscience and evolution to suggest that any attempts to move on from negative emotions must engage brain functions involved in generating compassion. Such a way of working could never be regarded simply as a matter of technique because emotions and relationships are so intimately connected, and so the perspective of compassion-focused work certainly must have implications for the therapeutic relationship. It is therefore no surprise that we find Paul writing and editing a book on the therapeutic relationship in CBT (Gilbert & Leahy, 2007) that suggests the desirability of being open to learning from other models of practice. Paul has chosen to develop his ideas by promoting another model – compassion-focused therapy (CFT). He does not seem to see this as an alternative (supplantive?) model but as a member of the CBT family of models, one that may perhaps be a somewhat 'semi-detached' family member – perhaps expressed in the final sentence of his excellent review, 'Moving beyond cognitive behaviour therapy': 'CBT is good at what it attempts to do, but (clinical) psychology as a science and service model goes way beyond it' (Gilbert, 2009b, p. 403).

Ann Hackman has been a pioneer in developing the innovative use of imagery techniques in cognitive therapy. Imagery techniques began with an early contribution by Beck (1970b) but were then neglected for several decades untill Ann and other colleagues developed a more systematic approach. Ann's interest in imagery began partly because images seem to have the ability to reach aspects of emotional experience that are beyond the realms of words and language. She has used concepts from the wider world of 'visualisation' and has some amusing tales to tell about some of her experiences while on this journey (personal communication). At the same time, she has also been insistent on staying true to the scientific methods of the Oxford tradition within which she worked, so that she can make empirically grounded contributions to the use of imagery with specific psychological problems (Hackmann et al., 2011). Despite her recent formal retirement she continues to be active in seeking yet more applications of imagery techniques to new areas of problems – such as their role in physical health care. Throughout this time, like myself, Ann has not felt it was necessary to develop an alternative model to cognitive therapy, and she has 'stayed with the programme' while being unafraid to explore and use options from other perspectives.

We have an interesting example of someone who became a kind of 'CBT apostate' in John Marzillier. I agree with Windy Dryden's comment on the cover of John's book that the account of John's development as a practitioner would be highly readable and instructive for most therapists (Marzillier, 2010). John portrays himself in the younger days of his career as a rather overconfident and bumptious practitioner. Yet he also displays the ability to be honest about his mistakes and limitations. He describes how he was able gradually to allow his clients to 'put him right' on a number of issues, especially on the importance of recognising their emotions and using what can be learnt from continuous interactions in the therapeutic relationship. Having been a thoroughgoing behavioural and then cognitive therapist, John retrained as a psycho-dynamic therapist in 1989. He charts this fascinating journey in the lively narrative of his 2010 book – including a classic account of his epic tennis match with Aaron Beck. For a time he tried to combine his new perspective with that of his old but eventually seems to have found himself turning more to the new. Some 'converts' are inclined to turn on their former allies but it is heartening to read that John retains respect for CBT, perhaps agreeing with John McLeod (2013b, p. xiii) that, 'Inter-school arguments are inward-looking, distract attention from the needs of clients, and are a waste of time.'

As I bring this section on expertise and mastery to an end, I realise that I have been avoiding something in these last pages. Perhaps my avoidance has been fuelled by some embarrassment of any suggestion that I know anything about mastery and/or by a sinking feeling that expertise and mastery have no ends: it is all just another ridge in hill walking I referred to earlier in the chapter. Even to imagine that one had achieved mastery seems like folly and perhaps points us towards a big potential downside to the licence that one can give oneself to be creative and to improvise – a lurch into a kind of slightly embarrassing 'I have been there and got the tee-shirt' attitude that may well show itself in our field as a form of 'wild eclecticism' (Dryden & Neenan, 2004). I think that if anyone were ever to convince me that this is what I had arrived at then I accept that it would be time for me, turning one last time to Shakespeare, to 'have my exit' (*As You Like It*, II. vii. 141).

I am, however, happy to be still on the CBT team – though I am also firmly of the view that psychological therapists and practitioners are at their best when they are open to learn from each other, and at their worst when they disrespect each other (Davies, 2013). There have been many hurtful actions and criticisms on all sides that have made this difficult to do at times. I end this book, though, standing by both my grounding in CBT *and* what I feel I have learnt from other models. Finally, may I appeal to other practitioners of good faith from all sides who feel similarly to consider exploring the idea that we should all be humble enough to learn from each other – because, apart from anything else, we all have much to be humble about.

FURTHER READING

Davies, E. (2013) Talking point: we are all on the same side. *Therapy Today*, 24(6). Retrieved from: www.therapytoday.net/article/show/3836

Gilbert, P. (2009) Moving beyond cognitive behaviour therapy. *The Psychologist*, 22(6): 400–403. (Available to download at: www.thepsychologist.org.uk)

Marzillier, J. (2010) *Gossamer threads*. London: Karnac Books.

Wills, F. (2008) The acquisition of competence during CBT training. Unpublished PhD thesis, University of Bristol. (NB: Visit the book's companion website for an extract from this thesis.)

(Continued)

(Continued)

See also the chapter on training and supervision lodged on the book's companion website.

Information on the CTS

The original CTS is available as a free download from the website of the Beck Institute: www.beckinstitute.org; follow 'CBT Resources'.

The CTS-R rating scale and manual are available from several different websites as free downloads by entering 'CTS-R' as a search term. One such website has many other helpful CBT materials: www.getselfhelp.co.uk

APPENDIX 1

RESOURCES FOR CBT MEASURES

As described within the text, a defining feature of CBT practice has been the use of psychological measures to assess problems and monitor client progress – classically using quantitative measures such as inventories to gauge the strengths of symptoms in anxiety and depressive disorders. The Internet has revolutionised access to such measures, many of which can be downloaded without any charge from various websites. Some measures, however, such as the Beck measures (see below), still require registration and payment – so users need to access some caution that they are legally using a measure that they come across.

PEARSON CLINICAL (WWW.PEARSONCLINICAL.CO.UK)

Therapists need to register so that they can purchase the following measures:

◆ Beck Depression Inventory II (BDI)

◆ Beck Anxiety Inventory (BAI)

◆ Beck Hopelessness Scale (BHS)

◆ Beck Obsessive & Compulsive Scale (BOCS).

These are also available as measures especially adapted for children and young people.

FREE DOWNLOADABLE MEASURES

It is now difficult to cover all the many available websites, and in any case they can be found via relatively straightforward searches by the use of key terms. One good starting point for aspirant CBT therapists is via the website of the Oxford Cognitive Therapy Centre (OCTC) where measures are downloadable without charge for a wide variety of problems that readers of this book are likely to be interested in: www. OCTC.co.uk/resources

APPENDIX 2

OTHER COGNITIVE METHODS USING COST BENEFIT ANALYSIS AND PIE CHARTS

It is sometimes said that there are three main ways of challenging negative thoughts:

◆ reality testing ('What is the evidence?')

◆ pragmatic testing ('Is that thinking justified when it makes you feel that way?')

◆ logic testing ('Does that way of thinking really make sense?').

Quite often a CBT practitioner will deploy all these three ways and then see which seems to be the most helpful to the individual client. Clients obviously have different ways of doing things within their own heads, and some ways of challenging thoughts will chime with their internal processes better than others. There is, however, usually no sounder way of finding this out other than by 'suck it and see'. It is probably also often a case of 'all hands to the pump' and 'we'll use whatever works'. From my experience with clients, however, I would say that, for most clients, logical challenges often have limited effects. Reality-testing challenges can work well but often they are helpfully reinforced by pragmatic challenges. Pragmatic challenges are often the ones that bring a commitment to thinking about things in a different way, because, the client might say, *they really work against me*. The CBA technique is probably the clearest and most parsimonious of the pragmatic challenges.

COST BENEFIT ANALYSIS (CBA)

CBA shows a subtle acceptance of the fact that sometimes the client's negative thinking may have some subtle pay-offs. Readers can probably all remember that before an exam, many examinees will be heard loudly declaring that they haven't done 'any revision at all!' Isn't it amazing how many then go on to pass? Similarly, some people who declare 'I'm such a failure' may be partly concerned to lower the expectations of others and also avoid later negative labelling by getting in first themselves. CBA helps to acknowledge these 'benefits' yet also set them against the context of their disadvantages:

Table A.1 CBA for the thought 'I'm such a failure'

Advantages	Disadvantages
I may avoid disappointment.	I feel depressed when I say this.
I may avoid people expecting too much of me.	I will avoid undertaking more challenging tasks and activities.
	My self-esteem will suffer.
	I may ignore some good aspects of what I can do.
	Other people may get fed up with me 'whining'.
	Other people may underestimate what I can actually do.

Problems with CBA can sometimes arise if clients are not willing to acknowledge that there are any advantages to negative thinking so we end up with a one-sided battle and an unsatisfying victory for the positive rational side. Clients can sometimes be helped to acknowledge 'benefits' by distinguishing between 'short term' and 'long term' cost and benefits. The advantages of negative thinking are heavily weighted towards short-term coping and against longer-term life development. It is probably easier to own a flawed coping mechanism as a way of coping in the short term, until a more positive longer-term strategy can be devised and implemented. Leahy (2003) suggests that the simple CBA above can also be used to review positive alternative thoughts. The CBA is really a form of problem solving and can be adapted to decision making. When problems with decisions arise they frequently involve other people, therefore it is useful to consider the costs and benefits for others as well as for oneself so that the matrix now looks like this:

	Advantages for self	Advantages for others
Decision A (or negative belief)		
Decision B (or positive belief)		

PIE CHARTS

When we discussed cognitive distortions in Chapter 4, we noted that one of the main 'serial offenders' was 'making over-statements'. These types of statements seem to result from negative attention bias – but they also reinforce it. It may well be that there is a form of 'special pleading' going on here. Special pleading is a well-known device to secure advantage by a selective review of the facts of the case. Here they seem to relate to securing disadvantage – unless we consider the case for 'subtle pay-off' made above.

The cognitive tactic is usually to get the client to see that their review of relevant factors is restricted and to explore whether a wider consideration of the facts may be helpful.

A flagrant distortion was immediately evident to me when one of my clients blamed herself for the fact that her husband had left her. It turned out that her husband had a gambling addiction and had over the years persuaded her to sign away all their joint money and assets to him, so that when he went away with another woman, my client lost everything including the roof over her head. We drew one circle in which she was attributed 100% of the responsibility for the break-up – 'If I had been a better wife, he wouldn't have got into gambling in the first place.' Then we listed some other factors that might have been involved so that a new 'pie chart' circle could be drawn. Leahy (2001) is spot on in suggesting adding 'bad luck' to the list – a more potent factor than most of us allow! The resulting list looked like this:

◆ My husband's gambling: 60%

◆ My husband's drinking: 20%

◆ The other woman: 10%

◆ The gambling and drinks industries: 5%

◆ Bad luck: 4%

◆ Not being a super wife: 1%

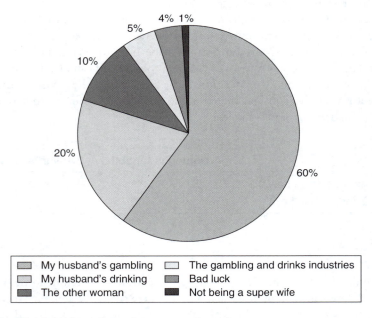

Figure A.1 Pie chart (based on above percentages)

Pie charts can have very powerful effects but, like all methods, sometimes run into problems. Therapists can sometimes feel a bit manipulative when they do the kind of pie chart described above – especially knowing that leaving the client's responsibilities until last virtually guarantees that only a tiny percentage of responsibility will be left by then. In the above example, we had to keep readjusting the previous figures to allow any percentage at all for the last few items. It can also be important for people to retain some responsibility, sometimes as a moral issue but also sometimes to be a player of some account. It strikes me in retrospect that this latter point was particularly true for this client after such a thorough 'disempowerment' by her husband. I wish I could record that I had registered this at the time – perhaps next time, eh?

FURTHER READING

Burns, D.D. (2001) Ten ways to untwist your thinking. In *The feeling good handbook.* Harmondsworth: Penguin.

Leahy, R.L. (2001) *Cognitive therapy techniques: a practitioner's guide.* New York: Guilford. (Chapters 2 and 6)

REFERENCES

APA (2000) *Diagnostic and statistical manual IV-TR*. Washington: American Psychiatric Association.

Anchin, J.C., & Kiesler, D. (1982) *Handbook of interpersonal psychotherapy*. New York: Pergamon Press.

Aristotle (2012) *Nicomachean ethics*. Chicago: University of Chicago Press.

Arnow, B.A., Steidman, D., Blasey, C., Mender, R., Klein, D.N., Rothbaum, B.O. et al. (2013) The relationship between the therapeutic alliance and treatment outcome in two distinct psychotherapies for chronic depression. *Journal of Consulting and Clinical Psychology*, *81*(4): 627–638.

Arntz, A., & van Genderen, H. (2009) *Schema therapy for borderline personality disorder.* Chichester: Wiley-Blackwell.

Ashworth, P., Williams, C., & Blackburn, I.-M. (1999) What becomes of cognitive therapy trainees? A survey of trainees' opinions and current clinical practice after postgraduate cognitive therapy training. *Behavioural and Cognitive Psychotherapy*, *27*: 267–277.

Atherton, J. (1999) Resistance to learning: a discussion based on participants in in-service professional training programmes. *Journal of Vocational and Educational Training*, *51*(1): 77–90.

Austen, J. (2014) *Sense and sensibility*. Harmondsworth: Penguin.

Bandura, A. (1997) *Self-efficacy: the exercise of control*. Basingstoke: W.H. Freeman.

Barlow, D.H., Ellard, K.K., Fairholme, C.P., Farchione, T.J., Boisseau, C.L., Allen, L.B. et al. (2011) *Unified protocol for transdiagnostic treatment of emotional disorders*. Oxford: Oxford University Press.

Bartlett, Sir F. (1932) *Remembering: a study in experimental and social psychology*. Cambridge: Cambridge University Press.

Beck, A.T. (1967) *Depression: clinical, experimental and theoretical aspects*. New York: Harper & Row.

Beck, A.T. (1970a) Cognitive therapy: nature and relation to behavior therapy. *Behavior Therapy*, *1*: 184–200.

Beck, A.T. (1970b) The role of fantasies in psychotheraphy and psychopathology. *Journal of Nervous and Mental Disease*, *150*: 3–17.

Beck, A.T. (1976) *Cognitive therapy and the emotional disorders*. Harmondsworth: Penguin.

Beck, A.T., Emery, G., with Greenberg, R. (1985) *Anxiety and phobias: a cognitive perspective.* New York: Basic Books.

Beck, A.T., Freeman, A., Davis, D.D., & associates (2004) *Cognitive therapy of personality disorders* (2nd ed.). New York: Guilford.

Beck, A.T, Rush, A.J., Shaw, B.F., & Emery, G. (1979) *Cognitive therapy of depression*. New York: Guilford.

Beck, J. (1995) *Cognitive therapy: basics and beyond*. New York: Guilford.

Beck, J. (2011) *Cognitive behavior therapy: basics and beyond* (2nd ed.). New York: Guilford.

Bennett-Levy, J. (2006) Therapist skills: a cognitive model of their acquisition and refinement. *Behavioural and Cognitive Psychotherapy, 34*: 57–78.

Beutler, L.E., & Harwood, T.M. (2000) *Prescriptive psychotherapy: a practical guide to systematic treatment selection*. New York: Oxford University Press.

Binder, J.L. (2004) *Key competencies in brief psychodynamic psychotherapy: clinical practice beyond the manual*. New York: Guilford.

Bolton, G. (2010) *Reflective practice* (3rd ed.). London: Sage.

Bond, T. (2010) *Standards and ethics for counselling* (3rd ed.). London: Sage.

Bransford, J.D., Brown, A.L., & Cocking, R.R. (2004) *How people learn: brain, mind, experience and school*. Washington, DC: National Academy Press.

Bransford, J.D., Franks, J.J., Vye, N.J., & Sherwood, R.D. (1989) New approaches to instruction: because wisdom can't be told. In S. Vosniadou & A. Ortony (Eds.), *Similarity and analogic reasoning* (pp. 470–497). New York: Cambridge University Press.

Bruch, W., & Bond, F.W. (1998) *Beyond diagnosis: case formulation approaches to CBT*. Chichester: Wiley.

Burdick, D. (2013) *Mindfulness skills workbook for clinicians and clients*. East Claire, WI: PESI Publishing.

Burns, D.D. (1999) *The feeling good handbook* (Rev. ed.). New York: Penguin.

Burns, D.D. (2001) Ten ways to untwist your thinking. In *The feeling good handbook*. Harmondsworth: Penguin.

Busch, F.N., Milrod, B.L., Singer, M.B., & Aronson, A.C. (2012) *Manual of panic focused psychodynamic extended range*. New York: Routledge.

Butler, G. (2009) *Overcoming social anxiety and shyness*. London: Robinson.

Casement, P. (1985) *On learning from the patient*. London: Tavistock.

Cash, A.H. (2007) *John Wilkes: the scandalous father of civil liberty*. New Haven, CT: Yale University Press.

Centre for Economic Performance (2006) *The depression report: a new deal for depression and anxiety disorders*. London: LSE.

Christie, A. (1976) *Sleeping murder*. London: Harper Collins.

Ciarrochi, J.V., & Bailey, A. (2008) *The CBT practitioner's guide to ACT*. Oakland, CA: New Harbinger.

Clark, D.A., & Beck, A.T. (2012) *The anxiety and worry workbook*. New York: Guilford.

Clark, D.M. (1996) Panic disorder: from theory to therapy. In P. Salkovskis (Ed.), *Frontiers of cognitive therapy* (pp. 318–344). New York: Guilford.

Coid, J., Yang, M., Tyrer, P., Roberts, A., & Ullrich, S. (2006) Prevalence of personality disorders in Great Britain. *British Journal of Psychiatry, 188*: 423–432.

Connolly, M.B., Crits-Christoph, P., Demorest, A., Azarian, K., Muenz, L., & Chittams, J. (1996) Varieties of transference patterns in psychotherapy. *Journal of Consulting and Clinical Psychology, 64*: 1213–1221.

Cooper, M. (2003) *Existential therapies*. London: Sage.

Cornell, A.W. (2013) *Focusing in clinical practice*. New York: W.W. Norton & Co.

Cummings, N., & Sayama, C. (1995) *Focused psychotherapy: a casebook of brief intermittent psychotherapy.* New York: Brunner/Mazel.

Damasio, A. (2000) *The feeling of what happens: body, emotion and the making of consciousness.* London: Vintage.

Davies, E. (2013) Talking point: we are all on the same side. *Therapy Today,* 24(6). Retrieved from: www.therapytoday.net/article/show/3836

DeRubeis, R.J., Siegle, G.L., & Hollon, S.D. (2008) Cognitive therapy versus medications for depression: treatment outcomes and neural mechanisms. *National Review of Neuroscience,* 9(10): 788–796.

Dobson, F. (2004) *Getting serious about play – a review of children's play.* London, UK: Department for Culture, Media and Sport.

Dryden, W. (1991) *A dialogue with Albert Ellis: against dogmas.* Buckingham: Open University Press.

Dryden, W. (2006) *Getting started with REBT* (2nd ed.). London: Taylor & Francis.

Dryden, W., & Neenan, M. (2004) *Rational emotive behaviour counselling in action* (3rd ed.). London: Sage.

Dryden, W., & Trower, P. (Eds.) (1988) *Developments in cognitive psychotherapy.* London: Sage.

Dryden, W., & Yankura, J. (1992) *Daring to be myself: a case study in rational-emotive therapy.* Buckingham: Open University Press.

Egan, G. (1975) *You and me: the skills in communicating and relating to others.* Monterey, CA: Brooks-Cole.

Egan, G. (2002) *Exercises in helping skills: a manual to accompany* The skilled helper (7th ed.). Pacific Grove, CA: Brooks-Cole.

Egan, G. (2013) *The skilled helper* (10th international ed.). Pacific Grove, CA: Brooks-Cole.

Ekers, D., Richards, D.A., McMillan, D., Bland, J.M., & Gilbody, S. (2011) Behavioural activation delivered by the non-specialist: phase II randomised controlled trial. *British Journal of Psychiatry, 198:* 60–72.

Elliott, R., Watson, J.C., Goldman, R.N., & Greenberg, L.S. (2004) *Learning emotion-focused therapy: the process-experiential approach to change.* Washington, DC: American Psychological Association.

Ellis, A. (1973) *Humanistic psychotherapy: the rational-emotive approach.* New York: Julian Press.

Ellis, A. (2000) *The Albert Ellis reader: a guide to well-being using rational emotive behavior therapy.* New York: Citadel.

Emery, G. (1999) *Overcoming depression: therapist's manual.* Oakland, CA: New Harbinger.

Epictetus (1995) *A manual for living (The Enchiridion).* San Francisco: Harper.

Epstein, S. (1998) *Constructive thinking: the key to emotional intelligence.* Westport, CT: Praeger.

Erikson, E. (1994 [1959]) *Identity and the life cycle* (Rev. ed.). New York: W.W. Norton & Co.

Fennell, M. (1989) Depression. In K. Hawton, P.M. Salkovskis, J. Kirk, & D.M. Clark (Eds.), *Cognitive behaviour therapy for psychiatric problems.* Oxford: Oxford University Press.

Fennell, M. (2004) Depression, low self-esteem and mindfulness. *Behaviour Research and Therapy, 42:* 1053–1067.

Fialkow, N.J., & Muslin, H.L. (1987) Working through: a cornerstone of psycho-therapy. *American Journal of Psychotherapy*, *43*(3): 443–452.

Flecknoe, P., & Sanders, D. (2004) Interpersonal difficulties. In J. Bennett-Levy, G. Butler, M. Fennell, A. Hackmann, M. Mueller, & D. Westbrook (Eds.), *Oxford guide to behavioural experiments in cognitive therapy* (pp. 393–412). Oxford: Oxford University Press.

Freud, S. (1914 [1991]) *On Metapsychology*, Penguin Freud Library 11. Harmondsworth: Penguin.

Gendlin, E. (1981) *Focusing*. New York: Everest House.

Gendlin, E. (1996) *Focusing oriented psychotherapy: a manual of experiential method*. New York: Guilford.

Gilbert, P. (2009a) *The compassionate mind*. London: Constable.

Gilbert, P. (2009b) Moving beyond cognitive behaviour therapy. *The Psychologist*, 22(5): 400–403.

Gilbert, P. (2010) *Compassion-focused therapy: distinctive features*. Hove, East Sussex: Routledge.

Gilbert, P., & Leahy, R.L. (2007) *The therapeutic relationship in cognitive behavioural psychotherapies*. London: Routledge.

Goldfried, M. (Ed.) (2005) *How therapists change: personal and professional reflections*. Washington, DC: American Psychological Association.

Gordo, A., & De Vos, J. (2010) Psychologism, psychologising and de-psychologisation. *Annual Review of Critical Psychology*, pp. 3–7. Retrieved from: www.discourseunit.com/arcp/8.htm

Greenberg, L.S. (2002) *Emotion-focused therapy: coaching clients to work through their feelings*. Washington, DC: American Psychiatric Association.

Greenberg, L.S. (2011) *Emotion-focused therapy*. Washington, DC: American Psychiatric Association.

Guidano, V., & Liotti, G. (1983) *Cognitive processes and emotional disorders: a structural approach to psychopathology*. New York: Guilford.

Hackmann, A. (1998) Cognitive therapy with panic disorder and agoraphobia. In N. Tarrier (Ed.), *Treating complex cases: the cognitive behavioural approach* (pp. 27–45). Chichester: Wiley.

Hackmann, A., Bennett-Levy, J., & Holmes, E.A. (2011) *Using imagery in cognitive therapy*. Oxford: Oxford University Press.

Hall, K., & Iqbal, F. (2010) *The problem with CBT*. London: Karnac.

Harris, R. (2006) *Imperium*. London: Arrow Books.

Harvey, A., Watkins, E., Mansell, W., & Shafran, R. (2004) *Cognitive behavioural processes across psychological disorders: a trans-diagnostic approach to research and treatment*. Oxford: Oxford University Press.

Hayes, S.C. (1999) Acceptance and Commitment Therapy (ACT): workshop given at the EABCT Annual Conference, London.

Hayes, S.C., Strohsal, K.D., & Wilson, K.G. (2004) *Acceptance and commitment therapy: an experiential approach to behavior change* (New ed.). New York: Guilford.

Hays, P.A., & Iwamasa, G.Y. (2006) *Culturally responsive cognitive behavior therapy: assessment, therapy and supervision*. Washington, DC: American Psychiatric Association.

Hazlett-Stevens, H., & Craske, M.G. (2008) Live (in vivo) exposure. In W.T. O'Donoghue & J.E. Fisher (Eds.), *Cognitive behavior therapy: applying empirically supported techniques to your practice* (2nd ed.) (pp. 309–316). Hoboken, NJ: John Wiley & Sons Inc.

Hick, S.F., & Bien, T. (Eds.) (2008) *Mindfulness and the therapeutic relationship*. New York: Guilford Press.

Hobson, R.F. (1985) *Forms of feeling: the heart of psychotherapy*. London: Tavistock.

Holmes, J. (1993) *John Bowlby and attachment theory*. Makers of modern psychotherapy. London & New York: Routledge.

Ilardi, S.S., & Craighead, W.E. (1994) The role of non-specific factors in cognitive behaviour therapy. *Clinical Psychology: Science and Practice*, 1(2): 138–155.

Inskipp, F. (1996) *Skills training for counsellors*. London: Cassell.

Inskipp, F., & Proctor, B. (1999) Post-tribalism: a millennium gift for clients. Keynote Address to the Annual Conference of the British Association for Counselling and Psychotherapy. University of Warwick, September.

Ivey, A.E., D'Andrea, M., & Ivey, M.B. (2012) *Counselling and psychotherapy: a multicultural approach* (7th ed.). Boston: Allyn & Bacon.

James, I.A. (2001) Schema therapy: the next generation – but should it come with a health warning? *Behavioural and Cognitive Psychotherapies*, 29(4): 401–407.

James, I.A., & Barton, S. (2004) Changing core beliefs with the continuum technique. *Behavioural and Cognitive Psychotherapies*, 32(4): 401–407.

James, I.A., Blackburn, I.-M., & Reichelt, F.K. (2000) *Manual of the revised cognitive therapy scale*. Newcastle upon Tyne: Cognitive & Behavioural Therapies Centre.

Kabat-Zinn, J. (2012) *Mindfulness for beginners: reclaiming the present moment and your life* (CD set). Boulder, CO: Sounds True.

Kagan, N. (1975) *Influencing human interaction*. Washington, DC: American Personnel and Guidance Association.

Kahn, M. (1991) *Between therapist and client: the new relationship*. New York: W.H. Freeman.

Katzow, A.W., & Safran, J.D. (2007) Recognising and resolving ruptures in the therapeutic alliance. In P. Gilbert & R.L. Leahy (2007) *The therapeutic relationship in cognitive behavioural psychotherapies* (pp. 90–105). London: Routledge.

Kazantzis, N., Deane, F.P., Ronan, K.R., & L'Abate, L. (Eds.) (2005) *Using assignments in cognitive behavior therapy*. New York: Routledge.

Kazantzis, N., & Ronan, K.R. (2006) Can between-sessions (homework) assignments be considered a common factor in psychotherapy? *Journal of Psychotherapy Integration*, 16(2): 115–127.

Keijsers, G.P., Schaap, C.P., & Hoogduin, C.A. (2000) The impact of interpersonal patient and therapist behaviour on outcome in cognitive behaviour therapy: a review of empirical studies. *Behaviour Modification*, 24(2): 264–297.

Kuyken, W. (2006) Evidence-based case formulation: is the emperor clothed? In N. Tarrier (Ed.), *Case formulation in cognitive behaviour therapy* (pp. 12–35). London: Routledge.

Kuyken, W., Padesky, C.A., & Dudley, R. (2009) *Collaborative case conceptualisation in cognitive-behavior therapy*. New York: Guilford.

Larkin, P. (2003) *Collected poems*. London: Faber & Faber.

Layden, M.A., Newman, C.F., & Morse, S.B. (1993) *Cognitive therapy of borderline personality disorder*. Boston, MA: Allyn & Bacon.

Leahy, R.L. (2001) *Overcoming resistance in cognitive therapy*. New York: Guilford.

Leahy, R.L. (2003) *Cognitive therapy techniques*. New York: Guilford.

Leahy, R.L. (Ed.) (2006) *Contemporary cognitive therapy*. New York: Guilford.

Leahy, R.L. (2007) Schematic mismatch in the therapeutic relationship. In P. Gilbert & R.L. Leahy (Eds.), *The therapeutic relationship in the cognitive behavioural psychotherapies* (pp. 229–254). Hove: Routledge.

Leahy, R.L. (2011) *Emotional regulation in psychotherapy*. New York: Guilford.

LeDoux, J. (1996) *The emotional brain: the mysterious underpinnings of emotional life*. New York: Simon & Schuster.

Levenson, H. (1995) *Time-limited dynamic psychotherapy: a guide to clinical practice*. New York: Basic Books.

Levinson, M. (2010) Working with diversity. In A. Grant, M. Townend, R. Mulhearn, & N. Short (Eds.), *Cognitive behavioural therapy in mental health care*. London: Sage.

Lewinsohn, P.M., & Gotlib, I.H. (1995) Behavioral theory and treatment of depression. In E. Beckham & W. Leber (Eds.), *Handbook of depression* (pp. 352–375). New York: Guilford Press.

Lilienfield, S. (2007) Psychological treatments that cause harm. *Perspectives on Psychological Science*, 2(1): 53–70.

Lindenfield, G. (2014) *Assert yourself: simple steps to build your confidence*. London: Harper Collins.

Linehan, M.M. (1993) *Cognitive behavioural treatment of borderline personality disorder.* New York: Guilford.

Linehan, M.M. (2004) Dialetical behavior therapy: synthesising radical acceptance with skilful means. In S.C. Hayes, V.M. Follette, & Linehan, M.M. (Eds.), *Mindfulness and acceptance: expanding the cognitive-behavioural tradition* (pp. 30–44). New York: Guilford.

Liotti, G. (2007) Internal working models of attachment in the therapeutic relationship. In P. Gilbert & R.L. Leahy (Eds.), *The therapeutic relationship in the cognitive behavioural psychotherapies*. London: Routledge.

Lively, P. (1977) *The road to Lichfield*. London: Heinemann.

Lovelock, J. (2014) *Rough ride to the future*. London: Allen Lane.

Mackay, H.C., West, W., Moorey, J., Guthrie, E., & Margison, F. (2001) Counsellors' experiences of changing their practice: learning the psychodynamic-interpersonal model of therapy. *Counselling and Psychotherapy Research*, 1(1): 29–35.

Mansell, W., Carey, T.A., & Tai, S.J. (2013) *A transdiagnostic approach to CBT using methods of levels therapy: distinctive features*. Hove, East Sussex: Routledge.

Martell, C.R., Addis, M.E., & Jacobson, N.S. (2001) *Depression in context: strategies for guided action*. New York: Norton.

Marzillier, J. (2010) *The gossamer thread: my life as a psychotherapist*. London: Karnac.

Masson, J. (1990) *Against therapy*. London: Fontana.

McCullough, J.P. (2000) *Treatment for chronic depression*. New York: Guilford.

McCullough, J.P. (2006) *Treating chronic depression with disciplined personal involvement*. Richmond, VA: Springer.

McGinn, R.K., Young, J.E., & Sanderson, W.C. (1995) When and how to do longer-term therapy without feeling guilty. *Cognitive Behavioral Practice*, 2: 187–212.

McLeod, J. (2010) *Doing case study research in counselling and psychotherapy*. London: Sage.

McLeod, J. (2013a) *Introduction to research in counselling and psychotherapy*. London: Sage.

McLeod, J. (2013b) *Introduction to research in counselling and psychotherapy*. Maidenhead: Open University Press.

Miller, W.R., & Rollnick, S. (2002) *Motivational interviewing* (2nd ed.). New York: Guilford.

Milne, D.L. (2009) *Evidence-based clinical supervision: principles and practice*. Chichester: Wiley.

Neenan, M., & Dryden, W. (2013) *Life coaching: a cognitive behavioural approach*. London: Routledge.

Nicholson, J. (2006) *The perfect summer: dancing into the shadow in 1911*. London: John Murray.

Orwell, G. (1953) *Such, such were the joys*. New York: Harcourt, Brace, Jovanovich.

Overholser, J. (1993) Elements of Socratic method: II. Inductive reasoning. *Psychotherapy: Theory, Research, Practice, Training*, 30(1): 75–85.

Padesky, C. (1993) Socratic questioning: changing minds or guiding discovery? Keynote address at European Congress of Cognitive and behavioural therapies, London, September.

Padesky, C. (1994) *Cognitive therapy for anxiety: audiotape*. Newport Beach, CA: Center for Cognitive Therapy.

Padesky, C. (1996) Developing cognitive therapy competency: teaching and supervision models. In P. Salkovskis (Ed.), *The frontiers of cognitive therapy* (pp. 266–292). New York: Guilford Press.

Padesky, C. (2004) Aaron T. Beck: mind, man, mentor. In R.L. Leahy (Ed.), *Contemporary cognitive therapy* (pp. 3–26). New York: Guilford.

Padesky, C. (2006) *Therapist beliefs: protocols, personalities and guided exercises* (2 CD set). Newport Beach, CA: Center for Cognitive Therapy.

Padesky, C., & Greenberger, D. (1995) *Clinician's guide to mind over mood*. New York: Guilford Press.

Papageorgiou, C., & Wells, A. (2003) *Depressive rumination: nature, theory and treatment*. Chichester: Wiley.

Pavlov, I.P. (1927) *Conditioned reflexes: an investigation of the physiological activity of the cerebral cortex*. London: Oxford University Press.

Persons, J.B. (2008) *The case formulation approach to cognitive-behaviour therapy*. New York: Guilford.

Persons, J.B., Gross, J.J., Etkin, M.S., & Madan, S.K. (1996) Psychodynamic therapists' reservations about cognitive-behaviour therapy: implications for training and practice. *Journal of Psychotherapy Practice and Research*, 5: 202–212.

Power, M. (2010) *Emotionally focused cognitive therapy*. Chichester: Wiley.

Rachman, S. (1997) The evolution of cognitive behaviour therapy. In D.M. Clark & C.G. Fairburn (Eds.), *Science and practice of cognitive behavior therapy* (pp. 1–26). Oxford: Oxford University Press.

Ramnero, J., & Torneke, N. (2008) *The ABCs of human behavior*. Oakland, CA: New Harbinger.

Reeves, A. (2012) *An introduction to counselling and psychotherapy: from theory to practice*. London: Sage.

Rogers, C.R. (1961) *On becoming a person*. Boston, MA: Houghton Mifflin.

Rogers, C.R. (1980) *A way of being*. Boston, MA: Houghton Mifflin.

Rothbaum, B.O., & Mellman, T.A. (2001) Dreams and exposure therapy in PTSD. *Journal of Traumatic Stress*, *14*(3): 481–490.

Safran, J.D., & Muran, J.C. (2000) *Negotiating the therapeutic alliance: a relational treatment guide*. New York: Guilford Press.

Safran, J.D., & Reading, R. (2008) Mindfulness, metacommunication and affect regulation. In S.F. Hick & T. Bien (Eds.), *Mindfulness and the therapeutic relationship*. New York: Guilford Press.

Safran, J.D., & Segal, Z.V. (1990) *Interpersonal processes and cognitive therapy*. New York: Guilford Press.

Sanders, D., & Wills, F. (2003) *Counselling for anxiety problems*. London: Sage.

Schon, D.A. (1994) *The reflective practitioner: how professionals think*. Farnham, Surrey: Ashgate.

Sciascia, L. (2002) *The Moro affair*. London: Granta Publications.

Segal, Z.V. (2009) *Mindfulness-based cognitive therapy for depression* (DVD). Washington, DC: American Psychiatric Association.

Segal, Z.V., Williams, J.M.G., & Teasdale, J.D. (2002) *Mindfulness-based cognitive therapy for depression: a new approach to preventing relapse*. New York: Guilford.

Servan-Schreiber, D. (2005) *Healing without Freud or Prozac: natural approaches to curing stress*. London: Rodale.

Shapiro, F. (2001) *Eye movement desensitization and reprocessing (EMDR): basic principles, protocols and procedures*. New York: Guilford.

Sherman, N. (2005) *Stoic warrior: the ancient philosophy behind the military mind*. Oxford: Oxford University Press.

Skinner, B.F. (1957) *Verbal behavior*. Acton, MA: Copley.

Skinner, B.F. (1965) *Science and human behaviour*. New York: Free Press.

Sloane, R.B., Staples, F.R., Cristol, A.H., & Yorkston, N.J. (1975) Short-term analytically orientated psychotherapy versus behavior therapy, *American Journal of Psychiatry*, *132*: 373–377.

Spiegler, M.D., & Guevremont, D.C. (2009) *Contemporary behaviour therapy*. Belmont, CA: Cengage/Wadsworth.

Stopa, L. (Ed.) (2009) *Imagery and the threatened self*. Hove, East Sussex: Routledge.

Strupp, H.H., & Binder, J.L. (1984) *Psychotherapy in a new key: a guide to time-limited dynamic psychotherapy*. New York: Basic Books.

Teasdale, J. (1996) Clinically relevant theory: integrating clinical insight with cognitive science. In P. Salkovskis (Ed.), *Frontiers of cognitive therapy* (pp. 26–47). New York: Guilford.

Teo, A.R., Choi, H., & Valenstein, M. (2013) Social relationships and depression: ten-year follow-up for a nationally representative study. *PLOS ONE*, *8*(4).doi: 10.1371/journal.pone.0062396.

Truax, C.B., & Carkhuff, R. (1967) *Towards effective counselling and psychotherapy: training and practice*. Chicago, IL: Aldine.

Tsai, M., Kohlenberg, R.J., Kanter, J.W., Kohlenberg, B., Follette, W.C., & Callaghan, G.M. (2009) *A guide to functional analytic psychotherapy: awareness, courage, love and behaviorism*. New York: Springer.

van der Kolk, B. (1994) The body keeps the score: the evolving psychobiology of post-traumatic stress disorder. *Harvard Review of Psychiatry*, *1*(5): 253–265.

Watson, J.B., & Rayner, R. (1920) Conditioned emotional reactions. *Journal of Experimental Psychology*, *3*: 1–14.

Wegner, D.M. (1994) Ironic processes of mental control. *Psychological Review*, *74*: 300–317.

Weishaar, M. (1993) *Aaron T. Beck.* Sage Modern Masters series. London: Sage.

Welford, M. (2012) *The compassionate mind approach to building self-confidence*. London: Constable and Robinson.

Wells, A. (1997) *Cognitive therapy of anxiety disorders*. Chichester: Wiley.

Wells, A. (2000) *Emotional disorders and metacognition: innovative cognitive therapy*. Chichester: Wiley.

Wells, A. (2006) Cognitive therapy case formulation in anxiety disorders. In N. Tarrier (Ed.), *Case formulation on cognitive behaviour therapy: the treatment of challenging and complex cases* (pp. 52–80). Hove: Routledge.

Wells, A. (2009) *Metacognitive therapy for anxiety and depression*. New York: Guilford.

Whitehead, E.E., & Whitehead, J.D. (2010) *Transforming our painful emotions: spiritual resources for emotional healing*. Maryknoll, NY: Orbis.

Williams, M.J.G., Teasdale, J.D., Segal, Z.V., & Kabat-Zinn, J. (2007) *The mindful way through depression*. New York: Guilford.

Williams, M., & Penman, D. (2011) *Mindfulness: a practical guide to finding peace in a frantic world*. London: Piatkus.

Wills, F. (2006a) Cognitive therapy: a down to earth and accessible therapy. In C. Sills (Ed.), *Contracts in counselling and psychotherapy* (2nd ed.) (pp. 41–51). London: Sage.

Wills, F. (2006b) CBT: can counsellors fill the gap? *Healthcare Counselling and Psychotherapy Journal*, *6*(2): 6–9.

Wills, F. (2008a) *Skills for cognitive behaviour counselling and psychotherapy*. London: Sage.

Wills, F. (2008b) The acquisition of CBT competence during CBT training. Unpublished PhD thesis, University of Bristol.

Wills, F. (2009) *Beck's cognitive therapy*. London: Routledge.

Wills, F. (2010) Yada, yada, yada: finding the missing bit of CBT – a call for more practitioner research. A paper given at the Annual Conference of the British Association for Behavioural and Cognitive Psychotherapies, Manchester, July.

Wills, F. (2012) Assessment and formulation, and CBT skills. In W. Dryden & R. Branch (Eds.), *The CBT handbook* (pp. 101–124 and 125–140). London: Sage.

Wills, F., with Sanders, D. (2013) *Cognitive behaviour therapy: foundations for practice*. London: Sage.

Winnicott, D.W. (1955–6) Clinical varieties of transference. *International Journal of Psycho-Analysis*, *37*: 316.

Wolpe, J. (1958) *Psychotherapy by reciprocal inhibition*. Stanford, CA: Stanford University Press.

Worthless, I.M., Competent, U.R., & Lemonde-Terrible, O. (2002) And finally, cognitive therapy training stress disorder. *Behavioural and Cognitive Psychotherapy*, *30*(3): 365–374.

Wright, J., & Bolton, G. (2012) *Reflective writing in counselling and psychotherapy*. London: Sage.

Wright, J.H., Basco, M.R., & Thase, M.E. (2006) *Learning cognitive behavior therapy*. Washington: American Psychiatric Association.

Young, J.E., & Beck, A.T. (1980) *The Cognitive Therapy Rating Scale manual*. Philadelphia, PA: Center for Cognitive Therapy, University of Pennsylvania.

Young, J.E., & Beck, A.T. (1988) *The Cognitive Therapy Rating Scale manual* (Rev. ed.). Philadelphia, PA: Center for Cognitive Therapy, University of Pennsylvania.

Young, J., Klosko, J.S., & Weishaar, M.E. (2003) *Schema therapy: a practitioner's guide*. New York: Guilford.

INDEX